FLEXIBLE STRATEGIC MANAGEMENT

FLEXIBLE STRATEGIC MANAGEMENT

Audley Genus

Brunel University, Uxbridge, UK

CHAPMAN & HALL

London · Glasgow · Weinheim · New York · Tokyo · Melbourne · Madras

Published by Chapman & Hall, 2–6 Boundary Row, London SEI 8HN, UK

Chapman & Hall, 2–6 Boundary Row, London SE1 8HN, UK

Blackie Academic & Professional, Wester Cleddens Road, Bishopbriggs, Glasgow G64 2NZ, UK

Chapman & Hall GmbH, Pappelallee 3, 69469 Weinheim, Germany

Chapman & Hall USA, 115 Fifth Avenue, New York, NY 10003, USA

Chapman & Hall Japan, ITP-Japan, Kyowa Building, 3F, 2–2–1 Hirakawacho, Chiyoda–ku, Tokyo 102, Japan

Chapman & Hall Australia, 102 Dodds Street, South Melbourne, Victoria 3205, Australia

Chapman & Hall India, R. Seshadri, 32 Second Main Road, CIT East, Madras 600 035, India

First edition 1995
Reprinted by International Thomson Business Press 1996

© 1995 Audley Genus

Typeset in 10/12 pt Palatino by Florencetype Limited, Stoodleigh, Nr. Tiverton, Devon
Printed in Great Britain by The Alden Press, Osney Mead, Oxford

ISBN 0 412 56400 9

CONTENTS

List of case studies   vii
Preface   ix
Acknowledgements   xi

PART ONE: The Nature of Strategy and Flexibility

1 What is flexible strategic management?   **3**
Learning objectives   3
1.1 Introduction   3
1.2 The nature of strategy   4
1.3 Models of strategic decision-making   10
1.4 What is flexible strategic management?   19
1.5 Summary   28
Study questions   29
Key readings   29
References   30

PART TWO: Why Flexible Strategic Management?

2 Uncertainty in the macro-environment   **35**
Learning objectives   35
2.1 Introduction   35
2.2 The changing macro-environment   36
2.3 Analysing the macro-environment   45
2.4 Summary   54
Study questions   54
Key readings   55
References   55

3 Uncertainty, industries and competition   **57**
Learning objectives   57
3.1 Introduction   57
3.2 Analysing industry structure   58
3.3 Industry evolution: the product life cycle   66
3.4 Evaluating competitive position: market share,
     strategic groups and competitor analysis   68
3.5 Summary   77
Study questions   77
Key readings   77
References   77

4 **Analysing and developing strategy in organizations**   **79**
   Learning objectives   79
   4.1 Introduction   79
   4.2 Flexibility and the analysis of strategic capability   80
   4.3 Defining the scope and direction of the firm   89
   4.4 Structure follows strategy?   98
   4.5 Summary   103
   Study questions   103
   Key readings   103
   References   104

PART THREE: Developing Strategic Flexibility

5 **Flexible management and strategic renewal: central issues
   and key activities**   **107**
   Learning objectives   107
   5.1 Introduction   107
   5.2 Capabilities and learning as sources of competitiveness   108
   5.3 The management of scope and scale   114
   5.4 The significance of organizational learning   118
   5.5 Summary   125
   Study questions   125
   Key readings   125
   References   126

6 **Flexibility between organizations**   **127**
   Learning objectives   127
   6.1 Introduction   127
   6.2 Strategic alliances: horizontal collaboration with competitors   128
   6.3 Vertical collaboration with suppliers   132
   6.4 Strategic networks   134
   6.5 Managing collaboration   139
   6.6 Summary   142
   Study questions   142
   Key readings   142
   References   143

7 **Flexibility within organizations**   **145**
   Learning objectives   145
   7.1 Introduction   145
   7.2 Product innovation   146
   7.3 Process innovation   155
   7.4 Managing the human side of the enterprise   161
   7.5 The dilemma of strategic control   169
   7.6 Summary   172
   Study questions   172
   Key readings   173
   References   173

   Index   175

CASE STUDIES

1.1 The nature of strategy: Tottenham Hotspur plc.   6
2.1 Honda: overseas investment and the limits to formalized
     monitoring of macro-environmental trends   49
3.1 The impact of government policy on the renewable energy
     industry   65
3.2 Problems with the product life cycle concept: the computer
     industry   69
4.1 The Icarus paradox: four trajectories   102
5.1 Logical incrementalism   122
5.2 An interpretative approach to strategic management   123
5.3 Collective entrepreneurship at Jaguar   124
7.1 Nintendo's 'outpacing' strategy   148
7.2 From tacit to explicit knowledge: product development at
     Matsushita   153

For my father, Mortie Genus

PREFACE

This book developed out of two concerns connected with the author's teaching and research activities. The first of these is the need to consider the relevance of flexibility to strategic management. Despite the significant degree of attention that notions of flexibility have received in other disciplines, it is an area that remains barely touched in strategy texts. Such a treatment of flexibility is appropriate for understanding the implications of strategic decision-making and change in uncertain situations.

The second concern addresses the contribution that a multidisciplinary perspective can make to illuminating some of the key issues of strategic management. Here, the development of a flexible approach to strategic management benefits from insights derived from the fields of operations and technology management, human resource management and economics, which might not typically be found in strategy texts.

The book makes no claim to be exhaustive. There are a great many strategy texts, a large number of which run into several hundred pages and cover a huge variety of 'classic' topics and analytical techniques. It was felt that the greatest need was not for another work of this type but for a textbook with a different character. So, the following chapters represent the recognition of process and resource-based perspectives on strategy development. This contrasts with many other texts which, despite disclaimers to the contrary, still take the reader through a 'formal planning' approach to strategic management. This book is selective. It tackles the principal topics and analytical tools relevant to strategic management, with an emphasis on implications for flexibility of decision-making.

The book is divided into three parts. Part One addresses the question 'What is flexible strategic management?' This is considered by way of an introduction to the nature of the concepts of strategy and flexibility. A framework for understanding the relevance of flexibility to strategic decision-making is provided, which informs the book as a whole.

Part Two of the book comprises three chapters that together consider why a flexible approach to strategic management is suggested. These chapters focus on the problems involved in adopting traditional approaches to strategic analysis. More specifically they relate the limitations of such approaches to the formulation and implementation of strategy.

Finally, Part Three considers the 'how' of the practice of strategic flexibility. This involves two main strands. The first is the strategic significance of organizational capabilities and intangible resources. Here, the relevance to strategic flexibility of employee knowledge and commitment, product and process technology, and issues of organization design is addressed. The second strand concerns the relationship of organizations to rival competitors and suppliers, for example. This presents a more collaborative view of inter-firm relations than is usually the case, including the relevance to strategic flexibility of a network perspective of these relationships.

Learning points are given at the beginning of each chapter. These are complemented by study questions and key readings at the end of chapters. These are intended to assist the reader to grasp the points being made in the text and to stimulate further thinking beyond the covers of this volume. In addition, a number of case studies help to consolidate the learning objectives of the book by bringing the theory 'to life'.

Audley Genus
Uxbridge, April 1995

ACKNOWLEDGEMENTS

The writing of this book has been the subject of a great many influences and contributions, too many and diverse to reflect properly here. So the following represents a small sample of the individuals to whom I owe a great debt.

First, I would like to thank David Collingridge for the many constructive insights he has given me, sometimes unknowingly. My thoughts on the matter of flexibility and strategic management have also benefited from the contributions and encouragement of: Peter Clark, Steve Conway, Keith Dickson, John Howells, Martin Harris, Peter James, Ian McLoughlin, John Quinn, Fred Steward and Ned Woodhouse.

In addition, the publication of the book has been facilitated by the efforts of Mark Wellings, my editor at Chapman & Hall, Lynne Maddock and Fiona Toms, who have attended to the sub- and copy-editing, and John Dixon, the production controller.

PART ONE

THE NATURE OF STRATEGY AND FLEXIBILITY

WHAT IS FLEXIBLE STRATEGIC MANAGEMENT?

1

Learning objectives

After studying this chapter you should be able:

- to understand the nature of strategy and strategic management
- to appreciate why strategic thinking is important
- to develop awareness of various approaches to the analysis, choice and implementation of strategy
- to understand the concept of strategic flexibility and the nature and significance of flexible strategic management.

1.1 Introduction

The emphasis of this book is the problem of maintaining or improving strategic performance in the face of continual change within an organization's internal and external environments. The central theme of the book is the pitfalls associated with adopting a 'rational', linear or deterministic approach to the development and implementation of strategy against this backdrop of flux. In the 1990s it is the persistence of such uncertainty, stemming from a variety of sources, that makes flexibility an attractive notion. Whether explicit or implicit, the strategy literature has recently shown an increase in attention on the problem of creating and sustaining 'flexible' organizations, and reference to the 'learning' or 'adaptive' organization is often made. Whatever the terminology, the message appears to be the same: organizations that are 'flexible' are likely to be better able to cope with change and modify their strategies than those that are not (Quinn, 1980; Harrigan, 1985).

The question at the heart of this book is, then, why flexibility has come to be seen as desirable and how it may be facilitated. There is, however, a danger that, in time, 'flexibility' may become as abused and overworked a concept as 'planning' was in the 1970s. Hence the chapters that follow seek to explore the key issues that highlight potential difficulties in developing strategic flexibility, as well as discussing the case for adopting a flexible approach to strategic management and some methods of doing it.

Before moving on to such matters, however, it is necessary to clarify what is meant by the concepts at the core of this book. Students and practitioners frequently ask such questions as: 'What does one mean by "strategy" and "strategic management"?', 'What does it [strategic thinking] have to do with the "real world"?', and 'How can I apply strategic management to my job or department?'. Section 1.2 provides a number of characteristics that typify strategy and the activities that reflect the importance of strategic management in practice. Section 1.3 then considers a variety of views relating to the process of making and implementing strategic decisions. Primarily, this involves establishing the distinction between 'rational' and more adaptive or behavioural approaches to strategic management and the management of strategic change. Following this, section 1.4 introduces the concept of flexibility as it applies to strategic management. The main aim here is to enable readers to grasp the nature and significance of 'strategic flexibility' and thus gain an initial understanding of the potential contribution of a flexible approach to strategic management. This is underpinned by reference to a framework for understanding the implications for strategic management that a lack of flexibility may have. A summary of the chapter is provided in section 1.5.

1.2 The nature of strategy

A number of characteristics may be said to reflect the essence of the concept of strategy and the main preoccupations of strategic management theory and practice. In order to gain some insight into the nature of strategy and strategic management, it is useful to consider these characteristics alongside definitions of strategic decision-making. The initial definitions below are given with the aim of illustrating the concept of strategy rather than for the sake of attempting to provide some once-and-for-all statement of what strategy and strategic management entail.

Chandler (1962) defines strategy as:

> ... the determination of the basic long-term goals and objectives of an enterprise and the adoption of courses of action and the allocation of resources necessary for carrying out these goals.

This view of strategy is in accordance with a linear approach to strategic management, which is discussed in section 1.3. Such a view considers strategy as a deliberate, systematic activity, where decision-makers know what their long-term objectives are and can plan to realize them.

For Mintzberg, however, it is necessary to consider the unintended and emergent nature of strategy, as well as its more deliberate quality. Mintzberg proposes a variety of ways in which strategy may be defined. These are known as the 'five Ps' (Mintzberg, 1991). Briefly, the 'five Ps' refer to:

- strategy as a plan
- strategy as a ploy
- strategy as a pattern
- strategy as a position
- strategy as a perspective.

Strategy as a plan refers to a consciously intended course of action or set of guidelines for dealing with a situation. A ploy is another type of deliberate plan but one with a shorter-term orientation than is usually associated with the term 'strategy'. So, when a firm threatens legal action to discourage imitation of its products by competitors, for example, it is the threat that is the ploy, rather than any actual behaviour to carry out the threat.

Strategy as a pattern, position or perspective reflects the less intentional nature of the concept, as defined by Mintzberg. Strategy as a pattern refers to the consistency of behaviour in organizations, whether or not this was intentional. Looking in from the outside, commentators or analysts often attribute a logic to past behaviour within organizations that makes it seem as though a pattern of decisions may be defined which reflects some intended plan. However, this 'pattern' may refer to the behaviour that emerged or the realized decisions of the organization, which do not have to match the decisions that may have been intended. Thus Mintzberg distinguishes between intended, realized and emergent strategies.

Strategy as a position refers to the location of an organization's resources within its environment, to do with whether businesses compete up- or down-market, for instance, or in a market niche. The use of such labels represents an attempt to establish the position of a firm within its market and to define its strategy. Again, the positioning of an organization within its environment may be a matter of intentional or unintentional decision-making.

Finally, strategy as a perspective relates to how individuals in organizations view themselves, the organizations they work in and the external environment. Strategy in this sense is about the values and attitudes that are held within organizations. These may be so strong as to define the *raison d'être* of an organization, the way in which internal activities are performed and how external events and conditions are interpreted.

Taken together, these definitions reflect the following characteristics of strategic activity and help illustrate the main topics of concern in the field of strategic management. Thus the concept of strategy and the practice of strategic management may be said to refer to:

- the scope and long-term direction of an organization's activities
- the fit between an organization's scope and direction, its internal resources and its external environment
- the values, expectations or ethical positions of individuals or groups within the organization, or of stakeholders to the organization
- the uncertainty and complexity posed by the above.

Case study 1.1 The nature of strategy: Tottenham Hotspur plc

The characteristics of strategy may be demonstrated by the example of Tottenham Hotspur plc during the past decade or so. The company is best known for its principal subsidiary, one of the biggest and most successful professional football clubs in the UK.

Scope/long-term direction   In October 1983, Tottenham Hotspur became the first English football league club to be floated on the London Stock Exchange. The football club became a subsidiary of the new group, which embarked on a substantial increase in the range of activities that the business as a whole engaged in and a new course of direction. Essentially, to counter the cyclical nature of earnings from football, the group entered new areas such as sports clothing and the import and export of ladies' fashionwear. Hence the extended range of activities was realized through a process of diversification achieved largely through acquisition.

Strategic fit   Throughout the 1980s and into the early 1990s, Tottenham experienced great difficulty in aligning its internal resources with its constantly changing activities. Despite success on the field (the football club won the FA Cup three times and the UEFA Cup once between 1981 and 1992), Tottenham found itself heavily in debt at the beginning of the 1980s and again by the start of the 1990s, with short-term debts in 1990 totalling over £22 million.

The move to diversify away from football had seemed logical in view of the uncertainties being experienced in that sector, such as generally declining attendances, increased demand for comfortable stadiums and the effect of hooliganism on crowd control and safety requirements. However, Tottenham's ability to manage its diverse portfolio was found wanting. Management expertise was lacking in the areas needed and financial control was poor. Indeed, despite the notion that football was the area where uncertainty necessitated a move into more reliable income-generating activities, it was the football club that ended up supporting losses in the other businesses in the group.

Eventually the diversification strategy was reversed and the acquisitions divested as the group focused on its core activity – football. At heart there was a lack of fit between the activities of the diversified group in the 1980s and its ability to manage those activities successfully.

Values, expectations and ethics   Of note here, is Tottenham Hotspur plc's connection with the late Robert Maxwell through Irving Scholar, a one-time leading shareholder, group director and club chairman. The group was the target of criticism and official censure for alleged behaviour that may have been unethical as well as against Stock Exchange and Football League rules. The main issue concerned rumours alleging secret negotiations took place between Maxwell and Scholar in mid-1990 about a rescue package for the debt-ridden group. These rumours prompted fears that shareholders, including most board members, had been kept in the dark about information that could be prejudicial to the holding company's share price. In the event, Maxwell withdrew his interest, there was a boardroom rift, and share dealing was suspended.

In addition, the aftermath of the split between Terry Venables and Alan Sugar, who had played major roles in the rescue of Tottenham, in the wake of the Maxwell affair was the subject of further allegations of unethical conduct. Venables, who was removed by Sugar from his post as chief executive in 1993, has been beset by accusations concerning his alleged conduct of business while at Tottenham. This has led to a number of investigations which have continued subsequent to his appointment as the England team coach. More specifically, Tottenham football club was docked six points from its 1994/5 Premiership total and banned by the Football Association from participation in that season's FA Cup for alleged irregularities in financial dealings over the past decade. However, these sanctions, which would doubtless have threatened the leading status of the club, were removed towards the end of 1994.

Uncertainty   Much of the activity that Tottenham Hotspur has engaged in over recent years has been the subject of great uncertainty. This is reflected in doubts concerning the future of football in England, particularly after the banning of English clubs from European competition after the Heysel tragedy in 1985, representing the loss for some years of a significant source of income. Another important event that increased uncertainty during the 1980s was the Hillsborough disaster, leading to the Taylor report, which in turn led to the recommendation of all-seater stadiums, a very large and unforeseen commitment that all clubs would soon have to undertake. Other difficulties included whether and how the value of players could be accounted for on the balance sheet, and the requirements for managing the various aspects of the group's activities. Many of these uncertainties (and others such as not knowing when the expensive East Stand would be completed, or how much it would cost) occurred at the same time, making it very difficult to get a fair picture of the group's strategic position and how it should proceed. In one sense, the realization that the group was in serious financial trouble at the end of the 1980s made life less uncertain since all aspects of its operations and strategy unquestionably needed rethinking.

Scope and long-term direction

Issues of scope and long-term direction are fundamental to the very definition of an organization and relate to its sense of mission and the broad means by which that is facilitated. 'Scope' is also a term that may denote the boundaries of an organization in the sense of how that organization views its relationship with customers, suppliers, other rival organizations within the same industry, governmental bodies and so on.

The experiences of Tottenham Hotspur plc during the 1980s (Case study 1.1) illustrate these issues of scope and long-term direction, together with the other characteristics of strategy listed above.

Strategic fit

Strategic management has tended to focus on the achievement of a 'fit' between an organization's mission or activities and both its wider environment and its resource capabilities. In terms of matching the activities and sense of mission that an organization has to conditions in its wider environment, numerous factors may be at play. For example, the implications of changing macro-environmental trends or industry-level trajectories of technological development, the state of the national or global economy or patterns of domestic or international competition, among others, may be relevant to the appropriateness of an organization's existing scope of activities and its direction. Key questions concerning the problematic notion of strategic fit include the extent to which the external environment of an organization can be analysed objectively. As we shall see, such issues have particular relevance for the applicability of competing approaches for understanding the nature and conduct of strategic management.

As for the matter of ensuring that there is a fit between organizational direction and resource capabilities, a number of points may be made. First, it is important to understand how the nature and deployment of resources within an organization impacts on the fulfilment of its current mission. Secondly, the extent to which organizational resources impede or stimulate change in the mission or direction of the organization, or in the manner in which existing objectives are to be achieved, is another issue that needs to be addressed. Thirdly, while the resources of an organization may be broken down into broad functional areas such as finance, marketing or production, the extent to which these are integrated to provide a product or service is a more relevant issue. Hence the standpoint of the performance of the organization as a whole is adopted, rather than the performance of stand-alone functions or departments.

A useful concept at this stage is that of 'strategic capability'. It considers the extent to which any particular organization is employing its resources to perform a set of activities in a manner that compares favourably with other organizations providing a similar product or service. The notion of strategic capability sits comfortably alongside the need to adopt a cross-functional integrated view of the resources of an organization and the role these have in the performance of the organization as a whole. Any consideration of the fit between organizational mission/direction and resources is therefore likely to focus on awkward questions about the co-ordination and control of resources. This is connected to the assignment of roles and responsibilities to various groups and individuals within an organization or the (re)allocation of major resources in it. For now it is only necessary to reiterate that notions of fit are problematic given changing internal and external conditions.

Values, expectations and ethics

Increasingly, the concept of strategy and the practice of contemporary strategic management have addressed values, expectations and ethics in terms of their relevance to organizational decision-making. Underlying this trend is the continuing debate surrounding the proper conduct of both private and public sector organizations and their role within wider society. The extent to which they exhibit social responsibility in areas such as the protection of the natural environment and fairness in competition may be considered in the light of general societal attitudes (e.g. the BA–Virgin Atlantic 'dirty tricks campaign' episode).

An important factor in attempting to come to terms with how decision-making evolves is an understanding of the power, values, expectations and influence of stakeholders inside and outside of an organization. External stakeholder groups (e.g. banks, customers, suppliers and trade unions) may take different positions on organizational activities according to their own interests. Similarly, the different nature of values and expectations held by internal stakeholders (e.g. senior and other managers and non-managerial employees) is also likely to impact on the course and conduct of an organization's activities, according to the relative power positions of those stakeholders. The recognition of different stakeholder groups pursuing competing objectives has implications for the strategy-making process. For example, such diversity might necessitate the making of trade-offs between the interests of the different groups variously affected by particular issues. Decisions to improve the community relations profile of a company, for instance, may not immediately translate into higher dividends for shareholders. Thus there may need to be some juggling of the stakeholder priorities that the firm is to address (for very large firms there will be a recognition of the need to satisfy institutional shareholders, who may own most of the voting rights).

Another related concern at board level is with corporate governance. This is connected to issues involving the composition, independence and organization of a company's board and its meetings. One aspect of this is the extent to which a very narrow range of stakeholder interests and values are catered for within strategy-making. The Cadbury Report, (1992), for example, highlighted the need for redressing the potential imbalance of power that resulted from having a combined chairperson/chief executive on company boards. This was seen as likely to affect adversely the ability of board members to influence the direction of companies, not least where the chairperson/chief executive was able to deny other board members access to relevant information.

As well as the matter of whether the roles of chairperson and chief executive should be split, the question of having external, non-executive or part-time board members also arises. There may be advantages, in terms of fresh insights on a company's position, to be gained from directors who are somewhat detached from its day-to-day management. However, there may also be some concerns about the contribution and remuneration of those who might be viewed as remote or not fully committed to the organization. Similar arguments may be advanced in support or criticism of interlocking directorates, where directors of different companies sit on each other's boards.

Another slant on the corporate governance issue is that given by industrial democracy or 'co-determination'. The issue here is the extent to which non-managerial employees have seats (and votes) on a company board. The legal framework of the German industrial relations system governs and protects co-determination, which may be viewed as an institutionalized sharing of responsibilities between management and labour. Such employee participation in company boards is rare in the UK or the USA (arguably except where employee buy-outs have occurred).

Values and expectations change within organizations, particularly where there has been a powerful stimulus for such change to occur. For example, organizations with a long history in the public sector have found that the transition to life in a more commercialized environment can be somewhat traumatic, involving a shift in orientation towards serving customers and managing budgets, following some change in national or local government policy.

Private sector business can likewise find difficulty in moving from a bureaucratic to a (presumed) more innovative, streamlined form. This is the case when, for instance, employees have to adjust from expecting close supervision from superiors to acting more autonomously within 'empowered' teams. Difficult issues about the management of values and change are thus central to the notion of strategic decision-making as they are likely to have organization-wide implications.

Uncertainty and strategic decision-making

In the light of the above, it is likely that strategic decisions are those that have a major impact on an organization as a whole. The extent to which such decision-making needs to recognize and integrate different functional interests and values within the organization, as well as to attend to a multiplicity of interrelated factors in a changing environment, indicates the uncertain nature of strategic decision-making.

1.3 Models of strategic decision-making

The aim of this section is to present a variety of approaches to the making of strategic decisions and the management of strategic change within organizations. There is a number of important areas of concern in reviewing these perspectives:

- How (ideally) should strategic decisions be made?
- How are strategic decisions and strategic change managed in practice, especially under conditions of uncertainty?
- To what extent do various approaches reflect a concern with the process and/or content of strategy (i.e. the 'how' of the development of strategy over time and/or the 'what' or substance of particular strategic decisions)?
- How do different views consider the extent to which strategy is deliberately made, emergent or accidental?
- What is the practical relevance of alternative models to the levels and elements of strategic management presented above?

Five models of strategic decision-making are considered below:

- linear (or 'rational') planning
- adaptive/incremental view
- interpretative view
- systems thinking
- 'garbage can' and population ecology views.

Linear (rational) planning

Labelled 'linear' by Chaffee (1983), 'rational' by Peters and Waterman (1982), 'formal' by others and the 'planning mode' by Mintzberg (1973), this approach states that the results of strategic decisions are the objectives and goals of the organization together with the means for achieving them. This process, according to Mintzberg (1978), is 'a highly ordered, nearly integrated one'. Moreover, the process involves a step-by-step planned search for optimal solutions to definable problems. Having analysed the extent to which action needs to be taken in order to fulfil pre-set objectives, strategy therefore concerns the consequent implementation of the means that have been decided upon for doing so.

The stages involved in the linear approach to strategy are shown in Figure 1.1. Such an approach treats strategy as an explicit, conscious process, where purposeful organizations make strategic decisions in advance of more specific business, or operational-level, decisions. Furthermore, a very important underlying assumption of this approach is that decision-makers have at their disposal all the necessary resources for understanding and analysing the problems at hand.

One of the most important criticisms of the rational approach to decision-making was made by Simon (1976), who developed the concept of 'bounded rationality' in recognition of the limited problem-solving capabilities of human beings in organizations. In particular, the quality of decision-makers' problem-solving capacities is often such that they are rarely able to cope with more than a limited range of analyses and information concerning the diagnosis of complex problem situations and potential courses of action relevant to these. Furthermore, the information required to undertake such comprehensive analysis, when it is not overwhelming, is simply often not available in the desired quantity or quality.

Another important consideration is the conflict between decision-makers (or stakeholders) over objectives, goals or values. It is assumed that these are shared, known and also capable of being quantified (e.g. by measuring profit

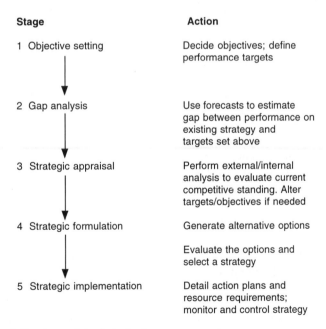

Stage	Action
1 Objective setting	Decide objectives; define performance targets
2 Gap analysis	Use forecasts to estimate gap between performance on existing strategy and targets set above
3 Strategic appraisal	Perform external/internal analysis to evaluate current competitive standing. Alter targets/objectives if needed
4 Strategic formulation	Generate alternative options
	Evaluate the options and select a strategy
5 Strategic implementation	Detail action plans and resource requirements; monitor and control strategy

Figure 1.1 A linear model of strategic management.

maximization through return on investment). It is as well to bear in mind that in business organizations there is a multiplicity of objectives that may be the subject of disagreement between decision-makers. For example, there may well be differences over the nature and scope of the firm's activities, its stance on ethical considerations, or the relative importance of market share or profitability goals. In public sector organizations, the extent of 'commercialization' of what may previously have been viewed as services for the public good may prove to be a bone of contention.

The extent to which strategy can be formulated in advance of implementation is indeed a problematic issue. For example, the employment of specialist planning departments may result in the preparation of strategic plans without the involvement of managers or others who might be affected by their implementation. As well as the loss of the vital expertise or information that these people may have brought to the process of strategic decision-making, such neglect may actually result in a degree of resistance to the planned changes, which might be perceived as not being 'owned' by those affected by them. Moreover, one of the most significant factors that makes the linear approach difficult to employ successfully in practice is the unforeseen problems that arise in the implementation of strategy. Such unanticipated events or crises can wreck even the most carefully thought-out strategic plan and can divert attention away from implementing a particular strategy, or considerably lengthen the time-scale for implementation beyond that expected.

Adaptive/incremental view

Research within this tradition tends to emphasize the extent to which linear/ rational models of strategic decision-making are unrealistic, either as ideals to aspire to or as descriptions of actual behaviour in practice. The focus of this approach is the unintended, emergent or implicit nature of strategy and the likelihood that 'rational' decision-making will be frustrated by conflicts of interest or lack of time, information or analytical capability. Overall, the adaptive perspective of strategic management considers strategy as a matter of evolution, which needs to be understood in terms of the actions that managers (and others) take to cope with an uncertain and complex external environment. In the organizational context, an adaptive approach recognizes the pervasiveness of social and political activities and their influence on strategic decision-making. The adaptive approach is arguably best explained by reference to the concept of incrementalism.

The starting point in this regard is the seminal work of Lindblom and his 'muddling through' thesis (1959). Given a situation of complexity and imperfect information confronting decision-makers, Lindblom argues for the value of an incremental strategy that emphasizes the choice of an option from among a limited range of alternatives and that differs only marginally from the status quo. In addition, Lindblom is keen to demonstrate the importance of the relationships decision-makers have with each other and the emergence of strategy as the unintended by-product of the political bargaining derived from these relationships. He is thus able to move beyond the conscious individual decider of the rational approach to a strategic decision-maker.

The incremental approach may be outlined as follows. Instead of attempting a comprehensive evaluation of possible strategies, decision-makers take as their starting point, not the whole range of hypothetical possibilities, but only the here and now in which they live. They then move on to consider how alterations can be made at the margin. This, then, is an approach that is adapted to the limited problem-solving capacity of human beings and also reduces the demand for information. It also takes into account the considerable costs of and time taken by analysis. Finally, incrementalism adapts to the fact that strategic problems are often fluid and that objectives are adjusted to available means or resources. This is in stark contrast to the rational view where objectives may be determined in advance of acquiring the means appropriate for achieving them.

Support for incrementalism comes from Quinn (1982), although not without some modification to Lindblom's thesis. Quinn developed his concept of logical incrementalism around his empirical study of strategic decision-making in a number of very large diversified firms. Essentially, Quinn's observations and findings led him to suggest that successful strategists purposely guide important actions incrementally toward strategies that embody many of the principles of elegant formal strategies. The approach is not 'anti-planning' as such. Indeed, formal planning is usually an essential building block in the step-by-step process executives use to develop overall strategies. However, for reasons such as the need to keep future options open or to secure individual or organization-wide commitment to new strategies, decision-makers using this approach must rely on more evolutionary practices than those using the rational model.

Logical incrementalism is therefore said to allow strategists to improve the quality of information used in decisions and deal with the practical politics of change, while building the organization's momentum towards the new strategy and providing the motivation to carry it through. In short, for Quinn, logical incrementalism is:

> ... a purposeful, effective, proactive management technique that is capable of improving and integrating both the analytical and behavioural aspects of strategy formulation.
>
> *Quinn, 1982*

In Quinn's incremental approach, unlike Lindblom's, some strategic alternatives can vary greatly from present policies. Here, as issues and possible strategies begin to become clearer 'persuasive data' is collected about the potential options. Only when decision-makers are confident that support exists for a particular course of action is it adopted and communicated. Indeed Quinn goes so far as to suggest that even quite radical changes never emerge 'full grown' and appear more as tactical adjustments. In this situation, advocates are cautious not to alienate allies, to carefully co-opt or neutralize strong opponents, and to seek out 'zones of indifference' where changes can be implemented without activating resistance. At the heart of it all is a process of learning and readjustment that enables the organization to keep itself in line with changes in its environment.

Interpretative view

This view comprises research that reports on and assesses the role of cognition and culture in strategic decision-making which, it is claimed, serves to cast doubt on the utility of decision-making approaches such as those discussed above. Indeed, the primary focus of such an approach is less prescription for making better strategy than an investigation and unravelling of the forces at work in actual decision-making situations.

Johnson (1988), for example, explains the process of strategy as the product of the 'political, cognitive and cultural fabric of the organization'. While Johnson does not deny that incrementalism typifies strategic development in organizations over long periods, he does consider that there may be a better alternative explanation of the actions of organizational participants in dealing with complex problem-solving situations. This explanation is provided in terms of the cognitive maps of managers and how these maps are related to their perceptions of their environment and to possible strategic responses. Central to the interpretation of environmental factors and alternative strategic responses, is the paradigm of the organization. This paradigm has been defined as:

> ... the set of beliefs and assumptions held relatively commonly through the organization, taken for granted and discernible in the stories and explanations of the managers.

Johnson, 1988

The paradigm held by the organization thus embraces assumptions concerning the nature of the macroenvironment and its industry, the capability of the organization, and the style of its managers or leaders and so on. The paradigm of the organization serves to filter signals about the various factors cited above and can be considered to be both a device for interpretation and for influencing actions.

Finally, the nature of the paradigm is likely to be more easily perceived by outsiders looking into an organization than by those who are inside it, for whom it may remain rather opaque. It is important to note that the paradigm is one, albeit integrating, component of the cultural web of organizations and that this as a whole can be a powerful stimulus or barrier to strategic change. Figure 1.2 and Table 1.1 provide a model of strategic management according to this interpretative view, and examples of different types of paradigm and cultural web. Part Three provides a more detailed discussion of incremental and interpretative views of strategy and of the role of aspects of culture in enhancing or constraining organizational learning and flexibility.

Systems thinking

The systems approach to strategic management addresses two main issues. The first of these is the notion that organizations are constrained by forces in their external environment, but also influence that environment. The other is how such interaction between a firm and the world outside occurs. This is based on

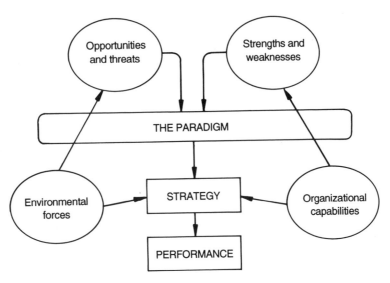

Figure 1.2   Strategy development – a cultural perspective. (Source: Johnson, 1992)

the recognition that organizations represent collections of different activities that require integration and co-ordination for effective performance to be realized.

Considering organizations, industries and the broader environment to be elements of a system, it is argued, can enable an understanding of how inputs and outputs from the various parts of the system are generated and transferred within it. It may also assist in clarifying how these system components are inter-related and interdependent.

The performance of individual organizations may be understood in terms of how they are affected by the behaviour of competitors, suppliers, customers and so on within an industry. This behaviour may be reflected in the strategic decisions that competitors make, the purchasing preferences of consumers or in the quality of components provided by suppliers, for example. More broadly, organizations may be constrained by factors in the general environment including government legislation or prevailing or prospective economic conditions.

As mentioned above, this is not a one-way street, so organizations, either individually or collectively, seek to influence the course of events in this wider environment, through political lobbying or marketing campaigns to stimulate demand, for example. Finally, the impact of environmental factors and the ability of an organization to influence them is likely to vary according to its size, nature and particular situation.

How a firm responds to or shapes events within the system is likely to depend on its ability to harness the different activities and functions within it. Considering organizations as a collection of subsystems of activity that require integration for overall effectiveness, emphasizes the manner in which activities are structured. Other important aspects of the management of these various activities relate to the pattern of communication and the systems of control within organizations.

Table 1.1   How managers define the cultural web – three cases*

A menswear clothing retailer	A consultancy partnership	A regional newspaper
Paradigm	*Paradigm*	*Paradigm*
We sell to 'the working lad's market' Retailing skills (as they define them) centrally important Retailing is about buying: 'we sell what we buy' Volume is vital Staff experience and loyalty important Low cost operations (eg distribution channels) important A 'big man' view of management (Note what is not here: retailing is not about shop ambience, service, etc)	We are the biggest, the best, certainly the safest Client satisfaction at all costs Any job is worth doing and we can do it Professionalism is important Avoid risks (The implication is that this consultancy aims to provide a very wide range of services, but is unlikely to provide services which are contentious or risky)	We are in the newspaper business Our paid-for daily will always be there Readers will pay for news Advertisers need newspapers
Power	*Power*	*Power*
The chairman regarded as all-powerful, but nicely Divisions of power significant: the major menswear business versus ('peripheral') businesses: head office operations versus field retail operations Insiders with experience traditionally powerful: outsiders without company experience not powerful and do not last long	Diffuse and unclear power base in a partnership structure However an external power base clearly important in the parent audit firm	The parent company – a newspaper group The autocratic chief executive Departmental rivalry between production, commercial and editorial departments
Organization	*Organization*	*Organization*
Highly compartmentalized operations with vertical reporting relationships (e.g. buying distinct from store operations) Every department with a director leading to a heavy superstructure Top down decision making with board 'fingers in every pie' Paternalistic	The regional partnership structure of the organization giving a flat if complex matrix Decision-making through a networking system, loose and flexible but based on 'who you know'	Vertical, hierarchical system with little lateral communication and much vertical referral Autocratic management style

Photocopy and Place
in Culture folder.

Control Systems

Margin control
Long established 'proven'
 rigid and complex systems
Paper-based control systems

Rituals and Routines

Long established merchan-
 dise sourcing in the Far
 East
Induction into the company
 way of doing things
 through attrition and
 training: 'outsiders serve
 an apprenticeship until
 they conform'
Emphasis on pragmatic rather
 than analytical decisions
Lack of questioning or
 forcing: 'you can challenge
 provided I feel comfortable'
Heavy emphasis on grading
 systems
Promotions only within
 functions

Stories

Big buying deals of the past
Paternalistic leaders (usually
 chairmen) of the past
More recent 'villainous'
 leaders who helped cause
 problems
'The Mafia' who excluded
 outsiders and achieved
 their exit

Symbols

The separate executive
 directors' corridor
Use of initials to designate
 senior executives and 'Sir'
 for the chairman
The dining room for directors
 and selected senior
 executives, but against
 what criteria?
Named and numbered car
 parking spaces rigidly
 adhered to

Control Systems

Emphasis on time control
 and utilization of
 consultants

Rituals and Routines

Writing and rewriting of
 reports, 'the product of
 the firm'
Partners signatures on
 anything that goes to
 clients
Gentlemanly behaviour,
 particularly with clients
 and partners

Stories

Big fee assignments
Big disasters and failures
Stories of the dominance
 of the audit practice
Mavericks who would not
 follow the systems

Symbols

The partnership structure
 itself
The symbols of
 partnership: the tea
 service, the office size,
 partners' secretaries,
 partners' dining rooms
One regional partnership
 that had always refused
 to integrate with other
 partnerships

Control Systems

Emphasis on targeting
 and budgeting to
 achieve a low cost
 operation

Rituals and Routines

'Slaves to time' to meet
 deadlines for
 publication
'Product' developed in
 hours and minutes, not
 days and months
Long working hours
 common
Ritualized executive
 meetings at senior level

Stories

Macho personalities and
 behaviour
Scoops and coverage of
 major events
Stories of the past
Major errors in print
The defeat of the unions

Symbols

Symbols of hierarchy: the
 MD's Jaguar, portable
 phones, car parking
 spaces, etc
The printing press
Technical production
 jargon
The street vendors

---

* Source: Johnson (1992).

The different activities relate to functions such as marketing, finance and production, and decisions within one function will often have implications for the others. Checkland (1981) suggests that the key issue here is the nature of the 'emergent properties' that result from the interaction of the different activities or functions.

The important thing to note is how these emergent properties relate to organizational performance. Where there is divergence in the view that different functional areas or departments take of their own role in an organization, these emergent properties may be harmful rather than beneficial, and may reflect a lack of integration and co-ordination of activities or values.

'Garbage can' and population ecology

Both of these perspectives on strategic decision-making impose limits on the notion of rational choice. Indeed, the garbage can model suggests that strategic decision-making is as much a matter of luck and timing as of rational planning. This view is most closely associated with the work of Cohen, March and Olsen (1972). They considered organizations and the situations in which strategic decisions arise as 'organized anarchies'. This term seeks to capture the ambiguity and instability of real-life decision-making situations that classical rational models underplay. Organized anarchies are characterized by 'fuzziness' (Eisenhardt and Zbaracki, 1992) and the objectives of an organization may thus be quite unclear or disputed. Furthermore, the underlying logic of decisions that are made may not be well understood. Finally, the amount of energy and time that participants are able to apply to particular problems tends to vary.

According to Cohen, March and Olsen, decision-making occurs with the random confluence of several relatively independent streams within an organization:

- problems that require attention
- answers that are looking for a problem to address
- participants who are able to devote time and energy to a particular problem
- choice opportunities, i.e. where a decision is expected to be made.

Again, the nature of decision-making in this approach is much more accidental than with the rational, linear view described above.

Population ecology is based on the natural selection model of biological ecology, having as its main focus aggregate populations of organizations rather than decision-making in individual organizations. The basis of population ecology is the view that environmental resources are distributed unequally between niches in the environment. Essentially, the survival, success and failure of organizations (as with biological organisms) depends on whether they find themselves in a resource niche that they can use or one that they cannot use (Aldrich, 1979).

As Aldrich notes, the population ecology model explains organizational change by reference to the nature and distribution of resources in an organization's environment. It is the environment, therefore, that is the central force in organizational change rather than internal leadership or participation in decision-making. The zone of discretion that strategic decision-makers have in this approach, is thus rather limited:

Environmental selection processes set the limits within which rational selection among alternatives takes place. Prior limits and constraints on available options leave little room for manoeuvring by most organizations ... strategic choice may be a luxury open only to the largest and most powerful organizations.

Aldrich, 1979, p. 160

Such limits and constraints exist in the form of ambiguity in the environment or barriers to entry into an industry, for example, which make the analysis and implementation of rationally devised strategies problematic.

Entrepreneurial strategy-making

It is important not to neglect the view of strategic management that emphasizes the role of entrepreneurial activity. This often focuses on the dynamic nature of bold, visionary, strategic leaders. In what Mintzberg (1973) calls the 'entrepreneurial mode' there is little role for formal analysis; organizational direction and success are much more to do with the leadership and risk-taking qualities of the firm's founder or chief executive/managing director. This heroic view of the role of strategic leader fits the popular image of entrepreneurs and corporate leaders such as Richard Branson at the Virgin Group, Lord Hanson of the Hanson Trust, or Rupert Murdoch of News International. However, this perspective may be countered by a concept of collective leadership and entrepreneurship, which recognizes the contribution of others to the development of strategy and a broader sense of organization-wide decision-making, as reflected in some of the approaches discussed above.

1.4 What is flexible strategic management?

The previous section described a variety of approaches to the management of strategic decisions. This section presents an emerging perspective on the formulation and implementation of strategy. Such an approach may be termed flexible strategic management and emphasizes the concept of strategic flexibility. A sample of views concerning the nature and aspects of strategic flexibility is given below. In addition to this overview of flexibility, various types of strategic flexibility are considered. Finally, a note of caution is offered as to the potential contribution of a flexibility-driven approach to strategic management.

The nature of strategic flexibility

Starkey, Wright and Thompson (1991) noted that:

Flexibility is at the heart of strategic decision-making.

p. 166

Moreover, according to Harrigan (1985):

> ... the essence of strategy is in the balance of focused, concerted commitments on the one hand and resource flexibility on the other.
>
> *(p. xiii)*

However, two questions need to be answered:

1. What is meant by flexibility?
2. How does the concept of flexibility contribute to furthering our understanding of strategic management or to the improvement of strategic decision-making in practice?

The first point to be made is that 'flexibility' and 'strategic flexibility' may not be the easiest of concepts for the uninitiated to understand fully because, as Evans (1991) notes:

> ... 'flexibility' is often used to mean different things in different contexts and, in the academic world is employed in a variety of ways, depending on the discipline in question.

Evans suggests that an initial appreciation of the concept of strategic flexibility may be gained by considering it alongside other concepts bearing a 'family resemblance' . Thus, for example, the concept of strategic flexibility may be explained in comparison with the following related concepts:

- adaptability
- corrigibility
- hedging
- reversibility
- learning
- renewal

Adaptability is a term often employed to mean much the same as flexibility. However, it should be noted that:

> ... adaptability implies a singular and permanent adjustment to a new transformed environment, whereas flexibility enables successive, but temporary approximations to this state of affairs.
>
> *Evans, 1991, p. 72*

Flexibility is thus a concept suited to dynamic environments where continual change is unlikely to make once-and-for-all adjustments an appropriate form of managing change. In fact, 'readaptation' , though not employed as commonly as 'adaptability', bears a closer resemblance to the concept of flexibility. Readaptation concerns the process by which 'the organization and the environment interact and evolve toward more mutually acceptable exchanges' (Lawrence and Dyer, 1981, quoted in Evans, 1991). This relates strongly to a notion of flexibility whereby the organization is capable of inflicting as well as responding to unanticipated changes.

'Corrigibility' and 'reversibility' refer to flexibility in the sense that errors associated with strategic decisions may be first detected and then remedied or ultimately completely undone to allow some new course of action to be pursued. Essentially, these concepts may be associated with flexibility in its more defensive or responsive meaning, as opposed to the more aggressive or anticipatory sense of the term. 'Hedging' (and also the holding of organizational 'slack', which is very similar) also relates to flexibility in the sense of protecting or insuring against error or risk. In everyday conversation, we speak of 'hedging our bets' and of 'not putting all our eggs in one basket' so as to attempt to minimize exposure to potential losses in a venture. 'Organizational slack' is often associated with the work of Cyert and March (1963) and refers to the extent to which organizational resources are not utilized to full capacity or efficiency (sometimes referred to as x-inefficiency). Such slack provides organizations with the capability to respond to suddenly changing conditions since they will not then always be operating at full stretch.

Two of the most significant emerging themes within strategic management in recent years have been organizational learning and organizational renewal. These exhibit a close resemblance to the concept of flexibility, as employed here.

Huff, Huff and Thomas (1992) note that the term 'strategic renewal' has begun to replace 'strategic change'. This is significant and more than just a matter of semantics. The growing concern with strategic renewal emphasizes the view that strategic development is evolutionary. Indeed, the redirection of strategy emerges from the present situation and is achieved over a period of time. Moreover:

> ... the need for renewal is never-ending. The viable organization must have the capacity to frequently improve its alignment with external and internal demands ... Renewal efforts are characterized as virtually continuous, but pulsing in ways that depart more and less dramatically from the status quo over time.
>
> *Huff, Huff and Thomas, 1992, p. 55*

Essentially, then, it is the dynamic character of strategic renewal that is of most interest to understanding flexibility. However, as well as reiterating that to be flexible implies some capability to adjust continually to, or shape, new circumstances, the issue of the scale of change is important. Thus, organizations that find themselves in crisis situations may well need to undergo fundamental and far-reaching strategic and operational change. For example, this may involve severe cutbacks in labour or a reduction in the scope of organizational activities. In these ways renewal efforts may be dramatic and reflective of a lack of flexibility or inertia on the part of the organization in question. This is especially pertinent if one considers flexibility in the sense of being able to make changes in course without incurring sizeable costs. The greater the renewal effort that is required, the more likely it is to prove to be demanding of time, money, commitment, expertise and so on.

Organizational learning has been seen as a process which, if properly managed, facilitates the flexibility of an organization (Senge, 1991). Organizational learning may be strategic or operational. Thus it may concern the development of cross-functional knowledge, skills and abilities that will be required for the future. It may also refer to the upgrading of practices with regard to the performance of specific tasks in a more immediate sense.

An important aspect of this is the existence and development of organizational 'routines' (Nelson and Winter, 1982). Organizational routines are the rules of thumb employed within organizations in the performance of everyday activities. Such routines become ingrained and condition the ability of individuals and organizations as a whole to perceive the need for, and to implement, new ways of performing such activities. This notion of routines is therefore central to an understanding of the possible constraints on, and development of, 'learning organizations'.

The essence of this section so far has been to present strategic flexibility as a capability that may permit some freedom of manoeuvre for organizations such that they may limit the extent to which they are hostages to fortune. The matrix in Figure 1.3 illustrates the point in terms of potential positions that may be associated with varying degrees of environmental uncertainty and organizational strategic flexibility. This framework provides a basis for considering the contribution of a flexible approach to strategic management.

The matrix is intended to be for illustrative purposes and so the variables that comprise the axes should be considered in a qualitative rather than quantitative way. The matrix is divided into four cells. These indicate the implications of different states of environmental uncertainty and organizational flexibility needed for an organization to be in control of its own destiny. This refers to the ability of an organization to shape its environment (e.g. through the exercise of market power or attempts to mould consumer or political opinion). Securing organizational control over its own destiny also relates to the ability to modify courses of action that prove to be simply erroneous or in need of some remedy, or when new information comes to light or circumstances change (Genus, 1992; 1993).

In cell 1, the flexibility of an organization relative to that of others in the same market or field of activity is high. This is against a background of low uncertainty in the external environment, i.e. important trends are relatively predictable and their relationship to each other is easily understood. Here, the potential exists for an organization to influence its market, it may enjoy a degree of dominance within a stable industry which permits a wide range of discretion. Furthermore, the low level of uncertainty in the external environment means that actions that

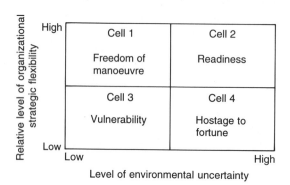

Figure 1.3   Understanding the need for strategic flexibility.

are taken, whether intentional or otherwise, will not be prone to sudden shocks which might render them suddenly inappropriate or obsolete. Thus cell 1 reflects the freedom of manoeuvre that a firm might enjoy. The danger, however, is that an organization currently able to act freely and relatively unhindered by external factors may find, eventually, that conditions in the external environment become increasingly complex and changeable. In addition to this increased uncertainty, the level of internal flexibility can deteriorate, such as when organizations become excessively attached to a previously successful formula.

If, against the background of increasing uncertainty, a high level of relative strategic flexibility can be maintained, a state of 'readiness' may allow for necessary changes of course. This may be related to the development of an enhanced capability to sense external change or to avoid internal commitments which comprise the future redeployment of resources. Cell 2, therefore, indicates that flexibility enables organizations to cope with increasing uncertainty. This does not necessarily mean that they will be successful; there are no guarantees. What it does signify is that a flexible organization may be able to keep pace with environmental change, sometimes acting proactively, sometimes reacting to external change that may not be at all easy to predict or analyse. Small-scale experimentation may be a useful source of trial and error learning here, enabling possible sources of difficulty in the real world to be identified without incurring the costs of full-scale implementation. So, arguably, flexible organizations can gain some measure of control over their destiny.

Cell 3 presents a rather different situation. Here, the relative level of organizational flexibility is low but so too is the present level of environmental uncertainty. An organization faced with this set of conditions may find itself vulnerable to future change. Such an organization might in the past have dominated its industry sector: it may have enjoyed a high market share and the power that may have accompanied this, for example. However, firms such as IBM have found that the factors that have contributed to success hitherto are not the ones that will serve them well in the face of external change. (In IBM's case this relates to an over-reliance on the mainframe aspects of its business and a neglect of the emerging personal computer segment.)

Cell 4 characterizes a very unwelcome situation. Here there is a combination of low organizational flexibility and highly uncertain environmental conditions. This would put an organization at the mercy of external circumstances. Where past decisions serve to restrict freedom of manoeuvre both internally and externally, any success that is enjoyed will be granted by good fortune rather than good management. Organizational performance therefore owes most to the course of environmental trends and events, an undesirable situation since it is essentially a hostage to fortune.

Aspects of strategic flexibility

Starkey, Wright and Thompson (1991) distinguish between two aspects of flexibility, a distinction having some significance for the conduct of strategy in organizations:

1. flexibility within firms
2. flexibility of relations between firms.

These aspects of flexibility reflect differing research approaches that need to be understood in order to improve one's insight into the appropriateness of various routes to achieving the flexibility required in dynamic environments. Hence the issue of flexibility within firms may be associated with a contingency view of the design of organizations. Such an approach emphasizes the relationship between the nature of environments and the manner in which organizations are designed (i.e. how roles, responsibilities and co-ordination/control systems are related within organizations).

Starkey, Wright and Thompson (1991) note two important contextual factors relevant to the issue of strategic flexibility within firms although these will also be relevant to the issue of strategic flexibility in relationships between firms:

1. the demand (customer) context
2. the supply (production) context.

On the demand side, flexibility within the firm may be associated with an ability to alter current strategies when existing markets being served become unattractive. This might mean changing the game plan at the business level or repositioning within declining markets to emphasize cost rather than brand superiority, for example. Or, it might refer to the ability to innovate and/or enter new markets when an existing one appears exhausted and incapable of revitalization. In terms of the supply context, new forms of technology may confer benefits associated with production cost savings or the facilitation of changes in output levels or materials usage.

The strategic issue at stake refers to what has been termed the transition to post-Fordism. The prevalence of bulk markets served by mass production of undifferentiated products (like the Model T Ford car which one could have in any colour as long as it was black) is seen by many to have significantly weakened over the past two decades or so. Similarly, the bureaucratic organizational forms emphasizing control and cost efficiency appear inappropriate to today's world where greater significance is being placed by consumers on non-price factors such as innovativeness, product quality or delivery time. The task of managing the transition between Fordist and post-Fordist paradigms is one which may be viewed as likely to make demands on the flexibility of organizations.

The perspective of flexibility pertaining to relationships between firms places greater emphasis on the market or contractual relationships inherent in the transactions that firms make with each other. In terms of its relevance to the internal flexibility of organizations, this approach seeks to address the apparent trend towards vertical disintegration, outsourcing and networking. Moreover, such a view of flexibility is concerned with noting the extent to which individual organizations are restructuring, divesting or demerging, so as to return to a core set of limited activities, managed in a less hierarchical, bureaucratic fashion than previously.

Supporters of this view would claim that such developments represent attempts by organizations to combat the rigidities or inflexibilities of the large, vertically integrated firm characterized by the Fordist mode of organization. Hence, the retreat to core activities (or to following Peters and Waterman's (1982) 'sticking to the knitting' principle) ought to involve less administrative burden for the individual organization. Furthermore, proponents of this approach would suggest that although organizational-level activities are restricted by such vertical disintegration, 'flexible specialization' (Piore and Sabel, 1984) may be enjoyed at the industry or multifirm level. Thus firms that are individually very specialized in terms of their activities and expertise combine together to create a network that is flexible overall. The flexibility of such groupings is based on the transactions and exchanges of information, materials, expertise and personal contacts that take place between organizations. This makes the relationship between organizations quite an important factor to consider in terms of the strategy and flexibility of organizations at the industry or multifirm level as well as at the individual level of analysis.

Slack and Correa (1992) and Camagni (in Bessant, 1991) identify different levels of flexibility that help to clarify the relevance of the concept to the strategic decisions that occur within organizations. Slack and Correa, for example, define what they see as representing three useful levels of analysis as far as flexibility within the firm is concerned.

1. At the level of the firm, flexibility is the ability of the whole organization to change its strategic position while keeping its functional strategies coherent.
2. At the functional level, flexibility issues relate to the ability of the operations function (for example) to change the nature, volume or timing of its outputs.
3. At the level of individual resources, flexibility issues might, for example, relate to the variety of tasks that individual people, machines or control systems can perform and the time, cost or difficulty of swapping between tasks.

Slack and Correa are keen to note the importance of the relationship between these various levels of flexibility. In particular, they stress the relevance of flexibility at the level of individual resources to functional and strategic flexibility. Slack and Correa also identify the need to think about flexibility more broadly than many practitioners and researchers (certainly within the operations management literature) do. Hence, they consider that there has been an over-emphasis on the flexibility of the 'structural' resources of organizations, i.e. the flexibility of technology or of the human resources of the organizations.

On the other hand, they consider that there has been a neglect of 'infrastructural' flexibility related to the systems, procedures and practices that bind parts of organizations together, often dictating what activities the organization or its functions can perform and how.

Camagni (Bessant, 1991) studied cases of flexible manufacturing in Italy, noting three different levels or 'stages' of flexibility that had implications for manufacturers' choices of production technology. Such choices can be viewed in terms of the extent to which they are of a strategic or more tactical nature. For instance, Camagni's 'substitution' stage involves the substitution of robots and machines for human beings within an existing system of production. The second stage Camagni terms 'production integration'. Here, different machines are integrated into flexible systems such as Flexible Manufacturing Systems, which may involve the redesign of plan layout or product components. Thirdly, the 'strategic integration' stage would see the redefinition of the nature of the product and its market image, according to the perception of opportunities offered to the manufacturer by the new technologies in question. This stage of strategic integration would most likely require substantial change on the part of the organization as a whole.

Thus cases of the introduction of new manufacturing technologies can help to demonstrate the various implications of such decisions (or the conduct of strategy in organizations). They also exemplify the significance of developing an awareness of different levels of strategy and flexibility, including the extent to which strategic and operational issues overlap and therefore need to be addressed in an integrated way.

Dimensions of strategic flexibility

Bearing in mind what has been said above about the nature of strategic flexibility, a number of different dimensions of flexibility might be the target of concern for strategic decision-makers. Thus it is possible to distinguish between what have been called the **temporal** and **intentional** dimensions of strategic flexibility. The temporal dimension concerns decisions that might be aimed at conferring flexibility through either the anticipation of possible future events or reaction to events that have occurred. More specifically, the temporal dimension can be thought of as comprising two modes. The **ex-ante** mode refers to preparations that might be made in advance of some future 'triggering episode' (such as suddenly intensifying competition, or changes in industry standard, where high technology is concerned). The **ex-post** mode refers to 'after the fact' adjustments made once such triggering episodes have occurred.

As for the intentional dimension, it is possible to distinguish between **offensive** and **defensive** modes of strategic flexibility. An offensive orientation to the achievement of strategic flexibility might be represented by attempts to outwit (or 'outpace') competitors through the facilitation of faster product or process innovation. On the other hand, the defensive mode would refer to measures to protect or to insure against risk or unforeseen circumstances or to correct serious errors once they have been committed. (Researchers such as Collingridge, (1992), Morone and Woodhouse (1986) and Genus (1992, 1993) have written about a variety of defensive methods for enhancing flexibility where the introduction of novel technology is concerned, including trial-by-error forms of implementing technology as a way of learning about the potential risks that might be involved in its introduction.)

One may distinguish between range flexibility and response flexibility. Slack (1983) considers these two dimensions of flexibility in terms of their application to various types of strategic and more operational activities that manufacturing organizations have to consider. Briefly, such activities might refer to a number of areas where flexibility may be critical to success, or at least to the avoidance of failure. These might be defined as follows:

- new product flexibility – the ability to innovate new products
- mix flexibility – the ability to produce a wide variety of products in a given period of time
- volume flexibility – the ability to change the level of aggregate output from the production system
- delivery flexibility – the ability to change, and meet changed, delivery dates.

Relevant to the above, range flexibility refers to the extent to which the organization and its production system can produce different types of product at various levels of output while satisfying different demands on delivery. Response flexibility describes the degree of comfort that is associated with making the change-over between different products, volumes of output and so on, within a particular range of activities. It is important to recognize that there are potential costs to organizations making such change-overs, which may represent time delays, commitment of organizational resources or financial outlay.

Response flexibility is primarily a short-term phenomenon since it refers to improvements that might be made within the current range of organizational offerings. Range flexibility tends to be a more long-term consideration since investments to achieve this are likely to be of a more fundamental nature. Such investments may involve decisions concerning capital equipment, labour and production organization, which may have an organization-wide impact. It should be borne in mind that apparently short-term decisions – concerning investments to improve change-over between different output levels, for instance – intended to enhance response flexibility, may have longer-term implications. Thus decisions to invest in new technology for facilitating change-over now, will most likely be made with the current range of products, product mix, output levels or delivery dates in mind. Where such decisions involve substantial commitments it may be that current response flexibility is being pursued at the expense of possible range flexibility.

Limits to the notion of strategic flexibility

Although there is clearly a contribution to be made to understanding the nature of strategic issues by invoking the concept of flexibility, this is not an unproblematic matter. It has already been noted that the literature on flexibility generally over-emphasizes flexibility at the level of individual resources within organizations, such as labour or manufacturing technology. Moreover, this literature has tended to focus on 'structural' rather than 'infrastructural' flexibility, thus neglecting the less visible aspects of organizations which impact on the performance and evolution of activities. Overall, the literature on flexibility needs to be treated with caution, since despite the relevance of the concept to strategic management, much of it has not sought to relate strategic flexibility within or between firms to the flexibility of individual resources or functions, which is often the main preoccupation of the studies conducted.

It is necessary to consider the lack of clarity that sometimes accompanies the use of the concept of flexibility. It is hoped that the above has provided sufficient insight into the various ways in which 'flexibility' may be understood and applied to strategic management. Nevertheless, it is appropriate to bear in mind the comment of Hill and Chambers (1991) that although flexibility is a concept with wide appeal, it is not always applied with a 'uniformity of interpretation', nor is it easily measured. Therefore, it is vital to be clear about what types of dimensions of strategic flexibility are most appropriate to the particular situation at hand, since this consideration is likely to have a bearing on the appropriateness of particular manoeuvres for achieving and sustaining such flexibility. Thus, rather than pursue flexibility as if it were some sort of panacea for all the various ills of an organization, it is necessary to consider most carefully the level or type of flexibility that organizations might require along the various dimensions discussed above (Hill and Chambers, 1991).

Starkey, Wright and Thompson (1991) address what they call the 'partial nature' of proponents of strategic flexibility. In particular, they note an emerging trend of research emphasizing market relations between firms that have become more vertically disintegrated, where in practice the reality is partly one of continuing vertical integration and merger activity. Starkey, Wright and Thompson (1991) also address the possible over-simplification of a 'back to basics' approach that stresses the notion of businesses retrenching to their core activities. This action may restrict strategic flexibility and the attainment of competitive advantage. Certainly, one could say that retreating to normally defined core activities might be tantamount to an organization putting all its eggs in one basket and therefore losing out on some of the perceived benefits of a broader portfolio approach to managing its activities. (This assumes that firms return to their original core activities following divestment or demerger since they may choose to emphasize certain segments or activities into which they had diversified.)

Another key concern is that the much-vaunted transition towards post-Fordist organizational forms and practices is illusory and that measures to improve labour flexibility, for example, in support of strategy, are more to do with increasing productivity and management control than employee commitment and autonomy. Hence, even where organizational change appears to be emphasizing innovativeness, learning and the strategic value of human resources, this may reflect a 'neo-Fordist' continuation of existing control relationships more than the emergence of a new paradigm. There is greater discussion of this issue in Part Three.

1.5 Summary

This chapter has provided an introduction to the field of strategic management and to the concept of strategic flexibility. Strategic decision-making may be seen as an activity having organization-wide significance, often taking place against the backdrop of great external uncertainty. Strategy is a concept that refers to the long-term direction and performance of organizations. The chapter has outlined a number of approaches to the process of strategic management, noting that it tends not to occur in practice in the deliberate, formalized manner of the classical, linear view. Alternative perspectives emphasize the role of political activity, interpretative mechanisms and sheer chance in the development of strategy. Also relevant to this discussion has been the extent to which changing external conditions may mediate the zone of discretion that strategic decision-makers enjoy. In particular, uncertainty makes the selection and implementation of strategy potentially hazardous and flexibility desirable.

This first chapter has introduced the notion of flexibility in relation to strategic decision-making. The 'family' of flexibility-related concepts has also been presented in a bid to clarify the usage of the term in this book. More specifically, flexibility was described in terms of an ongoing ability to respond to and to shape changing circumstances, a matter closely connected to the subject of organizational learning and renewal. The routines that exist within firms have been identified as influential on such learning, renewal and the development of flexibility. A framework has been provided to illustrate the potential contribution of strategic flexibility to the enhancement of the zone of discretion that organizations have. A number of aspects, levels and dimensions of flexibility have been identified and have been discussed in terms of intra-firm and inter-firm activities. The connection between such activities and the debate concerning 'post-Fordist' organizations has been made. Finally, it has been recognized that flexibility should not be treated as a panacea and that certain reservations may need to be acknowledged about this notion.

Study questions

1. Identify the relevance of different approaches to strategic decision-making to explaining strategic development in an organization with which you are familiar.
2. What is the significance of concepts of flexibility to strategic decision-making?
3. What is meant by flexible strategic management?
4. What factors may be considered to evaluate the degree to which an organization enjoys strategic flexibility?

Key readings

The Strategy Process: Concepts, Contexts and Cases (Mintzberg and Quinn, 1991) contains a wealth of articles on the concept of strategy, including Mintzberg's 'Five Ps for Strategy'.

Strategic Change and the Management Process (Johnson, 1987) similarly gives an overview of different approaches to strategic management while exploring the relevance of an interpretative perspective to the change at Foster Menswear.

Harrigan (1985) considers and defines 'strategic flexibility' in her book of the same name, and Bessant (1991) helps to pull together some of the meanings of flexibility in *Managing Advanced Manufacturing Technology*. A similar function regarding the 'family' of flexibility concepts is performed by Evans (1991) in his article 'Strategic flexibility for high technology manoeuvres' in the *Journal of Management Studies*.

Ansoff's *Corporate Strategy* (1965) is an early seminal strategy text.

References

Aldrich, H. E. (1979) *Organizations and Environments*, Prentice-Hall, Englewood Cliffs, NJ.

Ansoff, H. I. (1965) *Corporate Strategy*, Penguin, Harmondsworth.

Bessant, J. (1991) *Managing Advanced Manufacturing Technology*, NCC Blackwell, Oxford.

Cadbury, A. (1992) *Report on the Financial Aspects of Corporate Governance*, Gee, London.

Chaffee, E. E. (1983) Three models of strategy. *Academy of Management Review*, **10**(1), 89–98.

Chandler, A. D. (1962) *Strategy and Structure*, MIT Press, Cambridge, MA.

Checkland, P. (1981) *Systems Thinking, Systems Practice*, Wiley, London.

Cohen, M. D., March, J. G. and Olsen, J. P. (1972) A garbage can model of organizational choice. *Administrative Science Quarterly*, **17**, 1–25.

Collingridge, D. (1992) *The Management of Scale*, Routledge, London.

Cyert, R. M. and March, J. G. (1963) *A Behavioural Theory of the Firm*, Prentice-Hall, Englewood Cliffs, NJ.

Eisenhardt, K. and Zbaracki, M. J. (1992) Strategic decision-making. *Strategic Management Journal*, **13**, 17–37.

Evans, J. S. (1991) Strategic flexibility for high technology manoeuvres. *Journal of Management Studies*, **28**(1), 69–90.

Genus, A. (1992) The social control of large-scale technological projects: inflexibility, non-incrementality and performance in British North Sea oil. *Technology Analysis and Strategic Management*, **4**(2), 133–48.

Genus, A. (1993) Technological learning and the political shaping of technology: the management of R, D&D of wind and wave power in the UK. *Business Strategy and the Environment*, **2**(1), 26–36.

Harrigan, K. (1985) *Strategic Flexibility*, Lexington, Lexington, MA.

Hill, T. and Chambers, S. (1991) Flexibility – a manufacturing conundrum. *International Journal of Operations and Production Management*, **11**(2), 5–13.

Huff, A. S., Huff, J. O. and Thomas, H. (1992) Strategic renewal and the interaction of stress and inertia. *Strategic Management Journal*, **13**, 55–75.

Johnson, G. (1987) *Strategic Change and the Management Process*, Blackwell, Oxford.

Johnson, G. (1988) Rethinking incrementalism. *Strategic Management Journal*, **9**, 75–91.

Johnson, G. (1992) Managing strategic change, strategy culture and action. *Long Range Planning*, **25**(1), 28–36.

Lindblom, C. E. (1959) The science of muddling through. *Public Administration Review*, **19**, Spring, 79–98.

Mintzberg, H. (1973) Strategy making in three modes. *California Management Review*, Winter, 44–53.

Mintzberg, H. (1978) Patterns in strategy formation. *Management Science*, **24**(9), 934–48.

Mintzberg, H. (1991) Five Ps for Strategy, in *The Strategy Process*. (eds H. Mintzberg and J. B. Quinn), Prentice-Hall, NJ, pp. 12–19.

Mintzberg, H. and Quinn, J. B. (1991) *The Strategy Process: Concepts, Contexts and Cases*, Prentice-Hall, Englewood Cliffs, NJ.

Morone, J. G. and Woodhouse, E. J. (1986) *Averting Catastrophe – Strategies for Regulating Risky Technologies*, University of California Press, Berkeley and Los Angeles, CA.

Nelson, R. R. and Winter, S. G. (1982) *An Evolutionary Theory of Economic Change*, Belknap, Cambridge, MA.

Peters, T. J. and Waterman, R. H. (1982) *In Search of Excellence*, Harper and Row, London.

Piore, M. and Sabel, C. (1984) *The Second Industrial Divide*, Basic Books, New York.

Quinn, J. B. (1980) *Strategies for Change – Logical Incrementalism*, Irwin, IL.

Quinn, J. B. (1982) Managing strategies incrementally. *Omega*, **10**(6), 613–27.

Senge, P. (1991) *The Fifth Discipline: The Art and Practice of the Learning Organization*, Doubleday, London.

Simon, H. (1976) *Administrative Behaviour*, 3rd edn, Free Press, New York.

Slack, N. (1983) Flexibility as a manufacturing objective. *International Journal of Production Management*, **3**(3), 4–13.

Slack, N. and Correa, H. (1992) The flexibilities of push and pull. *International Journal of Operations and Production Management*, **12**(4), 82–92.

Starkey, K., Wright, M. and Thompson, S. (1991) Flexibility, hierarchy, markets. *British Journal of Management*, **2**(3), 165–76.

PART TWO

WHY FLEXIBLE STRATEGIC MANAGEMENT?

UNCERTAINTY IN THE MACRO-ENVIRONMENT

2

Learning objectives

Studying this chapter should:

- develop your awareness of the potential impact of uncertainty in the macro-environment on the management of strategy within organizations
- facilitate an understanding of approaches and techniques seeking to analyse or forecast trends in the macro-environment
- enable you to consider possible limitations to the employment of such techniques within a changing macro-environmental context
- enable you to discuss more flexible approaches to analysing and managing the macro-environment.

2.1 Introduction

This chapter, together with the others in this part, addresses the question of **why** a flexible approach to strategic management is advanced. All three chapters focus on the potential problems that might impact on organizational survival and well-being, which stem from overly mechanistic approaches to analysing or managing the various factors relevant to strategic decision-making. In particular, this chapter considers uncertainty within the macro-environmental context, in which all organizations operate.

Section 2.2. traces developments in the wider world over recent decades that have helped to shape the fortunes of whole industry sectors and, in part, made organizational flexibility at the strategic level all the more desirable. It may be seen that some of these developments are relevant to international competition between businesses, for example, while others may more narrowly affect domestic competition between firms or the activities of public sector/not-for-profit organizations. The types of factors in question at this macro-environmental level relate to uncertainties in the political or regulatory arena, trends in economic performance and economic management, ethical, demographic and socio-cultural change and the nature of technological development.

Section 2.3 presents a number of widely-taught tools and techniques for analysing current and future trends in the macro-environment. Such analytical devices are considered for their contribution to the task of comprehending or disentangling the myriad trends and signals at work in the wider environment.

The main focus is on the possible limitations to applying techniques that are essentially of more relevance to unchanging conditions than to the difficulties of strategic decision-making in an uncertain world. Central issues refer to the problematic nature of forecasting future trends and to potential difficulties in evaluating between many seemingly significant factors in a way that is manageable for strategy-making purposes. In addition, the extent to which such analytical exercises can, in their very conduct, become bureaucratic and thus rather inflexible over time, is another important area of concern. This calls in to question the nature of the processes by which analysis and management of the macro-environment occur, in addition to the matter of the content of the analyses performed.

Finally, by way of summary and in order to point the way to Part Three, section 2.4 considers possible avenues for dealing flexibly with uncertainty in the macro-environment. This preliminary discussion is presented in terms of the need to remedy some of the deficiencies of approaches discussed elsewhere in the chapter if organizations are to retain some confidence in their capability to manage strategically in a changing environment.

2.2 The changing macro-environment

The macro-environment provides the broadest, most general context for the activities of all organizations. It may be distinguished from the industry (or 'competitive' or 'task') environment and the internal organizational (or 'operational') environment (Figure 2.1). As such, events or trends within this macro-environment may sometimes appear remote to decision-makers within an organization, who might be tempted to devote greater attention and energy to the internal matters that are closest to home or to relationships and rivalries within their industry that often seem more relevant. However, the significance of the macro-environment to organizational strategy rests with the extent to which strategic performance is influenced by sudden shocks or newly emergent trends in the wider environment. This applies whether one views strategy as a matter of deliberate, anticipatory 'planning', as a more emergent politically- or culturally-driven response to change, or in some other way.

One way to develop an understanding of the degree of uncertainty that might characterize this macro-environmental context and its potential relevance to strategic decision-making is to describe the principal historical trends that have helped to shape the general business environment since reconstruction following World War II. It is worth noting the relationship of increasing change and uncertainty in practice to developments in the academic world as the study of organizations and decision-making progresses over the period.

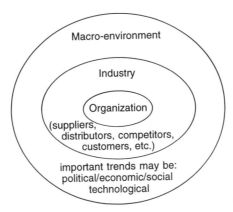

Figure 2.1 The environmental context of organizations.

The term 'uncertainty' is employed below according to the commonly accepted view expressed by Duncan (1972). Thus the degree of uncertainty posed to strategic decision-makers by forces or trends in the macro-environment will reflect the dynamism or the complexity of that environment; sometimes such dynamism and complexity may be present simultaneously.

The aspects of the macro-environment that can be said to be 'dynamic' are those which are the subject of rapid change. A low degree of dynamism may be said to be synonymous with the existence of 'static' conditions. 'Complexity' refers to the extent that factors within the macro-environment are interrelated, interdependent and difficult to evaluate or understand (especially with reference to their use in facilitating strategic decision-making). The prevalence of low complexity reflects the degree to which conditions are 'simple'. (NB these aspects of uncertainty may also be applied in considering the nature of industry sector environments, see Chapter 3.)

Broadly speaking, the nature of the contemporary business environment may be characterized as highly complex and similarly dynamic. In short, the uncertainty of this environment is such that it is difficult to imagine how most organizations and industry sectors could remain untouched by its potential impact. In the world of the 1990s, it would appear that the only trend about which one can have any degree of confidence is a trend towards ever-increasing uncertainty within the general business environment. This situation may be contrasted with earlier periods.

Harrison and Taylor (1991) have usefully distinguished between three 'planning styles' in the development of strategic management practice, which link to changing macro-environmental conditions and thus also to trends in industry-level competition. This evolution of planning styles roughly corresponds to developments in the academic literature:

- Phase 1 – long-range planning: 1950s/1960s
- Phase 2 – strategic planning: 1970s
- Phase 3 – strategic management: 1980s onwards.

Long-range planning: 1950s/1960s

As Harrison and Taylor (1991) note, this period following World War II was one in which a degree of relative stability and economic growth occurred. Planning within leading industrial organizations at this time proceeded by way of extending the usual one-year budgeting process to include five-year operating plans and a long-range forecast. Such longer-term planning was typically based on simple extrapolations of historical trends. Such analysis was based implicitly on what would now appear to be the rather dangerous premise that the economic boom experienced by 'Western' countries at that time would be continuous. The apparent prospect of continuing economic growth in the leading industrialized nations seemed to fuel an expectation on the part of producers that consumer demand for the products of industry was virtually insatiable (Harrison and Taylor, 1991).

The primary strategic requirement at this time appeared to be efficient production of the volumes demanded. Keeping costs low and productivity high thus entailed mass production and internal expansion in order to take advantage of economies of scale. Moreover, beliefs about the nature of economic growth and the general level of consumer demand meant that organizational growth through diversification or acquisition became favoured, a trend to which one may link the growing divisionalization of organizations during this period.

Strategic planning: 1970s

The 1970s saw a growing uncertainty in one critical area touching world politics and world economics. This uncertainty centred on what is sometimes viewed as the life-blood of the entire free market system, on which much of world trade is based: oil. Although the Organization of Petroleum Exporting Countries (OPEC) had been formed back in 1960, it was not until 1970 that the oil producing countries finally developed a consensus for action to control the price and supply of oil in the international market. As Odell (1986) notes, this objective was realized dramatically in October 1973 when the producing countries took advantage of supply restrictions, caused by renewed conflict between Israel and the Arab states, to control for the first time the amount of oil produced. This led to the oil crisis of 1973/74 and to fundamental changes in the international oil system.

The oil crisis of 1973/74 effectively ended the period of general economic stability and growth of the previous two decades. It also provided a potent new dimension to international politics and to relationships between the leading industrialized nations and other less developed or emerging economies, particularly those oil-producing countries of the Middle East and North Africa. Most Western countries depended on Middle Eastern oil: even those that had substantial indigenous reserves found them to be either of insufficient quantity (or quality) for self-sufficiency or, as in the UK, the reserves had only recently been discovered and were thus not yet fully developed.

As virtually every significant manufacturing or service-based sector required petroleum or its derivatives to function properly, the new higher price for crude oil had to be paid. This had a serious impact in a number of ways, perhaps the most significant of which, following this first oil 'shock', was a period of very high inflation in many Western economies during the middle of the 1970s. The price of crude oil more than quadrupled over the period 1972–74. Not surprisingly, annual rates of inflation in the UK did not average less than 10% between 1974 and 1977 inclusive as higher energy costs were passed on to consumers. Indeed, the average annual rate of inflation for the UK was nearly 25% in 1975.

Rapidly increasing inflation not only meant that energy costs and the price of finished goods and services rose, it also helped to stoke up unrest on the industrial relations front as workers sought to have their wages keep pace with rising prices. Governments were finding life difficult too, inflation was adding to the extent of welfare and benefits commitments, necessitating some rethinking about public finances (in particular the level of public spending) and the organization of public services. Businesses were now faced with a less predictable level of general consumer demand and the prospect, soon to be realized towards the end of the 1970s, of economic recession and stagnant, if not declining, industry sectors. In addition, new competition was emerging, particularly from South-East Asia and Japan, based on greater attention to customer needs and product quality.

Overall, the response to this change of circumstances was one of increased analysis concerning future strategy, based on a number of strategic planning concepts and techniques that had recently been developed. Some of the more influential analytical tools and concepts that have been employed to facilitate an understanding of the nature of the macro-environment are discussed in sections 2.3 and 2.4.

Strategic management: 1980s

If the 1970s could be referred to as 'uncertain', the 1980s could, arguably, also make a claim to that description. One aspect of this uncertainty relates to changes on the international and domestic political front. One example of this is the dramatic decline of Soviet military spending following the break-up of the Warsaw Pact and the thawing of East–West relations, which has provided new opportunities for expansion for western European companies. However, the same phenomenon has proved threatening to former Soviet organizations; thus it has been necessary for former suppliers of defence-related equipment to reinvent themselves as producers of goods for civilian use. This task has been made all the more difficult by the corresponding change towards reducing the role of the state in industries that were formerly centrally planned and supported, plus the continued poverty of Russian economic performance.

Another example of the potency of political factors may be found in the UK. The debate about the future survival of British Coal, which intensified following the announcement by Michael Heseltine, President of the Board of Trade, in October 1992 that 31 coal pits were to be compulsorily closed, is noteworthy. In particular, the cessation of the government subsidies that enabled British Coal to offer more favourable terms to its largest customers, the electricity generators, has been singled out as contributory to the closure move.

Furthermore, the impact of political factors on British Coal may be related to environmental considerations, demonstrating just how interrelated strategic considerations often are. In this case, the commitment of the UK government to a European Union policy of reducing carbon emissions may be cited. The environmentally unfriendly nature of coal-burning power station processes thus provided another potentially constraining factor to the activities of British Coal and the extent to which it could rely on governmental support.

The repercussions of the oil crisis and the changes to the supply and price of crude oil continued to be felt in this period, with two further 'shocks' in the international oil market occurring during the 1980s. The first, in 1979/80, was largely due to the 1979 revolution in Iran. Oil prices more than doubled compared with those in the period immediately prior to 1979. Once again, this helped to stimulate inflation in Western countries.

The second oil crisis of the decade was just as severe but the direction was different. This time the inability of OPEC members to agree on supply levels helped to produce a glut on the international oil market, with prices in 1986 dipping to below US $10 barrel compared with the peak in 1981 of over US $37 a barrel. Even though the demand for oil had been falling since 1979, and energy use had become more efficient, the instability of the oil market was still the source of great political and economic uncertainty, making it all the more difficult for businesses to plan long-term strategies confidently.

Having seen the post-war economic growth wither away during the 1970s, the 1980s saw a period of great volatility with successive bouts of recession, growth and, towards the end of the decade, signs once again of economic recession in the leading industrialized economies. Businesses, in the first half of the 1980s, were having to plan for rationalization, including often severe cutbacks in labour. In the UK, the sectors most affected tended to be those involved in manufacturing, and these areas declined as the importance of service industries and those based on innovative products began to emerge.

More specifically, a number of factors could be said to have played a significant role in the growing uncertainty on the national and international economic fronts during the 1980s and early 1990s (Grant, 1991). The intensification of competition as a result of growth in world trade, for example, has meant that business organizations have become increasingly vulnerable to changing trends in the international economic environment. Such vulnerability has clearly been exacerbated by the emergence of new successful trading nations from the Pacific Rim and the phenomenon of increasingly internationalized competition.

The increased interdependence of national economies resulting from the nature of flows in trade and capital has also been blamed for causing the import and export of economic problems, such as high inflation, from one country to another. This interdependence has also created instability, stemming from the divergence of economic policies pursued by different countries and the variations in economic performance that exist between nations.

This has been exemplified by the difficulties experienced in attempting to fix exchange rates within the European Union's (EU) Exchange Rate Mechanism of the European Monetary System. This is a task that has proved testing because of the different levels of inflation, interest rates, balance of payments surplus or deficit, and policy priorities among member nations, and, in particular, the interplay between German economic management and the economic performance indicators of the other member states. Indeed, the volatility of these various indicators (exchange rates, interest rates, etc.) in many countries testifies to the inability of those charged with managing national or international economic performance to secure the required level of control. Moreover, the effect of the liberation of Eastern Europe on the economics of Western Europe and the nature and policies of the European Union remains uncertain. Again, this has made for awkward decision-making at the strategic level in organizations.

Both the 1970s and the 1980s have witnessed increasingly globalized competition. This has applied to product markets and also to financial markets. Much of this growing globalization has been facilitated by developments in technology (discussed below) and the process seems likely to continue throughout the 1990s, though the requirements of organizations are likely to differ, in strategic terms, from those of the preceding decades.

The emergence and impact of globalized, or international, competition has been a significant factor in the macro-environmental uncertainty which has to be addressed by competitors in many industries. Failure to recognize or to influence such trends can spell disaster. For example, the UK, among others, was the mother of the machine tool industry and the market for textile machinery. Yet by the 1980s the UK share of both of these markets was negligible, largely as a result of failure to acknowledge the strength of emerging foreign competition. The story is repeated in a number of other sectors in which UK firms were once dominant, such as the car, steel and motor-cycle industries.

Similarly, where in 1970 the share of imports into the US automobile market was only 7%, by 1985 this figure had risen to 31%, with the principal factor cited being the relatively inferior product quality of US automobiles compared with those from Japanese producers. Moreover, whereas in 1979 US holdings abroad exceeded the value of foreign-owned assets in the USA by US $100 billion, by the end of 1986 this situation had reversed (Pearson, 1990).

A crucial factor in the economic performance of different countries, and one that plays a role in making firm-level strategic decisions subject to great uncertainty, is the nature of technological development. The management of technology is thus important in two principal respects. The first concerns the relevance of technological progress to economic growth at national level and how this link might be exploited. The second involves the capability of individual enterprises to transfer and harness technology in a bid to develop new products or production processes. In this case the central concern is with the trends in technological development that helped to shape the general business environment in the 1980s and are likely to do so during the 1990s and beyond.

A number of researchers have characterized a new 'paradigm' relevant to technological developments concerning the adoption of new modes of production and structure in organizations and the emergence of new industries and products. This new 'wave' of technological development has been associated with the 'post-Fordist' techno-economic paradigm. The uncertainties connected with such a revolution in technological development may be better understood by reference to different types of technological change and their relevance to the concept of 'long waves' of economic growth and recession. It is possible to differentiate between types of technological change according to their novelty and the extent to which they represent a fundamental change from the pre-existing state of affairs (Bessant, 1991).

In particular, four types of technological change can be identified:

- incremental
- radical
- new technology systems
- new techno-economic paradigms.

Incremental changes may be associated with relatively minor innovations that facilitate improvements in production or modifications in product design. They are minor in the sense that they involve the everyday process by which organizations learn to use or adapt technology to suit their own requirements. This does not mean that their impact is necessarily small over the longer term. Incremental changes of technology are also referred to as 'evolutionary', and are not likely to require significant organizational change or changes in consumer behaviour.

Radical changes in technology, as the term suggests, are likely to have a far greater impact than incremental ones. What Robertson (1967) refers to as 'discontinuous' innovations are likely to involve the introduction of quite novel new products or processes, necessitating a change in buyer behaviour. For instance, the compact disc or the innovation of nylon represent radical product changes, while on the process side, phototypesetting and the basic oxygen process for steelmaking have been singled out for their discontinuity.

New technology systems are characterized by the far-reaching changes they involve, which may affect more than one industry sector or lead to the creation of new sectors. Further changes that may be required often relate to the way in which production is organized, either within or between firms. The emergence of new synthetic materials in the post-war period provides one example of this type of technological change.

New techno-economic paradigms represent the type of technological change associated with the most fundamental shift from the status quo. This type of technological change can be characterized by major shifts affecting the entire economy as well as involving technical and organizational change, new products and processes, and the creation of new industry sectors. Technological change of this type is 'revolutionary' and is likely to involve the establishment of a new 'paradigm' that is likely to dominate for some decades.

The term 'techno-economic paradigm' (Freeman, 1982) refers to the taken-for-granted rules by which the relationship between technology, society, the economy and modes of firm organization is understood.

The current 'post-Fordist' techno-economic paradigm continues to unfold and so its implications for strategy-making are still somewhat uncertain. However, some of its characteristics may be defined and contrasted with earlier paradigms. In general, the new technologies that underpin the new paradigm include those connected with micro-electronics, biotechnology and information and communication technology. These technologies appear to form a cluster of developments offering opportunities for future growth based on emerging industry sectors, as proponents of the long wave model might suggest. Moreover, the emerging new paradigm may be viewed in the light of new forms of production that are increasingly reliant on networking and decentralization; these are deemed to confer the flexibility required to cope with more fragmented demand from, and greater emphasis on non-price factors by, consumers.

Proponents of the long wave model would point to the emergence of the current paradigm in terms of the growing inappropriateness of the previously dominant technologies and organizational forms to the newer challenges presented by the economic environment. In this instance, the limitations and problems associated with mass production and bureaucratic forms of organization in dealing with the need for product variety and smaller batch but still efficient and high quality production, may be cited.

The problem facing strategists in manufacturing organizations during the 1990s and beyond is the management of the transition in practice, based on the new technologies and on newer forms of organizing their activities. It is not clear how such transitions will best be effected. What can be said, however, is that a certain amount of trial and error may have to be undergone before appropriate solutions are discovered. Achieving this, considering the uncertainties involved, is likely to require a flexible approach to decision-making.

The 1980s witnessed many changes connected with social, demographic, ethical and cultural issues that helped to make the macro-environment more uncertain, particularly for organizations operating internationally. For instance, in the UK, the 1980s was a decade that witnessed changing trends in home ownership and personal shareholding as a result of certain political policies of the period. Expectations and attitudes concerning what constituted acceptable levels of unemployment and the role and control of trade unions were also the subject of change in the UK in the 1980s.

Significant demographic shifts have also occurred in the UK in recent years, particularly the general ageing of the population, a feature shared by many industrialized nations. The trend of increased life-expectancy has been exacerbated by the continued stagnation of the birth rate following the 'baby boom' of the post-war decades. The implications of this are potentially quite serious, and may affect the availability of young, skilled labour or the demand for products usually targeted at young adults, such as household goods and appliances.

Another area of increasing concern for strategic decision-makers during recent years has been the need to show that their organizations are behaving in a socially responsible and ethical manner. For private sector businesses, this consideration has been a matter of the extent to which they profit from illegal, immoral or unfair practices. For public sector organizations (or at least those entities providing the sort of services associated with, or formerly within, the public sector), the issue has been the extent to which 'value for money' considerations have infringed on their ability to maintain, or to improve upon, the quality of service given previously.

In both cases, social responsibility and ethics add another dimension of macro-environmental uncertainty for an organization to face – one that becomes all the more problematic the greater the number of national markets it operates in.

Perhaps the most important issue in business ethics to emerge during the 1980s concerned the stance that companies took with regard to the impact of their activities on the natural and physical environment. This raises the important question of whether there has been a fundamental change in the way industry views the protection of the environment. The extent to which this is true is debatable, partly because much of the adoption of 'environmentally friendly' practices, e.g. environmental audits, has been driven by government legislation and the pressure of public opinion.

It is interesting that in 1986 a survey by the European Commission showed that only 9% of Europeans thought that the development of the economy in the (then) European Community should take priority in policy, while 50% felt that protecting the environment was essential. In 1988, the environment was ranked as the second most important political issue facing the European Community, behind unemployment but ahead of inflation and arms control (Pearce, Markandya and Barbier, 1989).

There is a number of areas where the environmental impact of business has had to be considered. Such areas can be thought of as pertaining to the products that organizations sell or provide and to the processes by which these products are realized. Although far from new, the importance of such considerations has grown in recent years.

The 'greening' of business has been expressed by products and packaging that are environmentally friendly. Increasing awareness of potential global pollution stemming from the adverse effects of greenhouse gases (such as CFCs or CO_2) and the depletion of the ozone layer has stimulated the market for 'green' products. Firms such as the Body Shop are all but defined by their environmentally friendly image, selling products made only with natural and environmentally safe ingredients in containers that are similarly ecologically benign. The emergence of the market for lead-free petrol also exemplifies the effect of developing public opinion and political activity (through excise duty changes) on product decisions and strategy of business.

Both of these examples involve cases of emerging public opinion, although it has been suggested that public opinion has now rather tired of the environmental issue, and governmental action, demonstrating the uncertainty of strategic problems. In addition to the question of the resource capability of the particular organization involved, decisions about the products offered and the extent to which they are in tune with public opinion are necessarily a matter for quite delicate evaluation.

The processes by which products are made have also given cause for concern in terms of potential impact on the environment. One of the most potent issues here is the nature of inputs into the production process (e.g. whether they are recyclable); another has been the safety of the workplace environment and hazards that might be associated with the production process, transportation of the half-finished or final product, or the disposal of related waste materials.

Again, the existence of concerns about such matters is not a new phenomenon, but the emergence of environmental pressure groups has helped to focus public awareness on the issues involved. As well as the suspicion that has been directed at companies such as the Body Shop with regard to the truth of, and motives behind, its environmentally friendly image, uncertainty about the likelihood of imitation by other firms forms another potential threat.

The range and interconnectedness of all these factors make analysis an unenviable task. Strategic management and strategic thinking thus come to the fore, particularly when the ability to get a 'feel' for the uncertainty and potential implications of external factors, as an adjunct to, but not substitute for, decision-making is emphasized. Clearly, the long-range and strategic planning approaches that gained currency between the 1950s and 1970s (and still enjoy a dubious popularity) do not appear to be suited to the uncertain macro-environment conditions of the latter part of the 20th century. This issue is taken up in section 2.3 with more detailed reference to particular analytical techniques. In addition, in line with recent developments in strategic management, the discussion features some ways in which the ability of organizations to 'sense' external change is enhanced, but without the pretence of definitiveness or once-and-for-all accuracy of 'planning' perspectives.

2.3 Analysing the macro-environment

This section identifies a number of approaches that relate to the analysis of trends and influences on strategy which emanate from the macro-environmental context of the organization. The emphasis is on describing the various tools and techniques that have been employed or proposed for performing an appraisal of macro-environmental factors and their potential impact on strategic development in organizations. The discussion also centres on the extent to which such approaches are actually capable of being successfully applied in practice. This issue is especially relevant where the particular circumstances facing decision-makers may be said to be uncertain.

Much of this section refers to the task of forecasting trends in the wider external environment and of generating potential opportunities and threats to the organization from such forecasts. (The matter of attempting to define threats and opportunities from the industry environment, and thus from the external environment as a whole, is addressed in Chapter 3.)

Understanding the nature, extent and future path of opportunities and threats is commonly considered to form an important basis for gaining an appreciation of the strategic position of organizations (i.e. where an organization stands in relation to others that are in the same market or competing for the same customers). In a number of popular textbooks an analysis of strategic position proceeds by the identification opportunities and threats in the macro- and industry-environments, in part facilitated by analysing the competitive position of the organization (e.g. through market share analysis). The data thus gained is considered in conjunction with an examination of the relative strengths and weaknesses of the organization to give a 'SWOT' (strengths, weaknesses, opportunities and threats) analysis. This is intended to provide a means of comparing the external environment and internal strategic capability of the organization and is thus considered a very useful input into management thinking about future strategic decision-making.

This section links various approaches to the analysis of the macro-environment with the different planning styles and phases in the development of strategic management that were the subject of section 2.2. The extent to which they are limited in their practical applicability to the uncertainty of the contemporary business environment is indicative of the need for flexibility in management in such environments.

Long-range planning approaches

Approaches associated with long-range planning styles of strategic development emerged as the size of companies grew in the 1950s and 1960s, and as the early commercial computers arrived. As Pearson (1990) notes, much of the initial venture into formalized strategic planning was based on the accounting function within organizations. Thus, for companies with a number of subsidiaries, one popular approach was to make projections of consolidated accounts that shareholders would consider acceptable. Then, in order to produce financial targets for subsidiary companies, these projections were deconsolidated.

Such an approach tended to be quite demanding of analysis and to be based on a single long-range sales forecast that would be the main input for the derivation of very detailed annual budgets. The larger or more complex the organization, the greater the volume of data that would be produced. The strategic content and value of such an approach was limited. It could, however, be argued that the conduct of the long-range sales forecast shed some light on particular trends both in the industry-environment and in a wider context, and thus on potential threats and opportunities that might otherwise have been missed.

Strategic planning approaches

The limitations of the accounting-based long-range planning approach to analysing the macro-environment, in addition to the changing nature of the general business environment of the 1960s and 1970s, led to an increased desire to improve the quality of information being used as inputs into the process of strategic decision-making. In particular, the emergence of strategic planning techniques tended to focus on improving the nature of information for the purposes of strategic analysis and forecasting.

The strategic planning style that embraces such approaches still permeates many of the textbooks on strategic management, although the applicability or use in practice of many of the suggested techniques is not without question. As far as the analysis of factors in the macro-environment is concerned, a typical suggestion for carrying out such an appraisal is to conduct an audit of macro-environmental influences and then focus on a more explicit consideration of the most significant factors.

More specifically, 'PEST' analysis has been proposed as a method for auditing macro-environmental influences (Johnson and Scholes, 1993; Wheelen and Hunger, 1993). Here, trends in the macro-environment likely to influence the longer-term activities of an organization are identified (although its shorter-term operations may also be affected). The aim is to determine which factors have influenced strategic development and performance in the past and which are likely to do so now or in the future. 'PEST' factors are political/legal, economic, sociocultural/ethical and technological in nature (Table 2.1).

One aspect of PEST analysis is the general identification of key trends in the macro-environment, including the longer term shifts that may occur within it. Another aspect of this type of analysis is to evaluate the strategic significance of the most important factors from the analysis for a particular organization. Examples of techniques that seek to bring together the audit or list of PEST factors with the need to provide a more useful definition of organizationally-relevant trends are the matrix for environmental trend analysis and the issues priority matrix.

An outline of the matrix for environmental trend analysis is given in Figure 2.2. The method of analysis proceeds by first identifying, say, three important trends in each of the four PEST areas. Secondly, it is suggested that the likely impact of each of these trends on elements of the organization's industry-environment be evaluated. So, for example, a change in the law regarding the

Table 2.1   A PEST analysis of environmental influences*

1. What environmental factors are affecting the organization?
2. Which of these are the most important at the present time? In the next few years?

Political/legal	**Economic**
Monopolies legislation	Business cycles
Environmental protection laws	GNP trends
Taxation policy	Interest rates
Foreign trade regulations	Money supply
Employment law	Inflation
Government stability	Unemployment
	Disposable income
	Energy availability and cost
Sociocultural	**Technological**
Population demographics	Government spending on research
Income distribution	Government and industry focus of
Social mobility	technological effort
Lifestyle changes	New discoveries/developments
Attitudes to work and leisure	Speed of technology transfer
Consumerism	Rates of obsolescence
Levels of education	
Ethics	
Environmental protection	

* Source: Johnson and Scholes (1993), p. 82.

	Societal forces			
	Economic	Technological	Political-legal	Sociocultural
Task elements	1. 2. 3.	1. 2. 3.	1. 2. 3.	1. 2. 3.
Communities				
Competitors				
Creditors				
Customers				
Employees/ Labour unions				
Governments				
Special- interest groups				
Stockholders				
Suppliers				
Trade associations				

Figure 2.2 Environmental trend analysis matrix. (Source: Wheelen and Hunger, 1993, p. 93.)

protection of patents for technological inventions might have implications for the ability of competitors to imitate this source of potential competitive advantage for an organization.

How such technological imitation might be affected would depend on the direction and severity of the legislation in question. Nevertheless, it is possible that over the course of time, legislative action might reinforce the rights of patent or copyright holders, thus reducing the ability of others to imitate. In this case, the impact on parties in the external environment might be mapped out. Rival competitors might, for instance, be required to find alternative technological solutions to product or process development problems, while suppliers might find themselves unable to integrate vertically, due to the useful barrier to entry that enhanced patent protection now formed for the firm enjoying it. Following this approach, the other factors in the macro-environment would be similarly treated and the major trends linked to their likely impact on aspects of the organization's industry environment. In such a way, a picture of the general impact of macro-environmental factors might be built up.

In order to specify the opportunities and threats that apply to an organization's own strategic position it is deemed necessary to consider which of the developments presented by the environmental trend analysis are most likely to occur and most likely to have an impact on the organization. The issues priority matrix (Figure 2.3) has been proposed as a method for helping decision-makers to define which issues, stemming from the analysis of macro-environmental trends, are most deserving of attention. Those that are of lower priority are considered to warrant more generalized 'scanning' of the environment, whereas those that might be classified as higher priority issues are such that they require constant

		High	Medium	Low
	High	High priority	High priority	Medium priority
Probability of occurrence	Medium	High priority	Medium priority	Low priority
	Low	Medium priority	Low priority	Low priority
		High	Medium	Low

Probable impact on corporation

Figure 2.3 Issues priority matrix. (Source: Wheelen and Hunger, 1993, p. 94.)

monitoring. Higher priority issues are considered to form the key opportunities and threats in the macro-environment.

It has been noted that organizations rarely monitor these higher priority issues in their environment successfully. Apart from the methodological difficulty of assigning probabilities to the occurrence of environmental events and to the likelihood of their having some significant impact on the organization, there is another explanation. The values and perceptions of senior management or analysts will tend to distort the view of which issues in the macro-environment are worthwhile monitoring and the interpretations that are put on the outcome of any such monitoring.

The example of Honda's entry in 1962 into the European motorcycle market may help to demonstrate some of the issues around monitoring of the macro-environment (Case study 2.1). For Honda, the role of environmental monitoring, while it could conceivably have raised initial awareness of strategic issues and the quality of debate concerning their potential impact, was minimized by views within the firm concerning its perceived necessity.

Case study 2.1 Honda: overseas investment and the limits to formalized monitoring of macro-environmental trends

In 1962, Honda extended its activities to manufacturing mopeds in Belgium. The product was of high quality, Europe was a very large market for motorcycles and while this was said to be the first attempt at direct foreign investment by a Japanese corporation in an industrially advanced country, there appeared to be a considerable opportunity.

However, as former chairman Hideo Sugiara explained (1990), the result of the decision to manufacture in Belgium was a series of errors and miscalculations, with the Belgian plant turning in losses for more than 10 years. Problems noted were mostly connected with a failure by Honda to understand and to manage for differences, at the macro-environmental level, in history, culture and values. For example, the nature of European moped use was quite different from that in Japan and so the needs of the consumer were also different. In addition, differences in labour practices led to misunderstandings between management and local employees, resulting in unforeseen disruption to production activities. Finally, design of technological components is another activity that is deeply embedded in organization and national culture. Hence the design that was so carefully built into the moped in Japan, resulted in a moped for which there would be low component availability in Belgium.

Essentially, the nature of the values and perceptions of Honda's management, intertwined as they were with those of their national Japanese culture, influenced their view about the likelihood of the firm's experiencing difficulties with the move into Belgium. This could be interpreted as reinforcing the view that attitudes and beliefs, within managerial groups, influence the extent to which formalized monitoring is conducted at all, never mind the degree to which important future trends for the organization are defined.

Moreover, it is clear from what Sugiara has written, that Honda's problems in Belgium might not, in any case, have been properly understood or redressed by 'monitoring' of the macro-environmental trends in the host country; not, at least, monitoring in the formalized planning sense. Writing of the Belgian experience of the 1960s and also of later, more successful, ventures involving direct foreign investment in overseas manufacturing, Sugiara (1990) states:

> The lesson we [Honda] learned was that to invest and do business overseas, it is not enough to have abstract knowledge about the host country. It is essential to develop a deeper under-standing. This can be achieved only by immersion in local society and by working with the people in the country.

This approach, it is said, depends upon the development of flexible relationships between the corporation and various parties in the host nation, characterized by trust and mutual understanding of the different values and cultures involved. Thus for Honda, the role of environmental monitoring, while it could conceivably have raised initial awareness of strategic issues and the quality of debate concerning their potential impact, was minimized by views within the organization concerning its perceived necessity. Furthermore, defining and managing for the impact of macro-environmental factors appears to have been more a matter of organizational action with regard to, for example, relationships with customers, suppliers, employees and government, than one of attempted objective analysis by monitoring.

The role of forecasting in the analysis of the macro-environment

So far this section has concentrated on attempts to forecast future trends in the macro-environment and, in addition, to predict the impact of such trends on particular organizations. Indeed, the type of approaches referred to in the discussion of long-range and strategic planning could only be adopted against a measure of confidence in the specific forecasting techniques that have been, and continue to be, employed in the analysis of the macro-environment.

It is interesting to note that the continued use of certain forecasting techniques in today's changing world has led to a growing scepticism about their validity. Hogarth and Makridakis (1981) have found the general performance of fore-casting to be poor, casting doubt on the accuracy of the more sophisticated methods in particular. In addition to the increasing recognition of the limitations of forecasting, the more dynamic and complex contemporary business environment has prompted more genuinely strategic thinking by decision-makers in organizations.

Such thinking has focused more on the flexibility and general ability of organizations to shape and respond to external change, than on mechanistic analysis of their environments. Greater emphasis is being placed on the process by which views about the future are constructed as well as the actual content of the forecasts. The importance of recognizing and integrating the knowledge of organizational members into the forecasting process, and the need to synthesize forecasting into the strategy-making process, need to be stressed (Fahey and King, 1983).

How this emerging realization of the need for flexibility in management in a changing environment relates to the practice of strategic management is the basis of Part Three. For now, it is proposed to review some of the main forecasting techniques that have been applied to the analysis of external environment conditions, together with the principal limitations of forecasting in an ever-changing world.

Essentially, a forecast is an attempt to say what will happen in the future (Stacey, 1993). Many organizations use a variety of types of forecasts to say what will happen in their macro-environment and also in their industry. Forecasts are also employed to predict trends that are most closely related to the performance of an organization – sales volume for different products in a firm's product range, for example. The specific type of forecasting technique applied varies according to the dominant perception within an organization of the usefulness or relevance of a particular approach. Factors such as cost and the time required to conduct the analysis also come into play.

The wide variety of forecasting techniques may be classified according to whether their basic orientation involves either trend extrapolation or scenario building. The degree of use of various techniques of external environmental analysis in general is given in Table 2.2.

Table 2.2 Degree of use of forecasting techniques*

Technique	Top 1000 US industrials (n = 215)	Top 100 US industrials (n = 40)	Top 300 US non-industrials (n = 85)	Top 500 Foreign industrials (n = 105)
Trend extrapolation	73%	70%	74%	72%
Statistical modelling (e.g. regression analysis)	48	61	51	45
Scenarios	57	67	67	61
Relevance trees	5	3	7	4
Simulation	34	45	38	27
Brainstorming	65	61	69	52
Trend-impact analysis	34	33	31	29
Expert opinion/Delphi	33	42	24	35
Morphological analysis	2	0	0	5
Signal monitoring	15	19	14	18
Cross-impact analysis	12	22	11	5

* Source: Klein and Linneman (1984), *Journal of Business Strategy*, p. 72.

As Table 2.2 shows, trend extrapolation techniques have been widely employed by industrial and non-industrial businesses alike. Moreover, trend extrapolation has been revealed as the most popular form of forecasting used by corporations worldwide. In fact, according to one study, over 70% of companies used this approach either 'frequently' or 'occasionally', as opposed to 'rarely' or 'not used' (Wheelen and Hunger, 1993).

Trend extrapolation techniques are typified by relatively simple time-series methods which, for example, attempt to make forecasts of the future based on projections of historical trends. Extrapolation methods such as moving averages are problematic in that historical trends are the culmination of the relationship between many different variables. Thus a change in the relationship between variables can spell a change in the trend in question and thus render a forecast meaningless. This basic form of trend extrapolation is not appropriate for sudden shocks in the environment, such as the oil crises of the 1970s and 1980s referred to in section 2.2.

In addition, collecting the information required to establish a trend may be problematic. It may also be difficult to decide at any given moment what sort of information is likely to be of relevance for the future, an issue that will affect the design of information systems within the organization. Finally, the longer the time horizon that the forecast covers, the greater the chance that the historical relationship between variables will become outdated and the more likely that the forecast will prove to be inaccurate (Palmer and Worthington, 1992).

More sophisticated (though less popular) forms of trend extrapolation are those that attempt, through the use of statistical methods, to consider the historical relationships between variables and the significance of past trends to the future. Techniques that fall into this category include, for example, methods that involve regression or econometric models (as used by the UK Treasury and others to forecast the future state of the economy). As with the simpler trend extrapolation methods described above, the historical basis of these more involved techniques means that their reliability and accuracy will also be extremely limited.

Scenario building is a qualitative, rather than quantitative, approach to forecasting. Scenarios are alternative visions of the key future trends in the macro- (and micro-) environment. According to Wheelen and Hunger (1993), the use of scenarios has increased markedly in popularity since the mid-1970s. Developing scenarios can be done by using non-specialist organizational personnel or by consulting external (or internal) expert opinion. Scenario building may also be facilitated by making use of the product of more sophisticated or statistically-based analytical methods as part of a combined approach to forecasting.

One technique for developing scenarios that relies on the contribution of internal staff with some, though not expert, knowledge of the factors that might be relevant to the scenarios to be constructed, is brainstorming. In brainstorming, members of staff are encouraged to give vent to their opinions about possible alternative futures and trends in a freewheeling manner. The object of the brainstorming session is to facilitate an atmosphere of creative thinking where ideas may be generated without fear of adverse criticism and where eventually some consensus may be reached as ideas crystallize into alternative scenarios.

Another technique, using expert opinion, is the Delphi method. The experts concerned may specialize in particular areas of the macro-environment. They may be individual consultants, belong to consultancy organizations, or be specialists within the organization concerned. Specialisms may be in economic or consumer trends or related to technological forecasting, for example. The level and range of specialization may also vary between experts.

Whatever the nature of the participants, the Delphi method will typically involve a group of experts who do not know each other and who have no contact with each other during the scenario-building process. The panel members are asked, individually, to comment on the likelihood of a certain future scenario (or scenarios) actually occurring. On receipt of the comments of the various experts, the organization modifies the scenario accordingly and the process is repeated, until a consensus about the most likely scenario emerges.

The benefits of scenario-building may be expressed in terms of how it enables short cuts to be taken in picturing the future. Rather than attempting thorough-going statistical models and analysis of environmental trends, developing scenarios may allow the basic trajectory and drivers of change to be considered. Moreover, such an approach may facilitate the development of a range of views about the future in a manner that does not rely purely on the subjective hunches of participants. At the very least, managers and others involved will be encouraged to recognize their assumptions, to make them explicit and to debate the differences between their perceptions of the external environment and the implications of external change for the organization.

The danger remains, however, that the possible benefits of scenario-building approaches may be lost. In particular, an awareness of the extent to which the potential flexibility of scenario-building may be impaired has developed. Thus on the one hand, the use of scenarios may allow for a variety of potential organization positions to be considered, according to each of the scenarios that is made. This might lead to the eventual adoption of alternative contingency strategies, according to the realities of the actual situation that confronts the organization.

On the other hand, scenario-building (as with strategic analysis in general) is unlikely to contribute to a flexible approach to managing the external environment when the activity becomes bureaucratic or the preserve of specialist planners within the organization. Hence, one danger is that efforts to build scenarios will fail to involve staff from every level of an organization, who will tend to have different views about the key trends and likely changes in the external environment, but who may also view the strategic or operational implications of external change differently.

Furthermore, the process by which this (and other) types of forecasting is conducted may be adversely affected by dedicated planning departments. In this situation, planners may present a number of scenarios to senior management, having already decided what the important trends and changes might be. The problem here is that those located within specialist planning units may be unable to take a strategic, organization-wide view of the possible impact of environmental trends. Thus the input of operational staff from specialized planning departments may be limited in the strategic sense. The view that decision-makers take of the course of major environmental trends is, therefore, likely to be subject to their perceptions of the expertise and awareness of specialist planners.

2.4 Summary

This chapter has illustrated the different contexts in which organizational activities are performed, enabling a distinction to be made between the macro-environment, the industry context and the organizational context. The uncertain nature of the contemporary macro-environment, which affects industry and organizational activities, has been identified. Changing and interrelated trends carrying implications for understanding the nature of the general external environment have emerged since the end of World War II. These factors have related to political, economic, societal and technological conditions and have intensified in their complexity and dynamism over time.

It has been seen that methods for understanding the nature of the macro-environment and thus for providing an input into the process of the strategic decision-making process, have progressed in sophistication, particularly with developments in strategic planning in the 1960s and 1970s. By this time it had become increasingly clear that long-range forecasting techniques were inappropriate for constantly changing conditions. Hence, a growing preoccupation with quantitative forecasting techniques developed at this time, both in the academic sector and in large corporations (more of these are considered below as they apply to the analysis of industry attractiveness and organizational market positions).

The extent to which these developments in the strategic planning approach to understanding the nature of uncertainty in the macro-environment are also limited in their contribution to flexible decision-making, has been considered. Much of this discussion concerned the realities of organizational behaviour. As the Honda example demonstrated, the primary area of neglect in considering the use of monitoring and forecasting of external environmental trends involves the process by which analysis is actually conducted (or not) and the way in which organizations manage their environments.

This question of how organizations (and the individuals within them) learn about their environments, or seek to mould them to their own benefit, is addressed in Part Three. For now, however, it is useful to bear in mind the possible difficulties in attempting to analyse or forecast accurately a constantly changing macro-environment as a precursor to deciding on definitive strategic courses of action. In essence, this chapter has provided a means for understanding why it is necessary to adopt approaches to external environmental management that permit flexibility of thought about possible alternative futures and the strategies that might be developed therein.

Study questions

1. What factors may contribute to uncertainty in the general business environment?

2. Evaluate the relevance of long-range and strategic planning approaches to strategic decision-making under uncertain external conditions.
3. Discuss specific techniques that have been employed in order to aid forecasting of external environmental factors. What are their relative merits?
4. Consider the role of managerial judgement and intuition in understanding external trends and conditions.

Key readings

Harrison and Taylor (1991) give a good account of the evolution of long-range planning, strategic planning and strategic management approaches, in *The Manager's Casebook of Business Strategy*.

A quite detailed treatment of specific planning and forecasting techniques and the extent to which they are employed in practice is provided by Wheelen and Hunger (1993) in *Strategic Management*.

References

Bessant, J. (1991) *Managing Advanced Manufacturing Technology: The Challenge of the Fifth Wave*, NCC Blackwell, Oxford.

Duncan, R. (1972) Characteristics of organizational environments and perceived environmental uncertainty. *Administrative Science Quarterly*, 313–27.

Fahey, L. and King, R. (1983) Environmental scanning for corporate planning, in *Business Policy and Strategy: Concepts and Readings*, 3rd edn (eds D. J. McCarthy *et al.*), Irwin, IL.

Freeman, C. (1982) *Unemployment and Technical Innovation*, Frances Pinter, London.

Grant, R. (1991) *Contemporary Strategy Analysis*, Blackwell, Oxford.

Harrison, J. and Taylor, B. (1991) *The Manager's Casebook of Business Strategy*, Butterworth–Heinemann, Oxford.

Hogarth, R. and Makridakis, S. (1981) Forecasting and planning: an evaluation. *Management Science*, **27**, 115–38.

Johnson, G. and Scholes, K. (1993) *Exploring Corporate Strategy*, Prentice-Hall, Hemel Hempstead.

Odell, P. (1986) *Oil and World Power*, Penguin, Middlesex.

Palmer, A. and Worthington, I. (1992) *The Business and Marketing Environment*, McGraw–Hill, London.

Pearce, D., Markandya, A. and Barbier, E. B. (1989) *Blueprint for a Green Economy*, Earthscan, London.

Pearson, G. (1990) *Strategic Thinking*, Prentice–Hall, Hemel Hempstead.

Robertson, T. S. (1967) The process of innovation and the diffusion of innovations. *Journal of Marketing*, 3.

Stacey, R. D. (1993) *Strategic Management and Organisational Dynamics*, Pitman, London.

Sugiara, H. (1990) How Honda localizes its global strategy. *Sloan Management Review*, **32**(1), 77–82.

Wheelen, T. L. and Hunger, J. D. (1993) *Strategic Management*, Addison–Wesley, Reading, MA.

UNCERTAINTY, INDUSTRIES AND COMPETITION

3

Learning objectives

Studying this chapter should:

- develop awareness of the potential impact of industry-level uncertainties for strategic management in organizations
- help you to understand the contribution of techniques for analysing industry structure, evolution and competitive position
- give you an appreciation of possible limitations to the employment of such analytical tools

3.1 Introduction

This chapter considers the problems posed for strategic management by uncertainty and change at the level of organizations' industry sector (also referred to as the 'micro-' or 'task-' environment). Strategy texts typically distinguish between the macro-environment (Chapter 2) and this narrower industry environment, although in actuality the boundaries separating the two are rather blurred. For example, major technological shifts may be seen to pervade societies (i.e. at the macro-environmental level) but similarly to infuse specific industries. Nevertheless, distinguishing between these types of external environment is of some benefit in that it makes the analysis of a particular organization's position more manageable. Forces at work at industry level, such as the position and strategies of rival competitors, may therefore be considered as distinct from, say, pressures connected with national or global economic conditions, which affect all sectors.

The goal of industry analysis, in conjunction with an analysis of macro-level factors, is usually to evaluate the opportunities in and threats to a sector in general and specific firms in particular, depending on their competitive position within it. The main techniques for conducting such analyses emanate from the industry organization economics approach to understanding strategic development and competitiveness.

The work of one of its best known disciples, Michael Porter, is central to this chapter, drawing on Porter's 'five force' framework, an influential technique for assessing industry structure and attractiveness (Porter, 1980). The first part of the chapter introduces and illustrates the technique and reviews some areas of criticism of it. Subsequent sections deal with concepts and analytical techniques relevant to understanding industry evolution and the competitive position of organizations within their sectors, such as the product life cycle, market share analysis, and strategic group analysis. Again, some of the limitations and criticisms associated with these concepts and techniques are also considered. In particular, the focus is on the static and deterministic qualities of these tools.

Moreover, the extent to which certain features of organizational competitiveness are neglected or underplayed is addressed. Here, the nature and role of the resource base of the firm, or its collaborative or 'political' relationship with 'external' parties, assumes some relevance, as distinct from the antagonistic relationship with competitors that is typically portrayed.

The summary reiterates the central themes of the chapter, in terms of the limitations of the techniques referred to above and of the industry organization approach more generally. It also defines why a perspective on strategic management based on concepts of flexibility, learning and innovativeness may play a role in understanding industry sector dynamics and the performance of organizations therein.

3.2 Analysing industry structure

This section outlines one of the most commonly taught techniques for analysing industries and competition. This is Porter's five force model for analysing industry structure and profitability.

Porter's framework has become popular with academics and practitioners alike since the publication of his seminal book, *Competitive Strategy* (Porter, 1980). The five force model is displayed diagrammatically in Figure 3.1. The essence of the framework is its application to the analysis of industry structure, which in turn can be said to further the analyst's understanding of the profitability, and hence attractiveness, of an industry. As Porter himself puts it:

> The intensity of competition in an industry is neither a matter of coincidence nor bad luck. Rather, competition in an industry is rooted in its underlying economic structure and goes well beyond the behaviour of current competitors. The state of competition in an industry depends on five basic competitive forces ... The collective strength of these forces determines the ultimate profit potential in the industry, where profit potential is measured in terms of long run return on invested capital.
>
> *Porter, 1980, p. 3*

This profit potential varies between industries such that, for Porter, the key to competitive strategy for firms is:

1. to locate within an industry (or industries) that is attractive in profit-making terms
2. to find a position within that industry where the company can best defend itself against competitive forces or influence them in its own favour.

He cites sectors such as paper and steel as ones characterized by intense competition and where low profitability is common. By way of contrast, Porter suggests that competition is relatively mild in industries such as cosmetics, toiletries and oilfield equipment, in which high returns are 'quite common'.

In order to understand Porter's explanation for such possible differences, it is necessary to look a little more closely at the five force framework. First, three important points about the five force model need to be made. Porter adopts what he calls a 'working definition' of an industry which refers to:

> ... the group of firms producing products that are close substitutes for each other.

> *Porter, 1980, p. 5*

He recognizes that this raises questions about the meaning of 'close substitute' and the specification of boundaries, matters that will be taken up throughout the course of this book. The second point is that the framework is concerned with 'extended rivalry' within industries (however defined). What is significant about this is that suppliers, customers, substitute products and potential entrants are all recognized as potentially prominent players in addition to rival competitors as

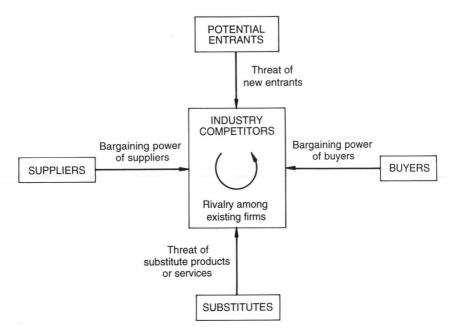

Figure 3.1 Porter's five force model for analysing industry structure. (Source: Porter, 1980.)

they are ordinarily considered. Hence the notion of competition is broad. The final point concerns the long-term orientation of the framework claimed by Porter. He states:

> The underlying structure, reflected in the strength of the [five] forces, should be distinguished from the many short run factors that can affect competition and profitability in a transient way ... Although such factors [such as short-term ups and downs in the business cycle] may have a tactical significance, the focus of the analysis of industry structure, or 'structural analysis', is on identifying the basic, underlying characteristics of an industry rooted in its economics and technology that shape the arena in which competitive strategy must be set.
>
> *Porter, 1980, p. 6*

Each of the 'five forces' is discussed below, beginning with the 'horizontal' forces of competition, which relate to the bargaining power of suppliers and buyers.

Bargaining power of suppliers

According to Porter, suppliers of raw materials or components to producers in an industry can exert bargaining power over those producers by threatening to raise prices or reduce the quality of goods or services supplied. In particular, profitability levels in an industry are under threat when firms are unable to pass on cost increases in the form of higher prices to consumers. A number of factors may lead to increased supplier bargaining power.

- The group of suppliers is dominated by a few companies and is more concentrated than the industry to which it is selling.
- The supplier group does not have to compete with substitute products that might also be sold to the industry.
- The industry in question is not an important customer to the supplier group.
- The product being sold to the industry is an important input to the business of the buyers, or is differentiated.
- The threat of forward integration from the supplier's group is a 'credible' one.

Bargaining power of buyers

The conditions that lead to increased bargaining power of buyers (e.g. manufacturers, service businesses, retailers, wholesalers and distributors), mirror those of suppliers to industries. Thus buyers 'compete' with an industry by forcing down prices, demanding higher quality or improved service or playing competitors off against each other. Such actions all have the potential to reduce industry profitability. More specifically, the following conditions can lead to high buyer bargaining power.

- The buyer group is concentrated or the volume of its purchases is large compared with the sales that the sellers make.

- The products purchased from the industry comprise a significant portion of buyers' costs or purchases, or is standard (undifferentiated).
- The threat of backward integration on the part of buyers is a credible one.
- Buyers earn low profits.
- The products of the industry are unimportant to the quality of buyers' products or services.

As for the 'vertical' forces that are said to drive industry competition, the threat of new entrants to an industry is discussed first, before moving on to look at threats to an industry from substitute products.

Threat of new entrants

New entrants may adversely affect industry profitability where competition for custom leads to prices being bid down, or where costs are inflated, through increased marketing spend, for example. Crucial to understanding the potential for new entrants into an industry are the barriers to entry that pertain to that industry and the likely reaction of existing competitors to the would-be entrant. Porter asserts a number of entry barriers, which, if high and/or combined with 'sharp retaliation' from existing competitors, will mean that the threat of entry is low. These six barriers to entry are:

- economies of scale
- product differentiation
- capital requirements
- switching costs
- access to distribution channels
- cost disadvantages independent of scale.

Somewhat ambiguously, Porter adds that government policy is another major (seventh) entry barrier (more of that below).

Threat of substitute products or services

The threat from substitute products in one industry comes from their potential to limit the returns that can be achieved in another industry by placing a ceiling on the prices that can profitably be charged in it. The identification of substitutes is a matter of defining products in rival sectors that can perform similar functions to the product of the industry (Porter, 1980). Two types of substitute deserve particular attention in the Porter framework:

- those that are improving in value, in price and product performance terms compared with the industry's product
- those that are produced in highly profitable industries, especially where developments there are threatening to reduce industry profits.

Intensity of rivalry among existing competitors

Central to the Porter framework (diagrammatically and conceptually) is the intensity of competitive rivalry among industry competitors. This can vary from mild (or 'polite and gentlemanly' in Porter's words) to 'war-like' or 'cut-throat', depending on the interaction of a number of structural factors. In short, highly intense rivalry is likely to pertain where the following conditions prevail:

- numerous, equally balanced or diverse competitors
- slow industry growth
- high fixed costs (relative to value added)
- lack of differentiation or switching costs
- capacity augmented in large increments
- high exit barriers or strategic stakes.

Limitations of the five force framework

The focus of criticism levelled at Porter's framework has been the problematic nature of industry boundaries, alluded to at the beginning of this section. Readers will remember that, for Porter, industries are considered in terms of groups of firms producing products that are close substitutes for each other. In addition,

> Structural analysis, by focusing broadly on competition well beyond existing rivals, should reduce the need for debates on where to draw industry boundaries. Any definition of an industry is essentially a choice between established competitors and substitute products, between existing firms and potential entrants, and between existing firms and suppliers and buyers. Drawing these lines is inherently a matter of degree that has little to do with the choice of strategy.
>
> *Porter, 1980, p. 32*

Thus recognizing these broad sources of competition and analysing their potential impact is of more strategic significance than the matter of drawing lines around the 'industry'. Porter also notes that defining the industry is not the same as defining where or how a firm can (or should) compete. This is an issue addressed by Levitt (1960) in his article about marketing myopia. Levitt proposed that wide definitions of the market served by a particular firm should be adopted. This view is exemplified by the firms in Table 3.1, which have all had a strategic focus on very broad target markets and customer needs, in contrast with others which have defined themselves in terms of the development of specific capabilities (such as Honda, Canon and Vickers) (Chapter 7).

Whereas Levitt suggested that a broad definition of the market served could be the key to flexible adjustment to changeable market conditions by allowing for early contemplation of potential substitute products, he is silent on the issue of the capabilities required to cater for the needs of the disparate customer groups to be served. Hence, with respect to the firms in Table 3.1, serving a wide range of market requirements in accordance with such broad conceptions of strategic

Table 3.1 Market served as the basis for strategy*

Companies pursuing market-focused strategies	Strategic focus	Comments
Allegis Corp.	Serving the needs of the traveller	Formed in 1986 from the merger of United Airlines, Westin Hotels, Hertz car rental; non-airline businesses divested in 1987
Merrill Lynch	Serving the investment and financial needs of individual and institutional clients	Between 1976 and 1982 diversified from stock-broking into insurance, retail and investment banking, real estate broking and relocation services. Financial performance during the 1980s was well below industry average and some activities were divested
Sears Roebuck	'Sears is where America shops'	During the 1980s, Sears' attempt to 'expand its special franchise with the American consumer' ran into trouble. In attempting to compete across a vast range of merchan-dise, for all ages and groups of people, while expanding aggressively into financial services, Sears was unable to develop the specialized resources and expertise needed to compete with more focused rivals

* Source: Grant (1991).

purpose and 'definition' of the businesses that each company was in, may be seen to have had disastrous consequences.

Levitt's more recent work invites similar debate, this time with respect to his 'globalization thesis'. In terms of international competition, Levitt considers that there has been a convergence in consumer preferences and lifestyles across the world which make it advisable to market products in a standardized way. Regional and national differences are superficial, and technology, communication and travel are deemed to be the force behind such convergence, as expressed by the observation that more and more people the world over wear the same brands of jeans and drink the same brands of cola. What is more, this standardization of demand has consequences for the role of multinational corporations. Indeed, for Levitt, the multinational firm is an anachronism; it is the global corporation that is the key to success for large firms in the modern world. Global companies, unlike multinationals, operate as if the world (or large parts of it) were a single entity, selling the same products in the same fashion everywhere. The multinational, in contrast, has different units, products and prices in a number of countries, and operates at high, rather than low relative costs (Levitt, 1991).

Such multidomestic firms – Hoover and General Motors during the 1960s and 1970s, for instance – might enjoy flexibility of response to local market conditions, especially where this approach allows for the differentiation of products according to local preferences. But, as Levitt would have it, the weakness of the multidomestic strategy rests with either the replication of the whole spread of organizational activities within each national subsidiary, or different national markets. This replication or differentiation would be at the cost of the reduced potential for exploiting scale economies that would be limited to the size of each particular national market.

So the essence of Levitt's argument is that those companies that treat the world as a single global market hold a distinct competitive advantage over those that compete on a national basis. The benefits of a globalization strategy may be obtained, Levitt claims, whether a firm decides to invest in manufacturing facilities in a number of different countries, or to maintain its manufacturing capability in its home base and export internationally.

Levitt's thesis has been the subject of great controversy. For example, it may be that, to be effective, a globalization strategy will require a great deal of centralized co-ordination of activities from corporate management, who may be somewhat remote from the national markets being served. Of particular note are the arguments of Bartlett and Ghoshal (1989) in their work on global competition and multinational organization. Their central position, somewhat contrary to that of Levitt, is that national and regional differences in consumer tastes do persist and that tastes are not becoming homogeneous in the way that Levitt suggests. Rather, they say, there remains, and is likely to remain, a high degree of heterogeneity of preferences among the world's consumers.

In these cases, Levitt's globalization thesis would appear to be at odds with flexible response at the level of national competitiveness and demand. This dilemma of the need to enhance efficiency through global integration, and yet enjoy flexibility and responsiveness to differences and changes in national product preferences, represents one of the key emerging trends of the 1980s and 1990s.

What of the potential significance of government policy to industries? Porter's view neglects this somewhat. For Porter, it is best to consider the impact of government policy 'through' the five forces, rather than as an especially influential force in its own right. A similar treatment is made of the role of labour within industries. In both of these areas, analysis is founded on the economic rather than the political or social dimensions of factors that are likely to be of serious import in many industries. For example, the nature of government policy can 'make or break' particular sectors: UK energy, science and technology policy, for instance, has been an important influence on the very existence and maintenance of the

---

Case study 3.1 The impact of government policy on the renewable energy industry

Michael Porter's framework (1980) for analysing industries (the five force model) does not recognize the potential impact of government policy as a 'force' in its own right. The example of state funding for renewable energy demonstrates how important governmental support can be for industry prospects.

Interest in various 'green' energy sources, such as wind and wave power, was rekindled in the aftermath of the 1973/74 oil crisis. In 1976, wave energy in particular, was considered to be the most attractive of these energy sources and so won a degree of governmental support for the funding of research and development. This move built some momentum for the development of offshore wave energy systems (as evidenced by the 'Salter Duck', for example). However, by 1983, wave energy research in the UK had all but closed down, with the decision by the (then) Department of Energy being described as one of the most prominent of turnarounds in the department's funding of research and development. Today, the establishment of the wave energy industry segment remains hardly any further forward than it was more than a decade or so ago.

Wind energy might be said to have experienced the reverse situation in terms of the willingness of central government to fund related research and development. In the 1970s, the prospects seemed gloomy as wind energy was seen as one of the least promising of the renewable energy sources. Now, it enjoys much greater support than (offshore) wave energy R&D. Nevertheless, the prospect for the development of this segment has stalled over the issue of actually installing wind turbines. In many cases, obtaining local authority planning permission has represented quite a stumbling block for developers (potential competitors) to surmount.

The establishment of a UK renewable energy industry generally has suffered noticeably in comparison with the nuclear energy sector, where governmental funding to resolve technical and economic performance difficulties has been, on average, 10 times greater. Clearly, the establishment of the nuclear energy sector has benefited greatly from government policy towards research and development funding in the energy area, while the renewable energy industry has not done so well.

Taken from Genus, 1993.

---

nuclear energy industry, which has benefited greatly from subsidies, whereas the domestic renewable energy sector has struggled to become established without such support (Case study 3.1).

Ultimately, the most severe difficulty that could be posed for the supporters of structural analysis, and indeed for the validity of any of the analytical techniques discussed in this chapter, is that it does not matter. The following quotation comes from the work of Richard Rumelt and is illuminating:

> The majority of the 'residual' variance [in the performance of different business units] is due to stable long-term differences among business units .. . Business units differ from one another within industries a great deal more than industries differ from one another.
>
> *Rumelt, 1991, p. 168*

The 'residual' variance mentioned refers to the fact that a study by Schmalensee had previously concluded that industry factors could only explain a very small portion of variance in performance between business units. This would therefore seem to have dealt a terminal blow to the classical portrayal of the importance of industry sector to firm profitability.

3.3 Industry evolution: the product life cycle

The product life cycle is closely associated with the work of Levitt. His seminal article, like that of Porter, has been very influential and his work on life cycle theory is widely taught in universities. Levitt's view was that the product life cycle concept was, at the time he was writing, 'almost totally unemployed and seemingly unemployable' (Levitt, 1965). In his view, the time had come for a familiar concept to be put to work. In order to turn knowledge of the existence of the product life cycle 'into a managerial instrument of competitive power', Levitt provides an elaboration and application of the product life cycle, described below.

The stages of the product life cycle are fourfold and are illustrated in Figure 3.2. In Levitt's words 'the life story of most successful products is a history of their passing through certain recognizable stages' (Levitt, 1965, p. 81). The first of these stages, Stage 1, is 'market development' (often referred to as 'introduction'). This first stage is when a new product is introduced to a market before demand for it has been proved, and often before all of the technical aspects relating to the product have been resolved. Sales at this time tend to be low and slow in growth. Stage 2 of the product life cycle is termed 'market growth' by Levitt. Demand 'takes off' and the total size of the market grows rapidly. The third stage is 'market maturity': market demand levels off, growing only at the rate of 'new family formation', or as existing customers replace items already purchased. Finally, Stage 4 is 'market decline', the phase of a product's life cycle where it loses appeal to consumers and there is a reduction in sales volume.

At each stage of the life cycle for an industry the way in which competitive conditions determine competitive strategies is as follows. In the introductory stage, the major issue is whether to 'lead' or to 'follow'; firms that are innovating bear the brunt of the initial risks that may be associated with introducing a new

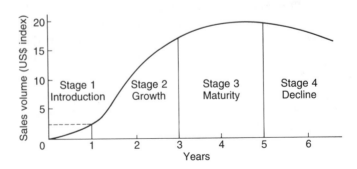

Figure 3.2 The product (industry) life cycle. (Source: Levitt, 1965.)

product to a market. There will not be much in the way of demand so there is the likelihood that marketing expenditure will have to be high to increase awareness of the product. In addition, the pressure will be on to recoup possibly very large outlays on research and development, when despite this there may still be uncertainties to resolve, concerning product technology and industry standards. One example of the latter is the video cassette recorder industry, where a number of years elapsed before VHS became the industry standard format, eclipsing Betamax and Video 2000.

In the growth stage many of the 'bugs' associated with initial development of the product will have been ironed out. As demand grows, the follower firms enter the industry; imitation of the product means that it becomes increasingly standardized. The task for the leading firm(s) is thus to ensure that consumers try their brand (as opposed to merely getting them to try the product). The fight for market share is now well and truly under way.

In the maturity stage, the emphasis switches from marketing as it will be difficult for firms to take share from others. Where an organization could expect its growth to parallel that of the market in the first two stages, now it has to improve its cost efficiency and price performance to be profitable. Differentiation may take the form of service and packaging.

Finally, in Stage 4, decline spells the exit of many firms. The industry becomes increasingly concentrated, passing into the hands of those most able to live with low prices and margins. Some organizations will be able to make something of life at this stage by harvesting carefully, selecting the customer segments and distribution outlets most likely to be profitable. Others may merge.

The life cycle concept has been the subject of a number of important criticisms, discussed below. The most basic line of attack against the life cycle concept is to focus on the degree to which it is deterministic. Essentially, this line of criticism questions the 'given' shape of the life cycle curve, compared with what is known of industry or product performance in practice. Moreover, to dispute the shape of the life cycle, is to dispute the length of the various stages within it. Finally, the idea that at each stage of the life cycle certain demand conditions exist which determine suitable competitive and operational strategies is the ultimate target for criticism.

These criticisms require further explanation. First, the duration of stages of the life cycle varies markedly between different industries. This, plus a certain lack of clarity about what stage an industry is in, blunts the usefulness of the life cycle as a tool for strategy formulation. In addition, growth in industries may not follow an 'S'-shaped curve at all, since some stage(s) may be skipped altogether. 'Fad' industries may see very rapid growth, little or no maturity stage and then 'decline', while other industries barely become established so that introduction is, to all intents and purposes, followed by decline. What is more, the nature of competition can be expected (and seen) to differ between industries that are nominally at the same life cycle stage.

A particularly important point is that companies are not necessarily 'sitting ducks' and can affect the shape of the life cycle, through marketing activity or new product innovations or refinements (Porter, 1980), for example. Examples of this include the 'mega-marketing' strategies and more political activities in which firms get involved. In one sector, one can cite collective action by US cigarette manufacturers in the 1970s and 1980s to lobby against the 'ethical' cigarette (i.e. containing no or low nicotine). In various countries such lobbying has aimed at maintaining pre-existing levels of advertising, sports sponsorship and the 'freedom' to smoke in public places. In these ways, extension of the life cycle beyond the point of decline may be achieved.

The relevance of process innovation and the dematurity of technological life cycles to such shaping of industry life cycles also merits attention. For instance, the diffusion of new technology (in the form of 'hardware' and organizational processes) throughout the world automobile industry has been quoted as one example of the way in which it was thought that a 'mature' technology had been refined. New practices and methods, largely arising from the operations and innovations of Japanese car firms, represent the dematuring of what was previously standard in the industry. Thus, in a general sense, the link between technological development (and redevelopment) and the evolution of an industry may be understood. This is in terms of the conventional wisdom of what constitutes the factors that must be got right if competitiveness is to be maintained (or at least not lost). This issue of technological dematurity as it applies to the internal strategic capability of firms, is considered in Chapter 4.

All of this assumes that the same unit of analysis is being considered. But a word of caution is warranted: the distinction needs to be made between 'industries', representing product 'classes' and 'forms', and, product 'brands' (Dhalla and Yuspeh, 1976).

Of these categories, 'product classes' represent the most general descriptor, referring to, say, 'cereals' or 'wine' (alcoholic) both of which have a life span measurable in centuries past and probably to come. Durable generic product classes such as these appear 'impervious' to the dictates of life cycle pressures, in the absence of technological breakthroughs, as long as they satisfy some basic need (Dhalla and Yuspeh, 1976).

'Product forms' tend to be more unstable than 'product classes' and correspond to what many commentators have in mind when they apply the life cycle concept to a 'product'. An example of the difference between 'class' and 'form' is the distinction that may be made between the 'class' of 'cigarettes' and product 'forms' such as 'filter' or 'non-filter', or 'high tar' versus 'low tar' cigarettes. Finally, brands should be a self-explanatory category, since brands refer to the particular individual products that firms sell, usually recognizable by their name and brand image conferred by advertising, promotion and reputation (such as Kellogg's Cornflakes, Cadbury's Wispa chocolate bar, etc.). Case study 3.2 illustrates the limitations of the product life cycle concept.

3.4 Evaluating competitive position: market share, strategic groups and competitor analysis

The analysis of market share and market power has long been a central strand in textbook treatments of the way in which the competitive position of an organization may be understood. It has also been the source of much contention,

Case study 3.2 Problems with the product life cycle concept: the computer industry

Some of the criticisms of the product life cycle may be illuminated by reference to developments in the computer industry in the 1990s. In particular, issues connected with the shape and stage of the life cycle and industry definition need to be considered.

The revolutionary rise of the personal computer in the early 1990s has contributed to what has been termed the 'chaotic nature' of the computer industry, with the wide availability of low-priced, 'clone' PCs. By 1992, the personal computer had become the mainstay of the computer industry, with PCs linked into powerful networks heralding a decline in the role of the mainframe and mini-computer. This was actually a process that had evolved, slowly at first, over the course of a decade, but that was not seen or accepted by the larger manufacturers, including IBM. To them, this was a 'shattering' development.

In life cycle terms the problems relevant to these changes are several. First, the matter of industry definition: is it defensible to talk of the life cycle for the computer industry as a whole when personal computers and mainframes are constituents within it enjoying vastly different fortunes?

This brings forth the issue concerning the distinction between generic product classes and product forms. This issue has implications for considering the stage of the industry life cycle (and therefore the requirements of competition). Considering the computer industry overall might suggest a product for which, arguably, there would be a continued need far into the future and which would enjoy gentle long-lived maturity after the initial satisfaction of basic demand. However, this is not necessarily the same for product forms (mainframe versus PC) or individual product brands. Within the computer industry, mainframes may be seen to have been in decline, whereas personal computers were in 'growth'. Major manufacturers are typically involved in both areas, so once again care needs to be taken: the two areas are connected and it is likely that actions taken in one aspect of the business will have spin-offs elsewhere.

Furthermore, the 'actual' and 'prospective' life cycle stage for a product (form or brand) may be as much to do with the perceptions of manufacturers as with sales figures. As mentioned above, the PC 'revolution' evolved over a number of years. The 'sudden growth' of the segment may not be merely a matter of the actual change in sales volume figures but an issue connected with the willingness of participants in the industry to envision it, or to accept the decline of their established mainframe business.

Information taken from the Financial Times, 30 September and 29 October, 1992, contributed to this case.

particularly regarding the relationship between market share and profitability. Studies under the Profit Impact of Market Share Programme (PIMS) and by the Boston Consultancy Group (BCG) have asserted and reasserted the relationship between market share and profitability. The BCG have underpinned this work with research on the experience curve concept (Henderson, 1979).

The role of experience here is important. Essentially, this is encapsulated by the BCG's 'law of experience' which relates to the observation from their studies of declines in unit costs with increases in cumulative production across a variety of industries. These reductions in unit costs amount to 20–30% with each

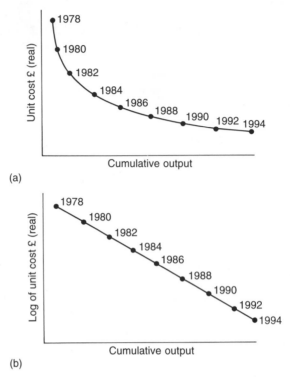

Figure 3.3   (a) The experience curve; (b) The experience curve (logarithmic scale).

doubling of cumulative production of a 'standard' product. A hypothetical experience curve is given in Figure 3.3(a), while Figure 3.3(b) shows the same curve translated into logarithms to give a straight line.

In Figure 3.4, the experience effect for Firm A is contrasted with that for Firm B, which is achieving more substantial cost reductions as a result of its faster growth in cumulative output over the years. Taking advantage of this superior cost performance should allow Firm B to price lower than Firm A. The benefits of experience may, then, be said to confer cost, price and ultimately profitability advantages for firms with large market share. It is on the basis of such analysis that the pursuit of market share is suggested as the primary strategic goal for firms.

There are certain weaknesses in this argument, however. Most notably, as with other concepts discussed in this chapter, the experience curve effect is assumed to be predictable, law-like and automatic. Little recognition is given to the possible centrality of learning processes and innovation which may underpin the experience effect, only cumulative output. For example, cost reduction may depend on the ability of individual organizations to assimilate new ways of doing things from competitors, – with regard to achieving cost and quality benefits from quality circles, say. The transfer and diffusion of such practices throughout the firm is unlikely to be frictionless and may involve a great deal of effort, negotiation and even failure before any cost benefits are realized. The

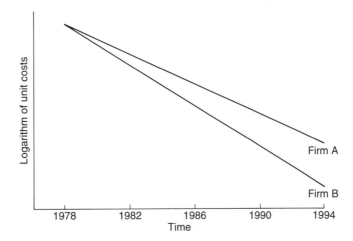

Figure 3.4 The experience curve effect for Firm A (slow growth) and Firm B (faster growth).

ability of an organization to produce internally improved work routines is also not a 'given' and is neglected in the experience curve approach.

More generally, the relevance of market share to strategic performance has been the subject of much debate. The validity of the expectation that large market share should bring forth strategic benefits, including higher profitability than low share competitors, has been called into question. Thus, while the evidence of a link between market share and profitability appears 'incontrovertible', there remains much disagreement about the interpretation of this relationship and, therefore, with the proposition that high market share should be the primary strategic goal for a firm to pursue (Grant, 1991).

A number of objections may be raised here. The first involves understanding the difference between 'association' and 'causation'. Hence, there is doubt that:

- market share confers (i.e. 'causes') superior profit levels
- profitable firms use their retained earnings so as to subsequently boost their market share
- both market share and high profitability are the consequences of some other third variable, say the outcome of innovativeness and learning capacity.

The basic point is that the extent to which high market share can be said to be the cause of high profitability is at best unclear (Grant, 1991).

It is also necessary to recognize that market share leadership is not, in any case, an intrinsically 'good' thing (Woo, 1986). Moreover, the fact and nature of effective businesses with low market share should also be addressed (Woo and Cooper, 1986). To deal with the first of these areas, it is possible to identify factors that seem to explain the performance of market share leaders experiencing low profitability (indicated by pre-tax returns on investment of below 10%; 'high' profitability for market leaders is denoted by pre-tax returns of over 40%).

The lack of flexibility of poorly performing market leaders operating in unstable environments is cited as a key factor. In particular, attempts to build internal synergy by sharing inputs across divisions (for example arranging the joint use of marketing resources) can have the effect of producing a similarity of outlook that leads to the neglect of underlying differences between divisions in terms of the abilities required for handling technological and market change. Moreover, commitments to internally negotiated pricing structures and sharing of facilities, especially for the low return market leaders, may have a restrictive bearing on decisions to exit declining markets because of the potential impact on other parts of the organization as a whole (Woo, 1986).

Some research into the strategies of low market share businesses has appeared in the small business literature (although the terms 'low market share' and 'small business' are not, of course, synonymous). Historically, this literature has tended to recommend firms with low market share to avoid head-on competition with larger rivals. Instead, they were advised to focus on selected product/market niches, localizing their operations and following a high quality, low volume business strategy. In essence, these prescriptions were the exact reverse of the orientation suggested for larger businesses (e.g. Hosmer, 1957).

Somewhat more recently, research such as that carried out by Hammermesh, Anderson and Harris (1978) and Woo and Cooper (1986) has considered how low share businesses have maintained their profitability performance by, effectively, not 'biting off more than they were able to chew'. Whereas ineffective low share businesses (i.e. those with a return on investment of less than 5% and market share of less than 20% over a specified four-year period) spread resources thinly over disparate activities including broad product scope, intense marketing and vertical integration, effective low share businesses competed rather differently. The latter showed less of a tendency to try to ape larger competitors. Instead, effective low share firms were characterized by 'selective focus' on key competitive activities crucial to success. In particular, such firms tended:

> To pursue a high quality, medium price policy complemented by careful spending on marketing, R&D and vertical integration.
>
> *Woo and Cooper, 1986*

These conclusions are of particular interest as they pre-date the emergence of work that emphasizes the definition of organizations in terms of their central 'core' activities, as well as countering the 'large-scale' philosophy of earlier contributions to strategic management. In short, then, market share may be an important indicator of competitive health but is not the be-all-and-end-all to understanding sources of profitability and, crucially, innovativeness and flexibility in industries characterized by changing fortunes and dynamics.

The final stop on this journey through analytical techniques for understanding industry structure and competitive position is with strategic group analysis, competitor analysis and market segmentation. Here, in particular, the focus is on Porter's work (1980) on strategic groups and competitor analysis. What these have in common is some attempt to combat the possible unwieldiness of the concept of 'industry' by allowing the strategist to construct more meaningful understandings of who or where competitors are and their relative position and strategies based on such insight.

Porter declares that characterizing the strategies of all significant competitors is the first step in structural analysis within industries, allowing the mapping of particular sectors into strategic groups. (Such characterization should involve the analysis of competitors' strategies, capabilities and the implications of likely moves, according to Porter.) A strategic group is 'the group of firms in an industry following the same or a similar strategy' (Porter, 1980). There may be only one group in an industry if all significant competitors are following the same strategy or, at the other extreme, every competitor might represent a different group if each has a different strategy. According to Porter, however, it is more usual for there to be a small number of strategic groups within an industry reflecting the essential differences in strategy followed within it.

An example of a strategic group map is given in Figure 3.5. It is constructed by selecting key dimensions of competition within a hypothetical industry to form the two axes that frame the map. These axes are: the degree to which a full range of products is provided ('specialization') and the extent to which competitors perform activities ranging from manufacture through assembly to sales ('vertical integration'). Other dimensions that could be used to construct a strategic group map include geographical coverage, marketing intensity, research and development (R&D) intensity and so on.

Porter is keen to stress that the dimensions chosen and the strategic groups thereby defined are not the same as the market segments that might be defined for competitors. Rather, a broader conception of the strategic posture of the competitors is involved, which may include their relationship to a parent if they are subsidiaries. For example, firms in the music recording and distribution industry may pursue different strategies depending on whether they are divisions of larger media and entertainment conglomerates or 'independents'. Porter also employs the concept of 'mobility barriers' to explain how the differences between strategic groups can create barriers to entry to those wishing to enter a group either from outside the industry or from another strategic group. Thus a strategic group enjoying high mobility barriers, by virtue of the importance of scale economies and marketing spend, for instance, will be better protected and more profitable than a strategic group where the minimum efficient scale of operation and reliance on marketing is lower.

In terms of the theme of the nature of industry boundaries and the specification of who 'competitors' are, the notion of strategic groups may be viewed somewhat differently, especially when considering the nature of strategic groups alongside the analysis of industry structure. For example, it is claimed that while Porter himself discussed the need for a dynamic analysis of industry, focusing on industry change and development, the popularization of the five force framework has emphasized a rather static view of its application. If this condition applies to the employment of strategic group analysis, which might otherwise provide a more manageable means of locating and understanding the more direct sources of competition within an industry as a whole, then some remedy is required. One suggestion is to use strategic group theory and Porter's notion of mobility barriers in order to develop the idea of 'strategic space' into:

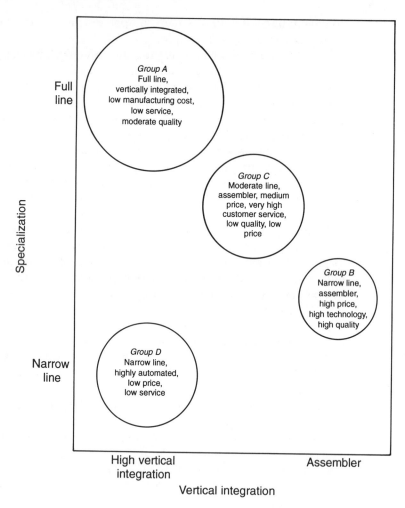

Figure 3.5   A map of strategic groups in a hypothetical industry. (Source: Porter, 1980.)

A framework with which firms can begin to map their strategies against the moving target of changing industry structures.

Segal–Horn, 1992, p. 97

Of particular note here is the fact that 'strategic space' refers to the areas of potential opportunity within an industry. These areas will not yet be available for exploitation by competing organizations, but as conditions develop they are likely to increase in potential. The feasibility of accessing this strategic space (or parts of it) depends on the effectiveness of the mobility barriers within different strategic groups. To reiterate, mobility barriers are those that might prevent the movement of the strategy of an organization. More specifically, and somewhat underplayed within the Porterian view, mobility barriers are supported by the assets and resources of members of strategic groups (Segal–Horn, 1992).

The nature of mobility barriers and the concept of strategic space have been investigated and developed on the basis of a study of the European food processing industry (McGee and Segal–Horn, 1988). The history of the sector has been characterized by shifts in the nature of competition based on the different asset bases and relative power positions of various wholesalers, manufacturers and retailers.

At the beginning of the 1990s, the character of the industry appeared to be shifting in a particularly fundamental way – in the direction of a truly 'European' industry. Previously, even multinationals in the sector organized themselves on a national basis, with activities from manufacturing to marketing being set up and operated on a domestic footing. Hence, the shift represented a move away from strategies geared towards serving specific domestic markets and facilitating local responsiveness, to serving consumer tastes.

Where do mobility barriers and strategic groups fit in? As far as strategic groups are concerned, the changing face of the food processing sector in Europe may be understood by reference to Figure 3.6. Strategic groups are mapped according to two dimensions reflecting the key bases of industry competition likely to be relevant to change in the sector: geographic coverage of EU territory; and brand (or product) strength, as indicated by marketing intensity, in terms of the ratio of marketing costs to total costs.

Constructing a map from these dimensions, and other information gained from interviews with executives in the industry, results in the definition of four strategic groups, A–D. The principal distinction may be made between group D firms, which supply mainly domestic retail outlets and whose brands lack a readily identifiable name (e.g. Hazlewood Foods), and those in group A where competitors such as Nestlé and Pepsico offer strongly branded products in a 'multidomestic' way.

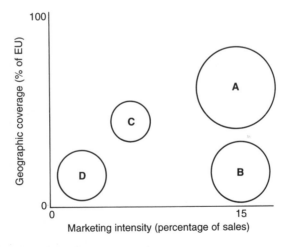

Figure 3.6 Strategic groups in the European food industry in the 1980s. A, multinational branders; B, national branders; C, weak national branders with direct (own) branding for retailers outside home territory; D, national direct (own) branders. (Source: Segal–Horn, 1992.)

The asset base of mobility barriers may also be explained by focusing on groups A and D. Group A firms are effectively able to thwart the entry of others into that group in a number of ways. In particular, marketing and R&D capabilities and brand identification stand out as being difficult to replicate. For group D, capabilities such as those embedded in local market knowledge are likely to impede the mobility of would-be entrants. However, those barriers that are associated with low-cost production and national scale economies are vulnerable to competitors with lower costs and higher volumes, for example. These might be similar firms operating in other national markets looking to develop new markets.

Finally, the concept of 'strategic space' needs to be related to a dynamic view of industry change (Figure 3.7 gives a matrix portraying possible future opportunities within the industries in terms of where existing strategic groups could move). For instance, for group D, the extent to which scale effects are critical to sustainable competitiveness, in conjunction with the ability of group members to manage growth in geographical coverage, indicates the likelihood that spaces X and V will be filled. For strategic group A, movement to space W would signal a shift to a more integrated pan-European strategy featuring common branded goods across the region, thus exploiting convergence of consumer demand in the area. For existing group A firms there could be a conflict between such a strategy of regional integration, and existing structures and commitments for serving their different national markets within multinational structures. However, there is the possibility that group A firms could use their existing position as cover, while gradually rationalizing and integrating production and marketing to make the transition towards space W. In these ways it may be possible to envisage future industry opportunities and change, recognizing the relevance of organizational assets and capabilities to the development of protective mobility barriers (Segal–Horn, 1992).

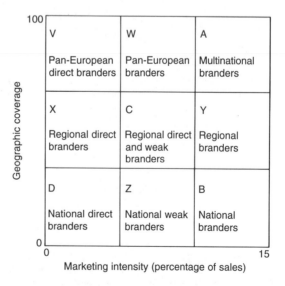

Figure 3.7 Strategic space analysis. (Source: Segal–Horn, 1992.)

3.5 Summary

The chapter has focused on the analysis of industry structure, evolution and competition and, in particular, the work of Porter. The techniques with which Porter is associated have been very influential, particularly, with regard to structural analysis, the five force model. However, a fundamental problem is that the application of this framework has been static in orientation. Moreover, there are considerable difficulties with the very notion of what an industry is and where its boundaries are. Worse still, despite all the tools described above, is the critique that says it is not so much the industry firms select that determines the performance of a business unit, but rather, that good performance is connected to what businesses do internally.

The chapter has also described the main features and limitations of the product life cycle, competition based on the attainment of large market share, and strategic group analysis. In addition to Rumelt's point, a number of objections – to do with determinism and the lack of recognition of the availability of a certain degree of strategic choice for organizations – have been identified.

Study questions

1. What is an industry?
2. What are the main conventional techniques for analysing industries and competitive position? What limitations are there to their application?
3. Consider the relevance of the experience curve to understanding sources of competitiveness in organizations.

Key readings

Porter's *Competitive Strategy* (1980) is essential here, as it includes his 'five force' model, a discussion of strategic group analysis and also the generic strategies framework (which we consider in Chapter 4).

For a consideration of the importance of market share as a strategic objective the article by Buzzell, Gale and Sultan (1975) is a must.

On the product life cycle concept, see Levitt (1965).

The article by Rumelt (1991) is a useful antidote to the view that emphasizes the importance of industries to competitive success.

References

Bartlett, C. and Ghoshal, S. (1989) *Managing Across Borders: The Transnational Solution*, Harvard Business School Press, Boston, MA.

Buzzell, R., Gale, B. and Sultan, R. (1975) Market share – a key to profitability. *Harvard Business Review*, **53**(1), 97–106.

Dhalla, N. K. and Yuspeh, S. (1976) Forget the product life cycle. *Harvard Business Review*, **54**(1), 102–12.

Genus, A. (1993) Technological learning and the political shaping of technology. *Business Strategy and the Environment*, **2**(1), 26–36.

Grant, R. (1991) *Contemporary Strategy Analysis*, Blackwell, Oxford.

Hammermesh, R., Anderson, M. J. and Harris, J. E. (1978) Strategies for low market share businesses. *Harvard Business Review*, **56**(3), 95–102.

Henderson, B. (1979) *Henderson on Corporate Strategy*, Abt Books, Cambridge, MA.

Hosmer, A. (1957) Small manufacturing enterprises. *Harvard Business Review*, **35**(6), 111–22.

Levitt, T. (1960) Marketing myopia. *Harvard Business Review*, July–August.

Levitt, T. (1965) Exploit the product life cycle. *Harvard Business Review*, November–December.

Levitt, T. (1991) The Globalization of Markets, in *Strategy* (eds C. Montgomery and M. Porter), Harvard Business School Press, Boston, MA.

McGee, J. and Segal-Horn, S. (1988) *Changes in the European Food Processing Industry: the Consequences of 1992*. Proceedings of the British Academy of Management Second Annual Conference, Cardiff.

Porter, M. (1980) *Competitive Strategy*, Free Press, New York.

Rumelt, R. P. (1991) How much does industry matter? *Strategic Management Journal*, **12**, 167–85.

Segal-Horn, S. (1992) Looking for Opportunities: the Idea of Strategic Space, in *The Challenge of Strategic Management* (eds D. Faulkner and G. Johnson), Kogan Page, London.

Woo, C. (1986) Market Share Leadership – Not Always so Good, in *Management Policy and Strategy: Text, Cases and Readings*, (eds G. A. Steiner, J. B. Miner and E. R. Gray), Macmillan, New York, pp. 394–9.

Woo, C. and Cooper, A. C. (1986) Strategies of Effective Low Market Share Businesses, in *Management Policy and Strategy: Text, Cases and Readings*, (eds G. A. Steiner, J. B. Miner and E. R. Gray), Macmillan, New York, pp. 385–93.

ANALYSING AND, DEVELOPING STRATEGY IN ORGANIZATIONS

4

Learning objectives

Studying this chapter will enable you to:

- consider the limitations of the linear approach to appraising organizational resources, and strategic choice and implementation
- understand the Porterian view of sources of organizational competitive advantage and the criticisms thereof
- develop an initial appreciation of transaction costs and evolutionary economics approaches and their relevance to the breadth and definition of an organization's boundaries
- consider the 'structure follows strategy' thesis in terms of its relevance to the strategy process as this occurs in practice

4.1 Introduction

In this final chapter of Part Two, the focus of attention turns to the internal aspects of organizational life. It is particularly concerned with the role played by organizational resources within the strategic management process. The aim of the following sections is to illustrate the conventional treatment of organizational resource analysis as this relates to the choice and implementation of corporate, competitive and operational strategies. Another important aspect of the chapter is to indicate possible limitations to such an approach to strategic management, where change and flexibility are prerequisites for survival, if not success. A number of important concepts and analytical techniques are either introduced for the first time in this chapter, or revisited from earlier chapters; several of these will be key to the discussions in Part Three.

Section 4.2 concentrates on the concepts and techniques that, most typically, are presented as the main ingredients with which to prepare an internal appraisal. Conventionally, this analysis is employed in order to facilitate a view of an organization's current strategic capability and overall strategic position (usually by considering its strengths and weaknesses in the light of external opportunities and threats). Some core elements of such an appraisal include product portfolio analysis, applications of economies of scale and the experience/ learning curve to understanding cost efficiency, value chain analysis, and the evaluation of 'synergy'.

Subsequent sections address aspects of the strategic choices that confront organizations and the consequences of these, from the classical viewpoint, for implementation. Thus section 4.3, for example, outlines some of the key issues associated with making strategic decisions that may affect the basis on which the scope of organizational activities is defined, or how the firm is to compete within its chosen markets. The work of Williamson on 'transactions costs' and Porter (again) on 'generic strategies' is considered in relation to the specification of organizational boundaries and competitive strategy.

Section 4.4 addresses the problems of implementing strategy according to the linear approach. This is of prime importance as it reflects practical and conceptual difficulties with this view of strategic management, partly because of the issue of how strategies are/should be made in practice, but also partly because of a lack of recognition of the degree to which strategy 'fails'. These matters are intimately linked to the view of strategy that puts resources, capabilities, change and flexibility to the fore, and which is at the heart of this book. In particular, the debate concerning Chandler's assertion that 'structure (i.e. resource deployment) follows strategy' (i.e. the choice of organizational objectives and goals) is central. A summary of the chapter as a whole is given in section 4.5.

important

4.2 Flexibility and the analysis of strategic capability

A central aspect of this book is the notion that continual and unpredictable external change serve to limit the application of the linear approach to managing strategic development. Instead, organizations that protect and nurture their flexibility are able to cope more easily with environmental uncertainty. Previous chapters have illustrated the failings of planning techniques with regard to the external context of organizations. This chapter, however, especially this section, looks at the approaches that have traditionally been advocated for the appraisal of internal activities.

First, a word about the role of such an analysis within the linear view of the strategic management process. Chapter 1 presented an outline of the linear approach to strategic management (Figure 1.1). Within this framework, the role of an internal appraisal can be seen as contributing to an evaluation of the competitive standing (or 'strategic position') of a firm. This is essentially a matter of comparing the strengths and weaknesses of the business unit in question with external opportunities and threats. The underlying philosophy of this type of approach is that strategy is about establishing, through formal planning and analysis, the nature of the external context of the firm and the 'gap' between existing and targeted internal company objectives and performance. It also incorporates the view that if current performance should fall short of meeting existing objectives, the latter will be reviewed in the light of such analyses. The contribution of this strategic appraisal is therefore to ascertain how well the firm is currently performing in terms of what future industry and macro-environmental trends are likely to be. It is also the basis on which alternative strategic options are to be generated and evaluated, with selected strategies necessitating implementation. Strategic implementation, in essence, is basically the means by which strategy is put into action, including decisions about the organizational resources that may be required in order to make the new strategy operational.

The internal aspect of strategic appraisal is invariably presented as comprising some analysis of the efficiency and effectiveness with which an organization utilizes its resources, plus an assessment of the balance of its resources. In addition, the need to adopt a comparative approach to these evaluations is usually stressed, in terms of how the same analyses match up to past performance in the same organization or to that of the competition, for instance. Typically, certain analytical concepts and tools feature an audit of resources, the experience curve and economies of scale, the BCG product portfolio matrix (or variations on it), financial appraisal, the value chain and synergy (e.g. Johnson and Scholes, 1993).

The resource audit is presented as a useful starting point for understanding strategic capability. The aim of performing such an audit is to identify the quality and quantity of resources available to an organization, and these may be grouped under the headings 'physical', 'financial', 'human', and 'intangibles'. Interestingly, for the perspective of this book, where recognition is given to intangibles, this tends to be superficial and be reduced to brief considerations of the goodwill value of brand names and companies targeted for acquisition (Johnson and Scholes, 1993). A similar point also applies to external sources of organizational resources. Both of these are given fuller discussion in Part Three.

More specifically than this, an analysis of the cost efficiency of the organization is suggested, sometimes (though not always) based on the concept of the experience curve and economies of scale. The experience curve concept was introduced in Chapter 3 in connection with the posited correlation between market share and firm profitability. Figures 3.3 and 3.4 illustrated the central argument underpinning the concept, essentially that firms with faster growth, and thus greater cumulative volume of output than their rivals, will enjoy the advantages of enhanced unit cost reductions obtained through the benefits of experience. This cost advantage would then allow such firms to undercut the competition. The implication of the experience curve concept is that high market share should thus be the central strategic objective for a firm.

While Chapter 3 was, in part, concerned with the limitations of market share as a strategic objective, it is necessary to say more at this point about the shortcomings of the experience concept, particularly with regard to the significance of the organizational processes that may underpin experience-based advantages.

The application of the notion of economies of scale also requires some scrutiny. Again, this was mentioned in Chapter 3 in connection with Porter's five force model, when the reference to scale economies was part of a discussion about the various barriers to entry that may prevent new competitors from joining a particular industry.

Figure 4.1 illustrates the hypothetical effect of economies of scale on the long-run average costs of a plant. Economies of scale occur whenever an increase in the inputs employed in a production process results in a more than proportionate increase in total output within a given period. Increases in scale thus give rise to decreases in unit costs. It is usual to consider economies of scale as arising from three principal sources. These may be technical input–output relationships such as where proportionate increases in inventory are not required to make up increases in output. Secondly, there may be indivisibilities, where inputs are 'lumpy' and thus not available in small quantities. Examples of such large-scale capital-intensive investment include the development or production of new aircraft or oil exploration equipment for inhospitable areas such as Alaska or the North Sea. Finally, specialization may be an important source of scale economies. This will occur when larger output permits greater division of labour within production so that individual employees become more expert at their specialized task and so perform that activity more time- and cost-efficiently (Grant, 1991).

There are three principal problems with applying this concept. Firstly, there is again the presumption that the management of cost and price factors should be the central preoccupations of the firm. The need for product differentiation from the customer's perspective plays no role here. This relates to the availability of product ranges with customized features in lot sizes that may be well below the minimum efficient size indicated by the curve of long run average costs.

The second problem relates to flexibility and the management of production and overall strategy when there are indivisibilities. Research in this area has shown how 'lumpy' investments in operational technology have reduced the scope for decision-makers to change course when unexpected events occur. Examples include highly capital-intensive investments in the platforms, pipelines and so on needed to get UK North Sea oil production underway in the 1970s. The scale of the sums invested (often billions of pounds per field in real terms) and the physical features of the technology, together with the lead time required for implementation (typically three to four years) and the commitment of the firms to their initial decisions, are all important factors. These meant that subsequent improvements in deep-sea oil production technology could not be easily incorporated into this first wave of pioneering exploration and that cash flow

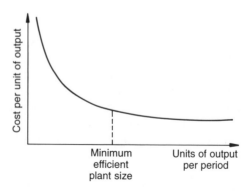

Figure 4.1 Economies of scale. A typical long run average cost curve.

from these early fields was especially sensitive to the instability of oil prices following the oil crisis of 1973/74 (Genus, 1992).

The third problem with economies of scale concerns the management of labour in large plant where this is heavily specialized. Such a Tayloristic division of labour is not likely to be appropriate for developing the motivation and participation that is often written about as being a requirement for contemporary organizations (although this is far from saying that it does not still occur).

An important technique for analysing the extent to which organizations are utilizing their resources effectively in terms of the products they offer, is the product portfolio matrix, (Figure 4.2). This analytical tool is primarily associated with the work of the Boston Consultancy Group (BCG) and is linked to the experience curve concept. The BCG product portfolio matrix emphasizes the importance of cash flow to a business: cash flow associated with the portfolio of products within a business unit, or cash flow pertaining to business units within a diversified firm.

The matrix includes cash generation and cash use, together with their relationship to the effects of experience, the relative level of market share held by a product or business unit, and relevant rates of market growth. Essentially, a balanced portfolio is one in which cash generation matches cash use, where the latter is for investing in future 'star' products/businesses that will be net cash generators rather than users. The framework may be explained in more detail.

Firstly, the matrix features axes of relative market share and real market growth rate. Relative market share is used to establish the position of the product/business in question against rival competitors. This is important since it suggests share advantage should be considered in terms of the leading competitors. (A 20% share where the next leading competitor has 10%, gives a relative value of 2, but where the second largest share is only 5%, the relative value of a 20%

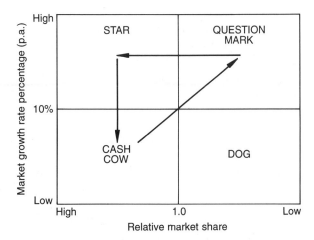

Figure 4.2 The BCG product portfolio matrix. (Source: Henderson, B. (1979) *Henderson on Corporate Strategy*, Abt Books, Cambridge, MA.)

share is 4; on the other hand, having a market share of 5% where the leading competitor has 20%, gives a relative share of 0.25.) Thus the significance of relative market share lies with the extent to which the relative share differential indicates experience and hence cost reduction advantages. This in turn suggests the extent of cash generation (bearing in mind the link between experience, share and profitability discussed earlier).

The other axis, real market growth rate, indicates the need for cash use, or investment. For example, a growing market (in product life cycle terms) should require investment in order to maintain current levels of share, never mind taking share from others (Chapter 3). A declining market might be expected to be less severe on investment; there should not be the same need for investing in productive capacity or marketing as when the market is growing.

Taking the above into account, the arrows on Figure 4.2 indicate the (ideal) direction of cash flow from 'cash cows' which are generators of cash, into the 'question marks' of today, so that the latter will become the 'stars' and cash cows of tomorrow. One of the most controversial aspects of the BCG framework is what should happen to 'dog' products or businesses. It is suggested that these be divested as they are a drain on cash resources which, unlike 'stars' and 'question marks', are unlikely to contribute to future cash generation.

A number of important criticisms have been levelled at this type of portfolio analysis. Some of these relate to technical difficulties that may be involved in constructing a matrix in practice, others to the general strategic implications of the technique. The measurement and definition of the 'market' and its rate of growth represent areas of concern, for example. The point about the uncertain and changeable definition of industry boundaries has already been made (Chapter 3). Depending on how narrowly or broadly this is conceived, a larger or smaller market share can be identified for the firm (e.g. should providers of bottled mineral water define their market as such, or as 'still soft drinks' or 'soft drinks' which, as a general category, would include carbonated products?). This is a matter of managerial judgement rather than hard-nosed analysis (McKiernan, 1992).

What makes for a high growth versus low growth market? In Figure 4.2, 10% is used to distinguish between the two. However, this is unlikely to be appropriate for all industries. What about the difference between growth rates in mature versus newly developed markets? Or the significance for the analysis of fluctuation growth rates or of periods of growth represented by the resuscitation of a declining sector?

In terms of the strategic implications of using the BCG matrix, a central issue is the focus on share relative to the market leader, which connects to the influence of the experience curve. As previously mentioned, this has the potential to blind analysts to threats from smaller-share, possibly more innovative or flexible firms. In short, this aspect of the matrix is not suited to facilitating a dynamic approach to competing. Another important issue is that products or business units may play a positive role within the portfolio, even if on their own account they are not generating positive net cash flows. For example, 'loss leader' products, such as bread or milk, may serve to entice shoppers into a supermarket to purchase more lucrative goods on the shelves. Hence 'dogs' may not be all bad. Further, where there is interdependence among products or business units, it may be impossible to define them as discrete units, as is required for the proper construction of the matrix.

Taken together, portfolio matrices, such as the BCG model, and production-oriented concepts, such as the experience curve and economies of scale, commit a fundamental sin: they ignore aspects of the interrelationship between product and process development. In particular, there is a tendency to treat product and process innovation as having almost law-like properties, where innovation is a 'thing' with a 'life', that occurs somehow independently of the specific context and behaviour of an organization (Clark and Staunton, 1989). This criticism is highlighted in Figure 4.3, which illustrates the Utterback–Abernathy model of technological change. Here, the interrelationship between product and process technology development is essentially characterized by the shape of the product's life cycle and the shape of the experience curve relevant to the production process. Basically, the 'birth' of the product is a dramatic event, removed from the routines and behaviour that characterize organizational processes, while the role of process innovation is to contribute to cost reduction as the product matures. However, it is necessary to keep in mind how the curves of the life cycle and experience are not 'given'. Chapter 3 outlined the ways in which organizations shape product sales through (re)innovation and 'leap-frogging' down the experience curve through assimilating new production practices. In addition to this, 'exnovation' may also be key, in that existing practices may need to be unlearned before new routines can become embedded within the fabric of the organization (Clark and Staunton, 1989). Finally, it would be as well to consider the contribution of process innovation product and general strategic needs more broadly than just in terms of improvements to cost efficiency. On this latter point, the work of those who have addressed the issue of the interplay and connection between production/operations activities, technology and strategic requirements for innovation, and quality, as well as efficiency, is relevant (Chapter 7).

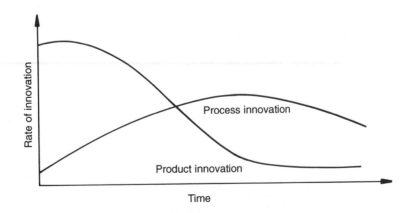

Figure 4.3 Not so dynamic product and process innovation. (Source: Utterback and Abernathy, 1975.)

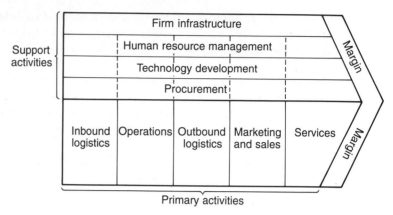

Figure 4.4 The generic value chain. (Source: Porter, 1985.)

Figure 4.5 The value system. (Source: Porter, 1985.)

A summary tool for drawing together the various analyses into a more holistic picture of a firm's strategic capability is the use of value chain analysis, as presented by Porter (1985). The value chain concept harks back to the work of McKinsey on the 'business system'. However, unlike the latter it is based on the activities performed by the firm, rather than on functions within it such as marketing, R&D, finance or manufacturing (Moore, 1992). Moreover, considering the value chains of a firm, its suppliers, distributors and end buyers, allows for the analysis of the wider 'value system' (Porter, 1985). A diagram of the generic (firm) value chain is given in Figure 4.4, while Figure 4.5 illustrates the value system concept.

Porter describes the analysis of a firm's value chain as:

> A systematic way of examining all the activities a firm performs and how they interact ... necessary for analyzing the sources of competitive advantage.

Porter, 1985

The generic value chain consists of primary and support activities, the performance of which may indicate the existence or potential for cost or differentiation advantage. The value that these activities generate is measured by total revenue. This reflects the price a firm's product can command and the units it can sell, which in turn depend on the willingness of buyers to pay the amount charged for what is provided. Crucially, the ultimate objective of any generic strategy is to earn a margin, i.e. the difference between total value and the 'collective cost of performing the value activities'. (Porter, 1985).

The five primary activities referred to in the generic value chain are:

- inbound logistics
- operations
- outbound logistics
- marketing and sales
- service.

Inbound logistics is a term that refers to activities connected with receiving or storing inputs into the production process; as such it may involve inventory management, handling raw materials or dealings with suppliers. Operations activities are those that revolve around the transformation of those inputs into the product that is to be provided. These activities relate to machining, assembly, packaging or the maintenance of operational equipment, for example. Outbound logistics activities are those linked to the physical distribution of the product to buyers, such as processing of orders, or delivery vehicle planning. Marketing and sales activities are those that ensure buyers are aware of the product, persuading them to buy it and making it available in the numbers and locations that will facilitate purchase. This includes selecting and managing relationships with advertising agents, wholesale distributors, and the firm's sales force, as well as attending to pricing and promotion activities. Finally, service refers to after sale activities that maintain or enhance the value of the product, such as in the area of installation, training, repair and spare parts availability.

The four support activities are:

- procurement
- technology development
- human resource management
- firm infrastructure.

Procurement activities are not the same as 'purchasing', according to Porter (1985). Procurement is a broader term that is intended to convey the extent to which purchasing is spread across the firm as a whole and not just limited to the buying in of raw materials for input into the production process. Procurement activities are thus apparent in a range of value activities including accommodation expenses for salespeople and management consultancy, as well as pre-production.

Technology development activities should similarly not be confused with or narrowed down to research and development. The term refers instead to the range of activities connected with attempting to improve the product, but also the process, of the firm. This therefore requires a broad view of 'technology' as not being restricted to its physical connotation or to the work of engineers or the product development department.

Human resource management is another activity that Porter sees as supporting the activities of the firm as a whole. It relates to the hiring, motivation, training, deployment and rewarding of employees. Some of the costs of these activities overall, as well as trade-offs that may have to be made between them, say between extra training and extra pay, are acknowledged by Porter as being notoriously difficult to measure or understand.

Finally, firm infrastructure activities support the entire value chain through the more specific activities associated with general management, planning, finance, legal, information systems and quality control functions.

It is the linkages between these various activities that, for Porter, suggest how the performance of one value activity affects the cost or performance of another. Important linkages may extend outside the firm and relate to its relationships with the value chains of suppliers and distribution channels in the wider value system.

The value chain is quite significant in terms of the development of Porter's work. One of the chief proponents of the industry organization economics approach, Porter, at least appears to be advancing an argument that suggests that the manner in which key activities are performed is fundamental to competitive advantage (quite a different argument from that usually advanced by the industry organization economics school, that it is the attractiveness of the sector that determines the profit potential for a firm). Indeed, it is the performance of these activities that dictates whether a business will be able to sustain a low cost or differentiated position. Thus, arguably, if it is borne in mind that the labels of the value activities or their order can be adjusted according to the needs of particular firms, the framework may be helpful in 'getting at' underlying strategic capability. In particular, the focus on activities and their combination in pursuit of a margin appears to relate well to a view of the capabilities of a firm that recognizes the importance of synergy. Moreover, the value system addresses the potential contribution to competitiveness of parties 'outside' of the firm, an aspect that is distinctly lacking in the other analytical frameworks discussed thus far.

However, like the other analytical tools described above, applying the value chain does invite the conduct of a 'snapshot'-type analysis. The underlying philosophy is one concerned with 'being' rather than 'becoming' (Pettigrew, 1992). It is one which emphasizes 'one-off' analyses of capability for the purposes of formulating strategy, rather than the understanding of sources of strategic renewal through time. There is therefore a marked neglect of the role of organizational learning and unlearning in conditioning the way that activities are performed and changed, which vitally underpins strategic flexibility.

Much the same criticism may be laid at the door of SWOT analysis. This comparison of the strengths and weaknesses of the firm with the opportunities and threats that it faces is all but ubiquitous in strategic management texts, the analysis often entailing long lists of the (supposedly) relevant factors. In addition, the view is given that SWOT analysis provides a means for objectively assessing a firm's overall strategic position. However, this position is undermined by factors that explain how subjective such analysis can be and by the neglect of the intangible resources of the firm.

For example, in terms of strengths and weaknesses, the issues considered are likely to vary according to what place in the corporate hierarchy managers hold. Also, it is possible for senior management to have an inflated or complacent view of how strong an organization is, compared with that of lower management.

Moreover, there may be differences in assessing opportunities and threats, with one research study particularly noting greater sensitivity to the latter (Whittington, 1993).

Interestingly, texts tend to treat issues of organizational culture and values separately from the principal discussion of strategic capability and SWOT factors. This, to be fair, is partly explained by the need to give these issues the attention they merit so that readers new to the strategy field are able to appreciate the influence of an organization's paradigm on the development of strategy. However, to be consistent, such treatments should cater for the nature of organizational culture as part of the assessment of strengths and weaknesses and overall strategic position, which then contributes to the framing and subsequent choice of strategy. A different approach, of course, is the one taken here that aims to circumvent the awkwardness of traditional ways of dealing with such issues. Thus, instead of grafting discussions of managerial judgement, expectations, values and the use of power as it occurs in practice on to the linear model of strategic choice, an alternative treatment is sought. This emphasizes how aspects of behaviour and understanding within (or between) organizations relate fundamentally to ways of learning about their context and capabilities and to their ongoing competitiveness.

4.3 Defining the scope and direction of the firm

The purpose of the internal and external analyses discussed above is to provide a clearer view of an organization's current strategic capability and overall strategic position. Conventionally, this type of appraisal is followed by a presentation of the strategic options open to a firm for a choice of strategy to be made.

These strategic options crystallize around certain key questions that are reminiscent of the fundamental characteristics of the strategy concept. Hence strategic options that may be available to an organization, invite decisions about its scope, nature and direction. Central to the analysis of these types of decision areas tends to be Porter's generic strategy concept and Ansoff's (1965) matrix of alternative strategic directions. In addition to this, 'methods' of development that concern boundary issues are sometimes referred to, i.e. whether the firm should proceed through its own internal means, make use of strategic alliances, or engage in merger/acquisition activity. Typically, relations between firms (in the form of alliances or networks) tend to be underplayed. In addition, the contribution that transactions costs and evolutionary economics perspectives can make to a fuller understanding of the choice issues referred to, is also often neglected or marginalized.

Porter's concept of generic strategies is employed in many texts as a device for considering the breadth of scope of organizational activities and the route that is to be pursued in terms of achieving a sustainable advantage at the competitive level. It is thus presented as being relevant to strategic decision-making at the corporate and competitive levels, with particular resource requirements for each generic strategy representing functional strategy needs.

Porter argues that firms need to choose a clear generic strategy as their primary route to outperforming other competitors in an industry (Porter, 1980). There are three generic strategies from which to select:

- overall cost leadership
- differentiation
- focus.

Rarely, he says, are firms able to follow more than one strategy as their primary target, or basis of advantage, although there may be combinations of either cost leadership or differentiation with focus. The generic strategies are presented in Figure 4.6. The first strategy is cost leadership. This is described as a strategy that has become increasingly common because of the growing popularity of the experience curve concept. Cost leadership entails managing costs so as to benefit from experience and scale effects. While Porter acknowledges that service and quality cannot be ignored, the thrust of the strategy is to achieve low costs relative to competitors. As discussed earlier, a low overall cost position is said to require a high relative market share, which might facilitate economies in purchasing, thus further contributing to cost reduction. It may also necessitate investment in capital-intensive equipment and start-up losses may need to be borne in order to gain share. An important point is that the strategy is about a firm's achieving the lowest cost position in an industry; there can only be one cost leader.

The differentiation strategy is one in which the perception is created, throughout an industry, that a firm's product or service is unique. Porter cites several different forms that this can take. These can be brand image or design (he uses the example of Mercedes), technology (Concorde), customer service (Marks and Spencer), or other dimensions. Clearly, there may be considerable overlap between these and firms may differentiate along a number of dimensions.

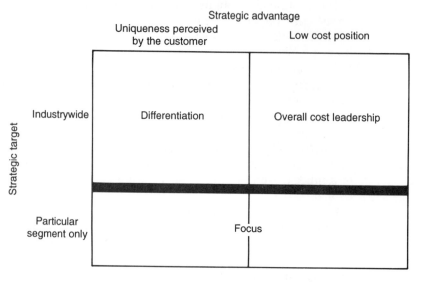

Figure 4.6   Porter's generic strategy framework. (Source: Porter, 1980.)

Differentiation succeeds as a generic strategy because the brand loyalty it engenders insulates the firm from its rivals. This loyalty is reflected in the degree to which customers become less sensitive to price. The higher prices that can be charged by a differentiating firm can permit high margins to be earned, but also allow for less attention to be paid to establishing a low-cost position. Finally, although competing broadly across an industry, a differentiating firm may sell products that have an air of exclusivity attached to them, the price of which may elicit a high margin but which may preclude a high market share.

The third generic strategy, focus, can be combined with either of the first two strategies. It is focusing that represents the narrowing of the scope of activities in the Porter framework; the central aim of the focus strategy is to serve one particular target very well. This target may relate to a particular buyer group, product line or geographical market and is in contrast to the industry-wide strategies of overall cost leadership or differentiation. For Porter, the essence of the focus strategy is that the focuser can serve the targeted niche more effectively and efficiently than can competitors who are competing more broadly. The focuser will thus be the cost leader or differentiator within its chosen target segment, even though it may not be so in terms of the market as a whole.

Perhaps the most contentious aspect of this area of Porter's work, indeed of all his work, concerns what happens to firms that do not follow his prescription to adopt a clear generic strategy, or to avoid mixing generic strategies. He sums it up thus:

> The three generic strategies are alternative, viable approaches to dealing with the competitive forces . . . the firm failing to develop its strategy in at least one of the three directions – a firm that is 'stuck in the middle' – is in an extremely poor strategic situation. . .The firm stuck in the middle is almost guaranteed low profitability. It either loses the high-volume customers who demand low prices or must bid away its profits to get this business away from low-cost firms. Yet it also loses high-margin businesses [*sic*] . . . to the firms who are focused on high-margin targets or have achieved differentiation overall.
>
> *Porter, 1980, pp. 39–42*

The position of being 'stuck in the middle' can be represented graphically, with the most profitable firms within an industry likely to be either the focusers or differentiators with low market share, or cost leaders and overall differentiators with high market share. As Figure 4.7 shows, 'stuck in the middle' firms, according to Porter, are likely to be the least profitable in an industry. (They will be at the bottom of the 'U-curve').

A number of criticisms have been made of the Porter framework. The most fundamental of these is linked to his assertion that successful firms are those that follow a clear generic strategy, not mixing cost leadership and differentiation. In the Porter framework these cannot be pursued simultaneously because of their very different organizational requirements (Table 4.1).

This internal incompatibility of resource and skill needs is what leads firms that attempt to pursue a mix of generic strategies to become 'stuck in the middle', with below average profitability. However, an increasingly common viewpoint

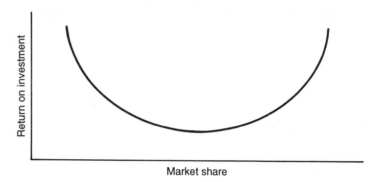

Figure 4.7   'Stuck in the middle'. (Source: Porter, 1980.)

is that the requirements for organizational success are such that both cost efficiency and differentiation need to be emphasized; indeed they are in practice being pursued simultaneously. In addition, even if either cost leadership or differentiation were to represent the underlying strategy of a firm, it is unlikely that such a strategy could be sustained indefinitely. Market fluctuations or the impact of changing macro-economic conditions mean that firms would need to be able to switch between emphasizing lowest-cost and differentiation bases of competition. This in turn suggests that flexibility would be warranted, an issue that does not figure in Porter's discussion of generic strategies; nor do capabilities in the broader sense.

Despite his recognition of the role that resource and skills play within the pursuit of particular generic strategies and his work on the value chain, the essence of his approach is on competitive positioning. The role of internal capabilities is to support the implementation of strategies that are made on the basis of the implications of industry analysis, which we have already seen to be subject to certain practical and conceptual limitations. Moreover, the source of these organizational skills and resources, is again not addressed by Porter. (This is analogous to the discussions above about how the benefits of experience accrue in practice.)

Finally, there are more specific problems with the way Porter argues his case in terms of the generic strategies. For example, he does not make clear the extent to which cost leadership is intended to confer price leadership. Does he mean this to be the case, or is cost leadership more about adopting a 'cost control orientation'? Also, there are various types of differentiation, including marketing and innovative differentiation. Arguably, innovative differentiation could be said to be more incompatible with a cost leadership strategy than marketing differentiation, especially if the latter is contracted out to be managed by an agency.

However, once again Porter is silent on this matter. Part Three considers alternatives to the Porterian approach with particular regard to the issues of capabilities, innovation and the simultaneity of cost and differentiation strategies.

A second area of concern involving the overall scope and direction of a firm relates to what products and markets it serves and the extent to which it is to be diversified. The Ansoff matrix is often employed to outline the various

Table 4.1 Required organizational skills, resources and policies for the three generic strategies*

Generic strategy	Commonly required skills and resources	Common organizational requirements
Overall cost leadership	Sustained capital investment and access to capital Process engineering skills Intense supervision of labour Products designed for ease in manufacture Low cost distribution system	Tight cost control Frequent, detailed control reports Structured organization and responsibilities Incentives based on meeting strict quantitative targets
Differentiation	Strong marketing abilities Product engineering Creative flair Strong capability in basic research Corporate reputation for quality or technological leadership Long tradition in the industry or unique combination of skills drawn from other businesses Strong co-operation from channels	Strong co-ordination among functions in R&D, product development, and marketing Subjective measurement and incentives instead of quantitative measures Amenities to attract highly skilled labour, scientists, or creative people
Focus	Combination of the above policies directed at the particular strategic target	Combination of the above policies directed at the particular strategic target

* Source: Porter, 1980.

strategic directions that firms may take. It is shown in Figure 4.8 (with the additions of consolidation and market withdrawal, to show that all options are not expansionist ones).

As described by Ansoff, the original matrix shows which paths (or 'growth vectors') a firm might take *vis-à-vis* its external environment, and the basis of its hoped-for advantage. Another important facet of this is synergy – the extent to which the firm will be able successfully to develop new product or markets, or diversify. Taken together, these factors, plus the objectives of the firm (as expressed by its required return on investment and sales growth rate), 'describe the concept of the firm's business'. They also describe the extent of growth for the organization and in what direction this is to occur (Ansoff, 1965).

The nature of the growth vectors warrants a little more explanation. First, market penetration is a strategy by which a firm emphasizes the pursuit of increased market share while maintaining its present product/market scope.

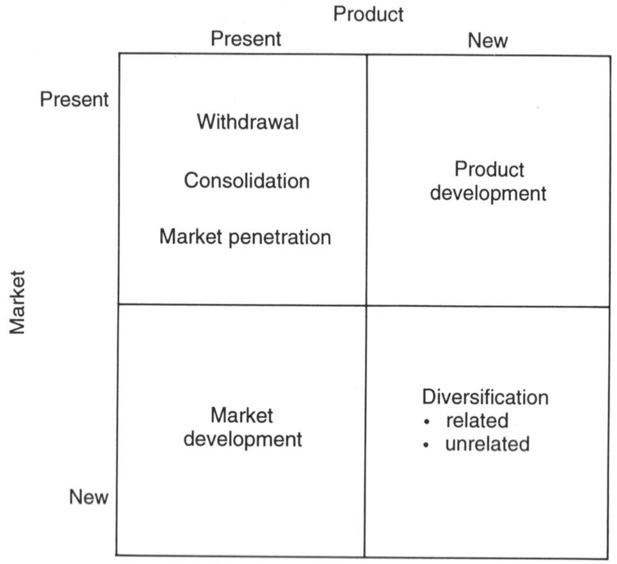

Figure 4.8 A matrix to show alternative directions of strategy development. (Adapted from Ansoff, 1965.)

Market development entails the finding of new markets for the firm's existing products. Perhaps the clearest case of this is the development of new geographical markets, such as the recent expansion of Western business interests into Eastern Europe or China, or the development by many South-East Asian companies of European or US markets. Product development is a growth vector that emphasizes product (or process) innovation, at least entailing substantial modification of existing products to be sold into current markets served by the firm. Finally, diversification is the only growth vector in the Ansoff framework that refers to a combination of new products and new markets being sought simultaneously. Ansoff says:

> The common thread [with existing activities] is clearly indicated in the first three alternatives, to be either marketing skills or product technology or both. In diversification the common thread is less apparent and is certainly weaker.

Ansoff, 1965

An important distinction to make is between related and unrelated diversification. Essentially, related diversification reflects some connection with the organization's existing activities. One example is that when vertical integration takes place, a firm will be extending its activities either backward or forward so as to undertake manufacturing or marketing functions that were formerly provided outside its boundary. Unrelated diversification, at its extreme, takes the form of conglomerate activity, in which there is little or no discernible synergy with current organizational activities. Conglomerate diversification activity is often associated with growth through acquisition and the risks that this tends to involve.

One of the aspects of this early work by Ansoff that tends to be neglected when the matrix is reproduced is its recognition of flexibility objectives being integral to the strategy of the firm. Indeed, the point is made that firms need to renew themselves continually so as to remain profitable in the longer term. Such renewal consists of the ability to bring in new resources and to develop new products and markets. However, opportunities for renewal along these lines can 'be upset by unforeseeable events', some of which may have a positive or negative impact on the profitability of the opportunity or of the firm as a whole (Ansoff, 1965). Such events may be 'acts of God', political change (e.g. war which causes the price of oil to rocket), or scientific breakthroughs. They may or may not be associated with the actions of competitors or customers, who may unexpectedly develop a new product or take their custom elsewhere. What is clear is that the prediction of 'revolutions or inventions is . . . a highly unproductive job'. This, for Ansoff, is where flexibility comes in.

Ansoff distinguishes between 'external' and 'internal' flexibility. What he calls external flexibility refers to the old adage of not putting all your eggs in one basket and suggests that firms can avoid this by being sufficiently diversified. Such diversification is required, it is argued, so as to minimize the effect of external shocks and/or to place the firm so that it can take advantage of future breakthroughs. Minimizing the impact of the unforeseen is a form of 'defensive' flexibility, while 'aggressive' flexibility captures the sense of preparedness for future breakthroughs. The essence of the argument is that organizations should avoid being captive to particular customers, geographical markets or technologies if they wish to sustain flexibility. (Readers may compare this to the discussion of the nature of strategic flexibility in Chapter 1.)

Internal flexibility is presented largely as the ability of the organization to absorb or provide a cushion against unexpected events. This, Ansoff says, may be measured by reference to financial liquidity so that greater flexibility is afforded by a low debt : equity ratio, for example, which retains greater borrowing capacity. (He does mention that a high debt policy may be used to permit the firm to invest in order to increase efficiency and the eventual return to shareholders.) The types of flexibility are related to the maintenance of returns on investment under unforeseeable circumstances, in what is termed the 'hierarchy of the flexibility objective'. This is shown in Figure 4.9.

Two additions to Ansoff's original matrix may be made – consolidation and withdrawal (sometimes a 'do nothing' option is also included). These serve to indicate non-expansionary alternatives that may be especially relevant to situations where existing product/market activities are underperforming or threatened by external change, recession or over-capacity in the sector, for example. Consolidation, for instance, may refer to efforts to restructure or 'turn around' an organization facing lacklustre performance, crisis levels of unprofitability, or lack of working capital. In the 1980s, such restructuring was often undertaken in the name of becoming 'leaner and fitter' and more customer responsive. There is therefore a clear relevance to strategic flexibility that is not always brought out. (There is more on this topic in Chapter 5.)

It is also necessary to consider the withdrawal option in terms of strategic flexibility as this is related to ease of exit from current commitments. Harrigan has observed:

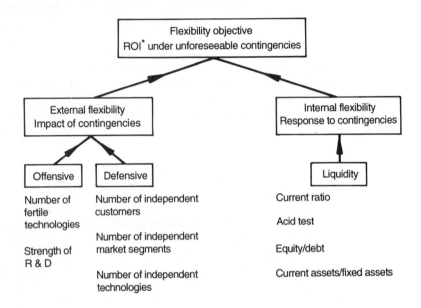

Figure 4.9   Hierarchy of the flexibility objective. * ROI, return on investment. (Source: Ansoff, 1965.)

> The timely extrication of a firm's resources from a business that is failing is a delicate manoeuvre.
>
> *Harrigan, 1985*

Such extrication is delicate partly because some of the sources of inflexibility may be structural in nature; for example, to do with the availability of a market for the resale of the assets of a business. However, exit barriers owe much to the resource base of the firm. Potential contributors to exit barriers thus notably include investments in highly capital-intensive automated production technologies, or a historical commitment to certain activities which decision-makers then become wedded to. (An example of the latter is where government support continues for struggling concerns that may have been great in the past or where closure may result in large job losses.)

It will be useful for the reader to keep in mind this discussion of (some of) Ansoff's work for later contemplation, especially where contemporary approaches to strategy based on the nurturing of core capabilities is concerned. Two areas to watch out for, more specifically, are:

- the sources of new products/markets, which on the capabilities-based approach are connected with fundamental and central key skills rather than with any dispersal of R&D or technology-related capabilities
- what is the connection between product/market developments and the design of organizations related to issues of hierarchical and lateral communication,

motivation, and worker autonomy and creativity? How do these in turn relate to the potential for improved organizational learning, innovation, flexibility and performance? On these counts, Ansoff is quiet.

Finally, in this section, it is necessary to look briefly at what are referred to as 'methods' or 'means' of strategic development (Johnson and Scholes, 1993 [the former]; Thompson, 1993 [the latter]). Typically, these terms are explained as part of the strategic choices confronting organizations which relate to whether they should proceed organically, ally with other parties in various ways or merge with/acquire others. Furthermore, they are presented as ways in which firms may go about fulfilling the Porter generic strategies and 'Ansoff' strategies discussed above.

The potential significance of these decisions should not be underestimated, however. The strategic importance of the method of development issue is the definition of the scope of the firm and its likely attitude towards 'external' relationships. As shown in Part Three, collaborative or contractual relationships with other parties may be an important source of shared learning and flexibility.

The contribution of institutional economists is worth considering here in view of their concern with the nature of the firm and how this changes. For example, the work of Williamson has been directed at explaining why organizations exist and their boundaries and structure. This emphasizes the notion of transaction costs, on which it is assumed that a firm will economize (Williamson, 1975). For our purposes, it is Williamson's continuum of governance structures that is of central importance. This ranges from the firm, on the one hand, to the market, where spot transactions with suppliers are made, on the other. In between these extremes are various types of intermediate governance structure, such as subcontracting or joint ventures (Chapters 5 and 6).

The internalization of activities by a firm (say by way of vertical integration and/or acquisition or merger) can be explained by the ability of the new entity to save on the transaction costs previously incurred. So, for example, US railroad companies merged in the late 19th century, leading to the creation of tracks that were hundreds of miles in length. Previously, tracks were about 50 miles long and were end-to-end systems with operators at adjoining ends engaging in contractual relationships (transactions), partly to co-ordinate policies aimed at winning the custom of users of the track as a whole. These relationships broke down when traffic volume slumped in the 1870s as operators engaged in price-cutting (Moore, 1992). The organizational response of merger of these operators into a new whole may thus be seen as a way of circumventing previous transaction problems. The new entity could be argued to enjoy the advantages of improved co-ordination of activities, at least partly linked to the reduced opportunism (i.e. price-cutting) of the formerly independent operators.

However, the recent vogue for externalizing activities may be viewed in terms of the control problems that face large, integrated and bureaucratic organizations. The internalization of organizational activities may lead over time to growth that is such that certain tasks may be allocated and performed more flexibly and efficiently outside of its pre-existing boundaries. The options then are whether an intermediate or market governance structure should be preferred as the vehicle of future transactions. A market solution may be appropriate where, for example, a standardized item is required that may be supplied by a plethora of bidding suppliers. However, where such an asset is more specific to the particular requirements of the externalizing firm, more continuous relationships with an individual supplier may be favoured.

A view from evolutionary economics may provide some contrast with the transaction costs economics approach. Here, rather than focus on the transaction as the unit of analysis, it is the firm as a 'repository of knowledge' that is the vehicle for explaining changes in governance structure (Nelson and Winter, 1982). In this view, such knowledge enables firms to perform or 'replicate' certain sets of activities, and it is learning, adaptation and experience (i.e. not the 'automatic' variety) that facilitate improved forms of organization or boundary definition. Vital to this process is the association of various inputs, especially human inputs.

Finally, the process of change is said to be a gradual, incremental one, occurring within an interdependent system – a point that is of particular relevance to the interrelationships that firms have with suppliers and competitors, for instance. In particular, this wider network context of existing transactions patterns the evaluation of the pros and cons of moving to new governance structures. So, for example, externalization in the form of 'contracting out' may become a popular option for organizations where existing internal routines are not available or are seen as no longer appropriate for performing the activity in question. This is essentially the rationale that underpins much of central government strategy towards privatization and local government reorganization in a number of countries.

4.4 Structure follows strategy?

The underlying philosophy implicit in the concepts and analytical tools discussed above concerns the notion of 'fit'. Two types of fit in particular pervade much of the literature on strategic management. First, one might refer to environmental fit, or the degree to which the strategy of an organization matches the situation identified from analyses of its external environment. In this connection certain texts speak of the 'suitability' or 'strategic logic' of alternative strategic options when discussing criteria for evaluating between them in order to facilitate the choice or selection of a strategy. Secondly, 'structural fit' is often at the heart of treatments of strategic implementation where the afore-mentioned strategy is made operational. Hence the linearity of this approach is presented as one in which the strategy of the organization is formulated and then appropriate actions are taken to ensure that the necessary resources are managed so as to implement the chosen strategy successfully. In this way, it is said that 'structure follows strategy'.

The 'structure follows strategy' thesis is identified with the work of Chandler (1962) and has been influential on strategic thinking. Essentially, what Chandler did was to study the relationship between changes in organizational form, strategies of growth and external change in relation to activities within four US industrial companies (Du Pont, General Motors, Sears Roebuck and Standard Oil of New Jersey). His definition of strategy was mentioned in Chapter 1, but may usefully be paraphrased here to underline his view of the strategy–structure relationship. Thus the analysis and selection of a strategy is what is being referred to when he writes of the determination of the long-term goals and objectives of the firm. However, 'structural' issues are meant when the specific actions and resource allocation necessary for carrying out (implementing) strategy are referred to.

An illustration of this structure follows strategy approach is given in Figure 4.10. In the view of Galbraith and Kazanjian (1986), a change in strategy requires change in all of the organizational dimensions identified in the diagram, so that the form of the organization remains consistent with its strategy. (Note that in Figure 4.10 one of the organizational dimensions is indeed 'structure', as used in its narrow meaning.) Moreover, there needs to be consistency across various of these dimensions if fit is to be maintained with the strategy. Hence change in the reward system will need to be accompanied by change in the nature of the task being performed, routes for career progression or the scope of autonomy implied in the way work is designed (Galbraith and Kazanjian, 1986).

The problems of applying such an approach in deliberately formulating strategy are many. Achieving fit between organizational strategy and the external environment is likely to be frustrated by constant change in the latter, a situation not helped by the methodological difficulties that characterize would-be analytical tools. It can be seen that real-world change, not least of all the moves of competitors and macro-level uncertainties, mean that the currency and consequences of particular strategies are not easily forecast before implementation. Hence many of the details of implementation can not be known a priori and are, in practice, worked out through action – action that often changes the course of a strategy. (This brings the difference between intended and realized strategy back to mind.) Of course, there may also be problems associated with poor communication of the intended strategy throughout the organization, or resistance to change.

Another set of objections to the traditional approach concerns the strategy–structure relationship more specifically. Firstly, aspects of the structure of an organization clearly do influence the content of its strategy and the way in which this comes about. Thus many aspects of an organization's 'structure' may be enabling and restraining for certain strategic trajectories that may be followed. In particular, existing power holdings, routines and organizational values condition the way in which activities are performed and the extent to which strategies that imply significant reorientation even appear on the agenda. Such structural factors also affect the type of intelligence data that is gathered – Texas Instruments, for example, emphasized cost data to the exclusion of information on what cost reduction was doing to customer satisfaction and product quality (Miller, 1992).

The 'Icarus paradox' underlines the point (Miller, 1992). The Icarus paradox is essentially concerned with how the ingredients of an organization's success may also be contributory to a subsequent deterioration in performance. In

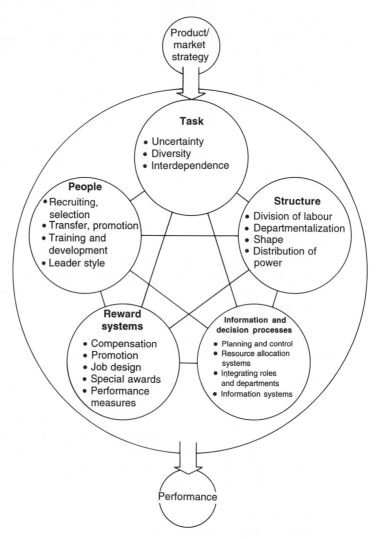

Figure 4.10 The structure follows strategy thesis. (Source: Galbraith and Kazanjian, 1986.)

a similar way to Icarus in Greek mythology, who flew too close to the sun and melted his wax wings, 'outstanding' companies can find that the primary sources of their success can also lead to their decline. An important aspect of this is that the interplay between strategies and structure (i.e. power-holders, leadership style, attitudes and routines) gives momentum to certain trajectories that succeed competitively. These trajectories are: focusing, venturing, inventing and decoupling. However, this momentum is problematic in that, for example, the organization's strong culture becomes rigid, thus inhibiting learning and contributing to strategic inflexibility as strategies of past success are increasingly reinforced. Unfortunately, the emphasis on previous strengths and successes blinds the organization to many current and future requirements, leading to a

Table 4.2   The four trajectories of the Icarus paradox*

<table>
<tr><td colspan="3" align="center">FOCUSING</td></tr>
<tr><td></td><td>*Craftsman* ⟶</td><td>*Tinkerer*</td></tr>
<tr><td>*Strategy*</td><td>Quality leadership</td><td>Technical tinkering</td></tr>
<tr><td>*Goals*</td><td>Quality</td><td>Perfection</td></tr>
<tr><td>*Culture*</td><td>Engineering</td><td>Technocratic</td></tr>
<tr><td>*Structure*</td><td>Orderly</td><td>Rigid</td></tr>
<tr><td colspan="3" align="center">VENTURING</td></tr>
<tr><td></td><td>*Builder* ⟶</td><td>*Imperialist*</td></tr>
<tr><td>*Strategy*</td><td>Building</td><td>Overexpansion</td></tr>
<tr><td>*Goals*</td><td>Growth</td><td>Grandeur</td></tr>
<tr><td>*Culture*</td><td>Entrepreneurial</td><td>Gamesman</td></tr>
<tr><td>*Structure*</td><td>Divisionalized</td><td>Fractured</td></tr>
<tr><td colspan="3" align="center">INVENTING</td></tr>
<tr><td></td><td>*Pioneer* ⟶</td><td>*Escapist*</td></tr>
<tr><td>*Strategy*</td><td>Innovation</td><td>High-tech escapism</td></tr>
<tr><td>*Goals*</td><td>Science-for-society</td><td>Technical utopia</td></tr>
<tr><td>*Culture*</td><td>R & D</td><td>Think-tank</td></tr>
<tr><td>*Structure*</td><td>Organic</td><td>Chaotic</td></tr>
<tr><td colspan="3" align="center">DECOUPLING</td></tr>
<tr><td></td><td>*Salesman* ⟶</td><td>*Drifter*</td></tr>
<tr><td>*Strategy*</td><td>Brilliant marketing</td><td>Bland proliferation</td></tr>
<tr><td>*Goals*</td><td>Market share</td><td>Quarterly numbers</td></tr>
<tr><td>*Culture*</td><td>Organization man</td><td>Insipid and political</td></tr>
<tr><td>*Structure*</td><td>Decentralized-bureaucratic</td><td>Oppressively bureaucratic</td></tr>
</table>

* Source: Miller, 1992.

down-turn in performance. A summary of the characteristics of the four trajectories is given in Table 4.2, while Case study 4.1 illustrates each of them.

So structure influences strategy. However, care needs to be exercised here. Much attention has been given to structure as culture in the strategy literature as well as in organizational theory more generally. While it is as well to consider structure as being more than merely the lines of reporting that appear on the chart that is often referred to as an organization's 'structure', seeing structure as culture can also be problematic. In identifying different types of organizational design there is a danger of short-sightedness concerning the nature of culture and the role that its management can play in managing organizational change. For example, much of the recent debate on organizational form and its relationship with flexibility, or employee motivation, tends to adopt a position in which it is assumed that change of form (e.g. of work group design or autonomy) will necessarily bring about change in culture (i.e. in attitudes to work and to the organization). This, in turn, is expected to have the desired effect on performance in terms of quality of work, efficiency and consistency with strategic requirements in general. It is this type of view that characterizes the writings of the Peters and Waterman variety. Here, achieving 'excellence' is largely a matter of attending to the inward-looking, over-bureaucratic organization so as to allow

Case study 4.1 The Icarus paradox – four trajectories

In his book (1992), Miller identifies four trajectories along which successful firms can get 'trapped' into eventual decline. These are as follows.

First, the example of Digital Equipment Corporation is used to illustrate the 'focusing' trajectory, where 'craftsmen' become 'tinkerers'. Digital made its name on the quality of the design of its computers, but turned in on itself as its engineering monoculture eclipsed marketing and financial considerations. This culminated in the development of a personal computer that was 'out of sync' with the budgets and needs of potential consumers.

The case of ITT demonstrates the venturing trajectory where 'builders' become 'imperialists'. ITT, under its chief executive Harold Geneen, had successfully pursued a diversification strategy, creating what in the 1970s was the biggest conglomerate in the world. But controlling a vast empire that employed more than one-third of a million people in over 80 countries became a matter of oppression from HQ 'hit-men' and an over-reliance on financial reporting in lieu of the substance of product and market issues.

Thirdly, the 'inventing' trajectory describes how 'pioneers' can become 'escapists'. Miller uses the example of a Minneapolis firm, Control Data Corporation, here. Perhaps more familiar to some readers is the example of inventor Sir Clive Sinclair, whose success with various products, from calculators to digital watches, was not matched by the launch of his C5 bike, where invention evidently dominated over market research.

Finally, the car firm Chrysler exemplifies the 'decoupling' trajectory. Here, 'salesmen' turn into 'drifters'. The success accorded to Lynn Townend, former chief executive of Chrysler, is of tripling of international market share within a five-year period. However, this has been seen to have been at the cost of engineering and production activities, as the firm's marketing/sales strengths became over-emphasized.

Adapted from Miller, 1992.

[handwritten margin note: Strong culture – success/failure Kay (1993)]

for the creativity of employees and get the firm 'closer to the customer' (Peters and Waterman, 1982). As noted above, this view of the culture–performance relationship can represent a double-edged sword; a 'strong' culture may be associated with failure as well as success.

Another view of structure and culture is anchored in the individual's interpretation of the meaning of events and language within and outside the organization. In this view, strategic change needs to be understood in terms of how those likely to sponsor or be affected by it 'make sense' of the situation with which they are confronted. This is reflected in the increasing use of metaphor and other symbolic language in the process of strategic transformation in which 'culture' may be thought of as the structuring of language and meaning (Wilson, 1992). More specifically, one expression of the use of symbolism relates to the enhancement of new product flexibility through the conversion of tacit into more explicit knowledge (see Chapter 7).

So, far from 'structure following strategy', the conduct of strategic change may be seen in terms of how individuals perceive, propose or resist the need for change. Of course, this occurs within the context of accepted ways of seeing or doing that characterize the organizations of which they are a part. This point has been underlined in this part of the book, where several of the analytical tools that are supposed to inform an objective appraisal of the external and internal factors affecting strategic choice have been shown to depend on the exercise of managerial judgement for their application.

4.5 Summary

This final chapter of Part Two has addressed the problem of conducting an internal appraisal of an organization in order to assess strategic capability and, in conjunction with external analyses, establish its overall strategic position. Two particular problem areas have been central to the discussion. The first has concerned technical issues involved in employing the concepts and analytical frameworks that typify traditional means of internal appraisal. As well as the difficulties in establishing and measuring variables (what is 'high' market growth or share, for example), more fundamental limitations linked to a second problem area have surfaced. This connects to the presumed sources of competitive advantage that underpin much of what has been discussed above. In short, the role of intangible resources, routines and other aspects of organizational knowledge and culture are inadequately treated, if they are addressed at all. This relates to views of strategy that are not founded on the need for learning/unlearning, since the environment is largely assumed to be static or amenable to accurate analysis. Finally, rather than to see strategic change as a linear exercise of analysis, choice and implementation this chapter has emphasized the interplay between strategic development and various aspects of organizational structure.

Study questions

1. Consider the limitations of the linear approach to analysing and implementing strategic decisions.
2. With reference to an organization with which you are familiar, discuss how far the value chain concept is able to explain current and potential sources of competitive advantage.
3. Using examples from actual practice, consider the merits and criticisms of Michael Porter's generic strategy framework.
4. To what extent do you agree with the statement that 'structure follows strategy'?
5. What factors and theoretical concepts may help to explain the determination of the boundaries of an organization?

Key readings

The work of Michael Porter, again, is essential: *Competitive Strategy* (1980) and *Competitive Advantage* (1985).

Ansoff (1965) gives a 'forgotten' section on flexibility objectives within strategy-making. A useful summary of the work of Porter, Chandler, Williamson, Ansoff and others is provided by Moore (1992).

References

Ansoff, H. I. (1965) *Corporate Strategy*, McGraw–Hill, New York.

Chandler, A. D. (1962) *Strategy and Structure*, MIT Press, Boston, MA.

Clark, P. and Staunton, N. (1989) *Innovation in Technology and Organization*, Routledge, London.

Galbraith, J. R. and Kazanjian, R. K. (1986) *Strategy Implementation: Structure, Systems and Processes*, West, New York.

Genus, A. (1992) The social control of large-scale technological projects: inflexibility, non-incrementality and performance of British North Sea oil. *Technology Analysis and Strategic Management*, **4**(2), 133–48.

Grant, R. (1991) *Contemporary Strategy Analysis*, Blackwell, Oxford.

Harrigan, K. (1985) *Strategic Flexibility*, Lexington Books, Lexington, MA.

Johnson, G. and Scholes, K. (1993) *Exploring Corporate Strategy: Text and Cases*, Prentice-Hall, Hemel Hempstead.

McKiernan, P. (1992) *Strategies of Growth: Maturity, Recovery and Internationalisation*, Routledge, London.

Miller, D. (1992) *The Icarus Paradox*, HarperBusiness, New York.

Moore, J. I. (1992) *Writers on Strategy and Strategic Management*, Penguin, London.

Nelson, R. R. and Winter, S. G. (1982) *An Evolutionary Theory of Economic Change*, Harvard University Press, Cambridge, MA.

Peters, T. and Waterman, R. H. (1982) *In Search of Excellence*, Harper and Row, New York.

Pettigrew, A. (1992) The character and significance of strategy process research. *Strategic Management Journal*, **13**, 5–13.

Porter, M. (1980) *Competitive Strategy*, Free Press, New York.

Porter, M. (1985) *Competitive Advantage*, Free Press, New York.

Thompson, J. L. (1993) *Strategic Management Awareness and Change*, Chapman & Hall, London.

Utterback, J. M. and Abernathy, W. J. (1975) A dynamic model of process and product innovation. *Omega*, **3**(6), 630–56.

Whittington, R. (1993) *What is Strategy and Does it Matter?* Routledge, London.

Williamson, O. (1975) *Markets and Hierarchies: Analysis and Antitrust Implications*, Free Press, New York.

Wilson, D. C. (1992) *A Strategy of Change*, Routledge, London.

STRATEGIC

Alternatives to the Porterian approach - particularly issues of Capabilities, innovation and the simultaneity of Cost + differentiation strategies.

FLEXIBLE MANAGEMENT AND STRATEGIC RENEWAL: CENTRAL ISSUES AND KEY ACTIVITIES

5

Learning objectives

After studying this chapter you should be able to:

- understand the strategic significance of organizational capabilities
- appreciate the potential contribution of intangible resources to developing organizational capabilities
- consider the relevance of 'externalization' and 'de-integration' to the performance of the organization
- relate the concept of 'momentum' to the capacity for organizational learning, strategic renewal and flexibility

5.1 Introduction

This chapter introduces a number of issues that are considered further later on. In particular, it provides the first step in addressing how a more flexible approach to management might be carried out in actual practice. The fundamental point to be made is that flexibility is a capability that organizations may have (whether or not they purposely do anything to foster it). Luck apart, an organization's performance is considered to be connected with the resources and capabilities it possesses or develops, and this is what distinguishes firms that do well from those that do not in the face of a similar external environment.

The nature of these capabilities is likely to be governed by the intangible resources available to the firm, and it is this issue that forms the early part of the chapter. An important area of this discussion centres on the potential for sustaining any advantage conferred by such capabilities – a condition that can not be assumed to be an enduring one. Another important topic, addressed in section 5.2, is the nature of organizational routines. Routines have a vital influence on the way organizational activities are usually performed, and breaking down old routines and developing new practices may be one of the key activities in effecting strategic renewal.

Later parts of the chapter relate recent trends in corporate restructuring and the nature of organizational learning with issues of renewal and flexibility. The restructuring issue is considered in terms of the relevance of the externalization of organizational activities (e.g. to contractors) to the achievement of improved efficiency and innovativeness. This connects with the discussion in Chapter 4 about the limitations of Porter's (1985) generic strategy framework and the 'productivity dilemma' associated with the work of Abernathy (1978). The main concepts addressed here involve economies of scope and of scale.

Section 5.4 outlines the notion of organizational learning and looks at the importance of 'unlearning' to managing renewal. The section moves on to consider the potential significance of 'momentum' and 'inertia' to achieving ongoing learning and incremental change. The likelihood that inability or unwillingness to learn may necessitate a more fundamental reorientation of values and transformation of routines is discussed in the light of an interpretative approach to strategy.

Finally, section 5.5 summarizes the main topics and the issues that pertain to them.

5.2 Capabilities and learning as sources of competitiveness

The importance of strategic flexibility to performance within changeable competitive conditions may be understood in terms of increasingly influential thinking regarding the underlying basis of organizational competitiveness. Thus both the need for and practice of flexible strategic management are related to a perspective that emphasizes the importance of developing strategic capabilities to the enhancement of organizational flexibility and performance. Of immediate concern, here, is the general distinction that may be made between capabilities-based approaches to understanding strategic management and the more static, industry organization perspectives that were the focus of Part Two. In particular, this distinction can be demonstrated in two areas: the definition of the firm's activities and boundaries; and the nature of the underlying sources of organizational competitiveness.

As far as the first of these two areas is concerned, it has been noted that the turbulence of external conditions makes the definition of organizational purpose and mission problematic. Where this is so, the changeability of customers, their needs and the technologies required for providing for those needs, suggests that a more appropriate basis for establishing corporate direction is required. In this light, the resources and capabilities of an organization may provide a more stable and manageable basis for establishing its *raison d'être* and direction.

With regard to the sources of organizational competitiveness, approaches that emphasize the role of resources and capabilities provide an alternative to the work of, for example, Porter. Readers will remember from Part Two that, for Porter (1985), the underlying sources of corporate profitability are the identification of attractive industries and the pursuit of one clearly defined 'generic strategy' (either based on cost leadership or differentiation, in conjunction with a decision about the degree of market focusing that should be followed).

Proponents of capabilities-based approaches to strategic management have two principal objections to the Porterian framework, in line with some of the common criticisms of this type of work. First, the empirical evidence of any link between the 'attractiveness' of an industry and the profitability of individual firms in it, is weak. Even if allowances are made for the difficulties of defining industry boundaries, there may be wide variations in the profitability performance of industry rivals, which should be faced with similar competitive conditions. Secondly, performance differences could be ascribed, in general, to the ability of rival competitors to position themselves appropriately, according to their analysis of industry structure and the definition of a generic strategy based on this. However, such a focus on industry structure or competitor analysis runs the risk of neglecting the capabilities that may be required to sustain the strategy in question. Such capabilities may relate to human, technological, financial or other resources and know-how. Moreover, these sources of strategic capability may be seen as fundamental to strategy development. This is in stark contrast to more traditional linear models of the strategic management process which view resources and capabilities rather as after-the-fact considerations relevant to the implementation of strategy.

Two key aspects of competing on the basis of capabilities are:

- the identification and evaluation of strategically relevant capabilities
- sustained and ongoing development of such capabilities for the future.

The second of these is especially relevant to the pursuit of a flexible approach to strategic management. Central to both aspects, however, is the consideration of capabilities in a strategic light, which stresses the process by which capabilities may be developed or deteriorate. Moreover, the role of intangible resources and organizational learning in this process must receive special attention. This is necessary to compensate for the deficiencies of the more conventional methods of resource analysis singled out in Chapter 4.

Figure 5.1 shows how the management of internal resources and capabilities may relate to strategic performance in a way that goes beyond the understanding given by the work of Porter. It should be noted that the relationship between resources and capabilities is not a straightforward one. The resources that may be at an organization's disposal can be defined as in Chapter 4. Hence, one might be able to perform audits or appraisal of the nature and deployment of resources classified as financial, human, physical (including technological) or product-market related. However, the key to understanding capabilities is to appreciate

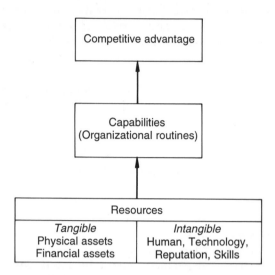

Figure 5.1   The relationship between resources, capabilities and competitive advantage. (Source: Grant, 1991.)

the manner in which organizational resources are co-ordinated or co-operate (Grant, 1991). In order to enhance such an awareness, the role of intangible resources (such as know-how) and the significance of organizational routines are in need of some explanation.

Some intangible resources refer to assets such as goodwill or company or brand image. These are given a value in company balance sheets or can be considered in terms of the difference between the stock market value of such assets (e.g. as paid for when one firm is acquired by another) and their book value. However, a much broader appreciation can be gained of intangible resources. Figure 5.2, for example, presents a framework for understanding various types of intangible resource as well as different kinds of capability differential with which they may be associated. The distinction is made between people-dependent and people-independent intangible resources, although in practice this distinction is not an absolute one. People-dependent intangible resources include the knowledge and accumulated experience of internal employees, plus the knowledge base of what are usually considered to be external factors, such as suppliers and distributors who can play an important part in the production and sale of the products of an organization.

There are also capabilities that stem from the reputation an organization enjoys, its networks or the possession of databases of knowledge. These intangible resources are somewhat dependent on the skills and know-how or personal contacts of the human resources within the firm, but may be thought of as amenable to externalized legal protection, too. Reputation, which relates to the image that competitors, customers or society at large have of the nature and conduct of a firm's affairs, may be developed through the inherent quality or service associated with a product. It may also be enhanced through promotion or advertising, or other forms of marketing activity. However, legal protection may be gained by recourse to laws and regulations that refer to breach of copyright (relevant to product design or name) or libel (relevant to product, brand or corporate image).

In a similar way, the network relationships of the firm may be an important source of capability as it pertains to the personal relationships that employees within organizations have with each other or with external bodies such as professional associations. 'Networks' is a term that also applies to relationships that the firm as a whole has with external parties such as competitors, suppliers, consumer groups or governmental and academic institutions. Taken together, these may form a vital source of new information that might input into the product development or production process activities of the firm. However, the ongoing nature of many of these links makes the sharing of information about certain aspects of the protagonists' activities all but inevitable. Here the role of legal protection, in the form of trade secrecy, patent, or other legislation, exemplifies the potential relevance of 'people-independent' sources of capability (or at least the defence thereof).

Perhaps more obvious forms of people-independent capability are those that relate to intellectual property rights: those intangible resources that firms may more easily be said to 'own' than, say, networks, reputation or know-how. In this regard, the extent to which organizations can buy or sell such assets as patents, copyright designs or trademarks is of significance, again in conjunction with the protective mechanisms embodied in relevant legislation (Hall, 1992). The knowledge associated with these resources is likely to be codified, for example where new product or process specifications are set down and registered with the Patent Office. Such intangible resources are therefore people-independent in that the potential for providing an edge in capability terms stems from their legal context and the nature in which they may be bought and sold. The application of such intangibles may be extended to the protection of tangible resources such as in the ability of firms to apply contracts to the leasing of machinery or motor vehicles. As indicated above, there is some overlap in the characterization of people-independent and people-dependent resources.

The capability differentials referred to in Figure 5.2 are fourfold. Functional differentials exist where an organization is capable of performing particular tasks better than its competitors. This relates to the operational activities of the firm, to do with its manufacturing ability or its skill at conducting market research, for example. As noted in Figure 5.2, this may be a source of capability differential that stems from the organization's relationships with others at its boundary (suppliers, distributors, etc.).

Cultural differentials are more to do with the attitudes and values that characterize the perception of those within the organization towards the need for learning and continual upgrading of performance. This is related to the likelihood that members of the organization will countenance or resist changes to the accepted way of performing existing activities.

Positional differentials exist when organizations are better placed (in space or time) to perform existing activities or improve on them than their rivals are. This advantage may be a firm's geographical location, or its position within a strategic network, which again may involve the proximity and quality of its

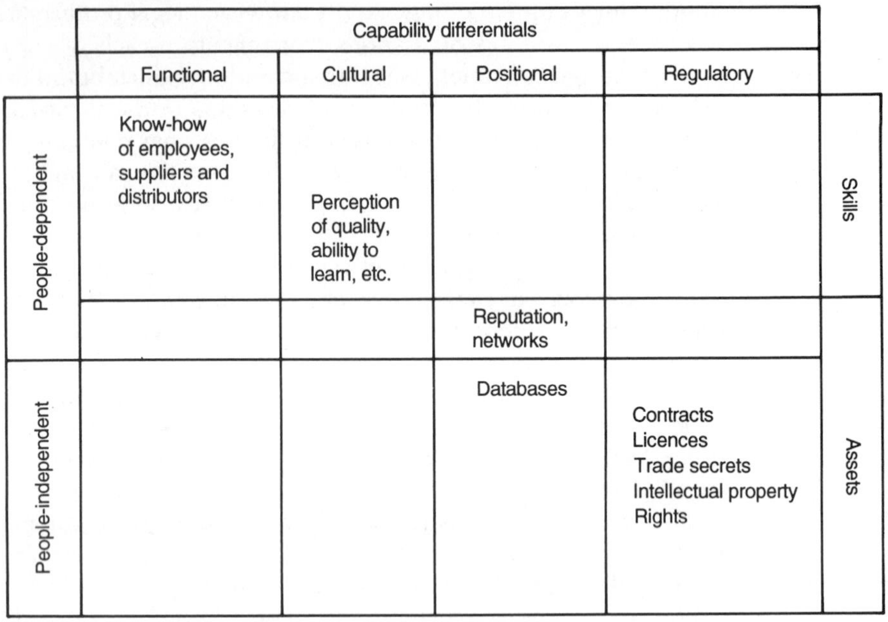

Capability differentials			
Functional	Cultural	Positional	Regulatory

People-dependent / People-independent (vertical left labels); Skills / Assets (vertical right labels)

	Functional	Cultural	Positional	Regulatory	
People-dependent	Know-how of employees, suppliers and distributors	Perception of quality, ability to learn, etc.			**Skills**
			Reputation, networks		
People-independent			Databases	Contracts Licences Trade secrets Intellectual property Rights	**Assets**

Figure 5.2 A framework of intangible resources and capability differentials. (Source: Hall, 1992.)

relationships with other firms, including rivals in strategic alliances. In addition, one can single out the capability of the firm to access knowledge databases and, more generally, to communicate with other parties via computerized information systems. The significance of reputation to the competitiveness of a firm is another type of positional differential that should be acknowledged. Positional differentials are the results of past activities which, it is argued, confer an advantage that would take rivals a long time to imitate (Hall, 1992).

Finally, regulatory capability differentials are reflective of the extent to which organizational assets may be protectable in law. As discussed above, such protection may be applied to trade secrets, intellectual property rights, contracts and so on. However, it should not be assumed that such protection will necessarily be strong; patent protection, for example, can often be easily circumvented.

To reiterate, the key aspect of this part of the discussion is the nature of sustainable competitive advantage and the role of intangible resources therein. It is necessary to introduce the nature of organizational routines at this point, in order to expand upon the sources of and barriers to developing sustainable strategic capabilities. Organizational routines are important to the learning facility (and hence strategic flexibility) of organizations.

Organizational routines pertain to the rules, standard operating procedures and socialization processes that govern the actions and interpretations of individuals in organizations (Nelson and Winter, 1982). As the term suggests, routines become embedded in the behaviour of those within organizations, so that they represent taken-for-granted, regularized ways of handling both familiar and unfamiliar situations requiring action or decisions. They are, therefore, quite an important type of intangible resource, and are linked to the cultural differential that the organization might possess. The nature of routines is sometimes referred to as capturing 'the way things are done around here' in an organization. Furthermore, routines may be said to arise out of the past learning of an organization.

> Individuals' interpretations of positive and negative feedback from the environment and causal relations between actions and results leads to the selection of specific patterns of behaviour, which are judged as more appropriate than others. These emerging behavioural patterns are the outcomes of ... learning processes, and are retained in the organizational memory in the form of rules, routines or standard operating procedures.
>
> *Borum, 1990*

The extent to which such routines are retained by organizations is linked with the sustainability of any strategic edge that may be conferred by capabilities based on routines. This issue also highlights the potential significance of continually being able to develop or upgrade capabilities based on the capacity to alter or modify existing routines.

The retention of advantageous organizational routines is influenced by a number of factors that may briefly be listed as the appropriability, durability, transferability and replicability of the capabilities based on those routines (Grant, 1991).

Appropriability relates to the ownership of the resources that generate rent (profit) for the firm. Clearly, firms own many tangible resources, such as plant or equipment. However, with respect to intangible resources the ownership issue is much less clear-cut. As discussed above, capabilities that are to do with intellectual property are intangible resources that can be protected in law, although the force of such protection is variable. Much of the capability of a firm can be argued to be resident in the skills and experience of its employees. However, this is not the same as its being in the ownership of the organization concerned. So a particular problem for organizations, particularly those whose product/ service is reliant on human expertise and judgement (such as high technology firms), is recognizing that valuable sources of competitiveness may be lost if employees leave the firm. This loss may be exacerbated if those employees then join rival competitors. A connected concern is assessing the extent of training that should be afforded to such individuals, lest the investment turns out to be one from which others benefit. Finally, those who are in possession of important skills for the firm are likely to be aware of that fact and may try to ensure that they receive the fullest recompense for their labour. Hence, the ability of an organization to appropriate the capabilities that may help to confer competitive advantage, may be a critical factor in sustaining that edge.

Durability concerns the longevity of resources. It is widely accepted that the life cycle of technology is shortening so that physical capital equipment is not as durable as hitherto. However, intangible resources are not necessarily in the same position regarding life span, especially where brand image or corporate reputation is involved (Grant, 1991).

The transferability of capabilities relates to those that can be bought on the open market and are not embedded within a particular firm. Transferability, therefore, is a matter of the degree to which rivals can imitate the success of a leading firm by external means, such as the purchase or hire of software, or by poaching senior management, for example.

By contrast, the replicability of resources and capability is more to do with internal imitation of others' capability. This characterizes attempts by Western companies in recent years to mimic Japanese practices, by implementing quality circles or just-in-time inventory management. In general, broadly-based capabilities are more likely to confer an advantage that is sustainable than ones that are dependent on a narrow base of skills or resources (such as might be implied in an over-emphasis or commitment to capital-intensive technology). Furthermore, the latter situation will be more likely to compromise flexibility of manoeuvre because of the sunk costs and physical 'lumpiness' associated with the investment (Genus, 1992).

5.3 The management of scope and scale

Issues of scope and scale are key to understanding the development of a flexible approach to strategic management for two reasons. First, a contemporary view holds that the emergence of new advanced technologies makes possible the efficient production of small batches of multiple products within a production system. In addition, the matter of scale economies, where there is globalization of competition, can be catered for by strategic alliances or the specialization and flexibility granted by de-integrated networks. Considerations of volume of production or investment in capital equipment may be addressed by either of these routes, with a reduction in the role of the large, integrated organization. The second aspect revolves around a broader, longer-term perspective of the dynamics between the economies of scale and scope (Clark and Staunton, 1989). This type of view serves usefully to remind us of the ongoing interplay between the significance of scale and scope economies.

One example that demonstrates this interaction centres on the evolution of the international automobile industry. In the speciality niche, scope and scale have changed markedly. For example, in the late 1920s, specialist producers in Europe were assembling in the region of 20 000 cars, across several varieties of a core model, employing a small-batch production mode. However, some 30 or so years later, in the 1960s, the likes of Volvo were rapidly shifting production up towards 200 000 speciality cars, across distinct product ranges (as opposed to variations on one core model). By contrast, the generalist producers such as Ford may be said to have focused on scale economies at the beginning of the same period, with the oft-quoted switch in emphasis towards scope economies emerging from the end of the 1970s onwards. The changing significance of scale and scope economies within one sector, along with the unevenness of this change across different segments of the industry, can readily be seen (Clark and Staunton, 1989).

With this note of caution in mind, we must now consider the implications that the increased significance of economies of scope seem to have for the definition of organizational boundaries. In particular, this calls for a consideration of the possible strategic advantages that may be afforded through de-integration of organizational activities. In turn, this involves a discussion of the various means by which 'internal' and 'external' organizational activities and relationships may be managed.

The notion of de-integration relates to the externalization of activities that were formerly performed in-house. Externalization is therefore connected to the types of ownership and control that apply to the performance of production and other activities and to the manner in which they evolve. Essentially, the externalization of activities may be contrasted with their integration (or internalization) within the 'boundary' of an organization. So, rather than integrate all activities from purchasing of raw materials to manufacture to sales/distribution and thence service, firms may opt to externalize one or more of these activities, either by 'arms-length' transactions with other firms or by closer relationships with other parties. These may be gained by adopting some kind of intermediate transactional relationship – somewhere between pure integration and the distance of spot-market transacting (Thompson and Wright, 1988).

Such intermediate transactional relationships deserve greater discussion as they connect closely with preceding discussions of capability, as well as with the substance of debates concerning the redrawing of organizational boundaries. Examples of intermediate transactional relationship include:

- contracting out
- co-contracting (e.g. joint ventures)
- franchising.

Contracting out involves the provision of goods and services by an agent (or agents) for a 'principal' organization within the context of an ongoing, recurrent relationship (Thompson and Wright, 1988). This kind of relationship is addressed in Chapter 6 with reference to vertical collaboration within an industry sector. The potential benefits of contracting out may be discussed where tasks requiring specific skills or expertise are involved, especially where an atmosphere of trust exists among the protagonists. In such cases, contracting out activities to other, specialist firms may be advantageous over in-house production.

Co-contracting relates to horizontal collaboration (again discussed in Chapter 6). This is exemplified by joint ventures, where two or more rival organizations carry out R&D, production or marketing jointly, often setting out a separate legal entity to perform the functions involved. In this type of transactional relationship, pooling of resources and know-how can enable the application of more diverse capabilities than would otherwise be the case, to difficult, risky projects (such as those potentially involving capital intensive technology development).

Finally, franchising/licensing typically takes one of two forms. The first type involves a continuing contractual relationship between, a franchisor and franchisee, where the latter is usually a small independent firm operating under the name of the franchisor and producing or marketing goods or services already market-tested by the franchisor. Fast food outlets provide the most obvious examples of this. The second type involves the auctioning or award of franchises or licences which confer the exclusive right to produce goods or a service for a specified period. Examples here include the brewing of beers or lagers under licence in countries other than the country of origin, or the exploration and production of petroleum from licensed UK North Sea oil territory by oil companies under licence from the UK government.

The virtue of such externalized forms for producing products and services is often at the heart of the debate about 'flexible specialization', a term associated with the work of Piore and Sabel (1984). Essentially, flexible specialization can be described as a form of production process that facilitates responsiveness to changing demand for varied, customized products. This is made possible by the recent advances in micro-electronics for communications and manufacturing purposes, and stands in contrast to standardized mass production (Piore and Sabel, 1984). Indeed, it is argued that there is an 'industrial divide' between 'mass production' and 'flexible specialization', an argument that is closely linked to that which asserts that a new paradigm for production, associated with fundamental technological change, is emerging.

An example that Piore and Sabel use to illustrate their argument is that of the Italian textiles industry, centred on the district of Prato. Between 1966 and 1982, exports boomed and employment remained steady at a time when, elsewhere in Europe, business was floundering. (In 1977, exports of textiles from the region totalled about US$ 800 million, rising to roughly US$ 1.5 billion in 1982; about 45 000 workers were employed by more than 10 000 firms.) In Prato, such comparative success could be explained by two factors: one, a long-term shift from standardized to fashionable fabrics; and the second, a corresponding reorganization of production from large integrated mills to smaller, more technologically sophisticated units, specializing in particular phases of production.

Part of the Prato success story is explained historically: owing to the ravages of the Depression in the 1930s, the large textile firms in the region had laid off many workers, or lent or hired them equipment to do subcontracting work. As a result, a vast network of small textile shops grew up, the owners of which became increasingly comfortable with bearing the risks that their former employers had done previously. Moreover, the larger firms were able to increase their flexibility by being able to convert what had been fixed costs into variable costs, since the new subcontractors could be used as a buffer against falling demand or to absorb increases in demand.

A similar crisis in the 1950s led to further fragmentation of the industry as the larger firms repeated the response of 20 years earlier, creating an even more dispersed web of small family-run companies. Any over-dependence of the smaller firms on the larger ones was countered by the co-ordination of the former into autonomous federations. This co-ordination was facilitated by someone known as the *impannatore* – a designer whose central responsibilities were to create designs according to the dictates of fashion and to encourage the firms to experiment with materials and processes of production. The firms' successes fuelled the creativity of the *impannatore* whose demands on the firms grew in turn. The result of the process as a whole was that by the late 1970s there was only one surviving integrated firm in the region, employing just a few hundred workers (Piore and Sabel, 1984).

The notion of flexible specialization, as expounded by Piore and Sabel (1984) in particular, has attracted much debate. Some of the chief criticisms relevant to externalization and strategic flexibility may be summarized (Hyman, in Pollert, 1991).

First, the continued power and influence of the large multinational conglomerate over national and international economic activities is undervalued. Similarly, the role of financial and governmental institutions is neglected in favour of an orientation towards an analysis of small-scale production based upon the deployment of new technology and the serving of non-standardized markets. Secondly, there remains a question mark over the notion that consumer markets are now becoming fragmented and customized. Hence one may consider that niche markets have existed in a number of sectors (such as automobiles) for several decades. Moreover, mass production (which may or may not equal 'Fordism') is not dead; witness the standardized production of many domestic and leisure electronics products. Indeed, the dichotomy between 'mass production' on one hand, and 'flexible specialization' on the other may be seen as being overly simplistic. A more balanced view of the emergence of new patterns of consumption and production and of the continuity of 'older' ones would seem to be warranted, therefore. Finally, the extent to which the concept revolves around an analysis specific to a particular geographical location in Italy, represents another limitation in terms of the generality of the phenomenon of flexible specialization and the extent to which it is possible to replicate it elsewhere.

What all this means, from the point of view of developing strategic flexibility, is that relations between a whole range of actors need to be addressed and in context. For example, the role of government in facilitating R&D and inter-firm collaboration, and the nature of producer–supplier relationships both feature in Chapter 6. Hence it is recognized that development of capital-intensive or experimental technology, for instance, may well be the subject of relations between a range of organizations, large and small, corporate and non-corporate. Again, the cost/quality aspects of production may be crucially affected by the ways in which (larger) producers relate to (smaller) suppliers and the degree of mutual dependence which characterizes this relationship. So, once more, the relevance of the flexible specialization thesis to strategic flexibility needs to be treated with caution.

Moving away from the topic of externalization, what about the organization of activities that remain in-house? It has been noted that at the same time as the pre-existing conventional wisdom about the nature of economies of scope and the extent to which diversified companies were able to capture them was under challenge, many large firms were rethinking their positions (Goold and Campbell, 1989). The strategic initiatives of many large companies during the last two decades have thus featured the following: decentralization, where the locus of decision-making responsibility shifts 'down' the corporate hierarchy to 'empowered' business units or worker teams; 'downsizing', where staff numbers are reduced at all levels; and 'de-layering', which is a reduction in hierarchical levels within the organization (Legge, 1993). Examples of these activities are many and include General Electric's 1981 'de-staffing' exercise, the unprecedented shake-out of employees in the UK banking industry over the past decade and de-layering in companies such as British Petroleum and British Telecom.

These activities are the stuff of strategy gurus such as Peters. For instance, in *Thriving On Chaos* (1989), Peters' 'handbook for a management revolution', he declares:

> Excessive organizational structure is a principal cause of slow corporate response to changed circumstances. We must . . . radically reduce layers of management . . . No more than five layers of management are necessary.
>
> *Peters, 1989, p. 354*

Moreover, he goes on to state:

> [Firms] are being strangled by bloated staffs, made up of carping experts and filling too many layers on the organization chart. Today's structures were designed for controlling turn-of-the-century mass-production operations under stable conditions, with primitive technologies. They have become perverse action-destroying devices, completely at odds with current competitive needs.
>
> *Peters, 1989, p. 355*

While the 'doing more with less' message will appeal at least intuitively to many, the pain associated with actually managing such restructuring is rarely so appetizing (and interestingly rather marginalized in Peters' writings). Thus the transition towards more flexible organizational forms and behaviour faces a number of difficulties.

First, there are the quantifiable costs of such activities which are certain to harm corporate profits in the short term; and it is not just the costs of redundancy payments for staff – the redeployment and retraining of the remaining staff also needs to be considered. In addition are the costs, such as lower morale, that may not be directly quantifiable but have the potential to hurt organizations nevertheless (e.g. through lower work quality, absenteeism, high labour turnover and so on). This is of particular significance at a time when some of the key business 'buzz' words involve a notion of changing antagonistic relationships between employers and employees. This issue of attempting corporate restructuring while seeking to develop employee commitment is returned to in Chapter 7. In addition, there may well be scepticism about management's motivation for making changes, not the least of which may be the notion that such moves are little to do with enhancing flexibility and much more to do with increasing control over employees, through fear of redundancy, for example.

Another important aspect of internal organization with regard to economies of scope is the co-ordination of activities and functions, and the role of technology management in facilitating this. This is of great significance if internal activities in organizations are to be managed in more decentralized and autonomous ways. At stake is the way in which product innovation is fostered and new production processes absorbed and dispersed within the company. Furthermore, the relationship between such co-ordination, the learning capability of the organization and its design or structure will be critical to strategic performance and change. These issues are discussed in the next section and are considered more fully in the remaining chapters of the book.

5.4 The significance of organizational learning

This section addresses the role of learning within a flexible approach to strategic management. It extends the work of the previous sections in this chapter by considering the relevance of learning to the development of strategic capabilities and issues of organizational scope and (de)integration. The heading of this section specifies organizational learning and so it is learning capacity of organizations as a whole and of individuals within organizational settings that is of issue, not individual learning *per se*. Moreover, this focus on organizational contexts stresses learning as a processual phenomenon, rather than the one-dimensional perspective represented by work on the experience learning curve, for example.

It is necessary to outline the connection of organizational learning with strategic capability and flexibility at this point. Such a link may be understood by reference to the following definitions. The first views organizational learning as concerning:

> [the changing] routines [that] are independent of the individual actors who execute them and are capable of surviving considerable turnover in individuals.
>
> *Levitt and March, 1988*

The second refers to how those within firms:

> collectively change their knowledge, values and shared mental models of their company and its markets.
>
> *Pettigrew and Whipp, 1991*

It is important that any notion or discussion of learning relate to the competitive situation an organization faces. A key aspect of this revolves around the idea of organizational learning as a process and, in particular, the means by which new routines and strategically-relevant knowledge are acquired and embedded in organizations. This process will vary between firms and industry sectors, of course, and even within one organization over the passage of time. Nevertheless, some general points may be made. First, the nature of the learning process is likely to comprise the following elements (Dodgson, 1991).

- search
- accumulation
- diffusion
- review.

These refer to how new knowledge is discovered and acquired by the firm and also to the manner in which new routines are dispersed throughout the various functions or department of the organization. Finally, the element of review is suggestive of the process by which existing and perhaps out-moded routines are identified and ultimately upgraded.

Next, a number of sources of learning may, broadly, be defined as follows (Pavitt, 1991):

- learning by doing (i.e. by producing)
- learning by using (a new product/process)
- learning by trial and error
- learning by studying, analysis or research
- learning by imitation
- learning through sharing/collaboration
- learning through luck or serendipity.

It is important to recognize the different contexts within which learning may take place. As typically presented, work that has been done on the learning curve or economies of experience reveals a preoccupation with the 'inner' context of organizational life and, more specifically, with the realm of production/ manufacturing. Even in this limited, though important, sphere, some issues for learning tend to be neglected. For example, if one is to go beyond the view that learning occurs 'naturally' as a function of cumulative experience or scale of production, it is necessary to consider a more multifaceted and problematic view of organizational learning.

This partly relates to activities 'external' to the organization, but as far as it is possible to separate out 'internal' learning processes, the following appear to be significant. Firstly, it is reasonable to expect that within different organizational activities the aims of learning may vary from the strategic to the tactical and that, accordingly, such factors may have implications for the nature of learning processes. Hence, 'learning by doing' may not be suitable for situations where safety procedures are at stake, such as with the storage of chemical waste where smaller scale laboratory trials or simulations may be more advisable than a 'live' demonstration without such preparation.

In terms of a more cross-functional, strategic perspective, it is important to note how learning may be encouraged, although not in any sense be formally planned. In particular, two areas have been suggested as being relevant to organizational learning about knowledge existing outside the firm and also to the generation of knowledge that is new to the firm and its industry sector or society in general (Dodgson, 1991).

One area pertains to the structure of organizations, referred to above in the discussion of the management of scope and organizational form. The essential point to grasp here is that 'structure' is considered as being to do with the relationships between various organizational participants and functions. Hence at issue is a concept that addresses both the formal chart, or 'map', of organizations, their departments and reporting relationships, but also more informal aspects of organizational relationships as revealed by the climate that influences actual behaviour within them. The other area concerns the degree of support that the organization offers in the form of time, training, access to sources of specialized knowledge, finance, autonomy and so on.

The competitive context of organizational learning can be appreciated where, for instance, such learning involves imitation of the products or processes of industry rivals. The common practice of 'reverse engineering', for example, refers to a method of learning in which one firm takes apart the product of a rival in order to find out about its physical construction and likely cost of manufacture. Of increasing importance, however, are the ways in which competitors share information or learn collaboratively. This brings to the fore the nature and management of strategic alliances and other forms of competitor collaboration, which may be seen as potentially enhancing mutual learning, for the purposes of technology or new product development, for example. It also calls for some understanding of ways in which organizations are learning from and with their customers and suppliers, in some contrast to the typical textbook approach to environmental analysis. A similar point applies to the ways in which relationships and trends at the macro-environmental level are being handled by firms in practice.

Having outlined certain aspects of the processes and contexts that have an impact on organizational learning, it is as well to reflect on some problematic issues associated with learning. Firstly, such learning is likely to need to develop amidst a continually changing scene of competition. This means that the outcomes of the learning process (in terms of new products and processes among others) need at least to keep pace with changing competitive conditions. The potential difficulty, however, is that changing the knowledge base of the organization is not a straightforward matter. It is not merely a matter of adding or diffusing new knowledge, it will most likely also involve the shedding or modification of existing ways of doing things (or of learning to do them differently). Here, the matter of 'unlearning' processes is at issue and parallels discussions of flexibility that centre on the reversibility of decision-making. Unlearning therefore refers to the process of breaking down existing organizational routines, a vital element in the facilitation of learning and the management of strategic renewal.

This parallels the work of Lewin (1951, see also Burnes, 1992, who gives a useful summary), who suggested that the management of change can be modelled as a process involving the following three elements (or 'stages'). These are:

- unfreezing
- moving
- refreezing.

Unfreezing refers to the undoing of existing attitudes and practices within the firm, including developing an awareness that such change is warranted. This may necessitate the demonstration of a potential crisis in order to facilitate a consensus that 'something must be done'. In practice, this may be intertwined with 'moving', which relates to the implementation of structures and processes for improving the capability and ultimate performance of the organization – for instance by the introduction of teamworking or new patterns of employee–management relations. This needs to be accomplished in such a way that the firm does not retreat back to habitual, uncompetitive behaviour. Refreezing concerns the need to reinforce and support the changes that have been made so that some stabilization of new organizational routines is achieved, again so as to prevent a slide back into the pre-existing way of doing and seeing things.

The way in which Lewin's 'three-step' model is presented emphasizes the importance of refreezing activities to the permanence of a change programme and, indeed, the establishment and securing of a new equilibrium for the organization (Lewin, 1951; Burnes, 1992). However, like the linear model that implies that changing organizations is a matter of adjusting structure so as to facilitate the implementation of a 'correct', pre-planned strategy, there is a danger that such an approach to change will neglect the continuing and uneven nature of organizational transformation (Pettigrew and Whipp, 1991). Thus, even if change is viewed as 'one-off' episodes, there is a likelihood that the path towards improvement will not always run smoothly; there may be 'blips' along the way. Taking the more ongoing perspective of organizational renewal, it seems improbable that any 'level of equilibrium', or established routines, will be capable of serving an organization well indefinitely. Recognizing this raises the issue of how organizations can engender more gradual, progressive learning, which can feed an improvement of routines over time and help to combat the need for more radical and painful

Case study 5.1 Logical incrementalism

The seminal work of James Brian Quinn has served to illustrate the nature of continual consensual strategic change for which he coins the term 'logical incrementalism'. The following quotations capture the manner in which firms blend the need to ensure that overall their employees are pulling in the same direction. At the same time, however, the organization maintains an ability to look at the external environment in a fresh and flexible way. The first quotation comes from a chief executive and the second from a chairperson, both of companies that formed part of Quinn's research sample (these included Exxon, IBM, and General Motors).

If good people share the same values, they will instinctively act together ... We work consciously to understand each other and where we are going. If we know these things and communicate openly, our actions will be sensible and cohesive. Yet we'll have the flexibility to deal with changing environments. These – and the choice of top-flight people – are our real controls for co-ordinating strategy development.

How do you manage the strategic process? It all comes down to people: selecting people. First, you look for people with certain general characteristics. They have to be bright, energetic, flexible, with high integrity or they won't be adaptive and last in the long run. Among these you look for the best people with the kinds of experience and interests likely to lead the company in directions you want it to go. But you have to be careful with this. You don't want just 'yes men' on the directions you believe in. You want people who can help you think about new approaches, too. Finally, you purposely team people with different interests, skills and management styles. You let them push and tug a bit to make sure different approaches get considered. And you do a lot of chatting and informal questioning to make sure you stay informed and can intervene if you have to.

Source: Quinn, 1982.

turnaround measures. In part this requires the conflicts and 'failures' of everyday organizational life to be viewed as opportunities for experimentation and reflection. Fundamentally, the management of momentum becomes central.

It has been argued that the key to avoiding the dangerous momentum that leads to organizational short-sightedness and eventual inertia is the ability to encourage self-criticism within the organization while maintaining cohesiveness and coherence about its direction (Miller, 1992). This does not mean doing without a central theme to direct and harness activities around particular sets of capabilities. Rather, it is suggested that in order to avoid the myopia associated with a kind of unheeding momentum that turns a firm's strengths into liabilities:

Managers must begin to reflect about their basic assumptions, about their deep-seated views of customers, strategies and corporate culture. They need also to search for the underlying goals and presumptions that drive their organizations. It is only after they become conscious of such inbred premises for action that they can begin to question and alter them.

Miller, 1992

So, self-reflection about the fundamentals of organizational strategy is prescribed as a preventive remedy for complacency. This questioning of deep-seated values

Case study 5.2 An interpretative approach to strategic management

Research by Gerry Johnson in three British retail clothing companies exemplifies the role that the interpretation of signals from the external environment, in conjunction with the organizations' paradigm, plays in strategic change. One of the sites of the research is 'Coopers'.

For Coopers what, at first sight, seems to be an incremental process of moving from the lower-end of menswear clothing, through retail diversification, to a strategy based on younger, more fashion-oriented clothing plus discounting and cost-cutting, can be accounted for differently.

There was little evidence of the environmental scanning and deliberate experimentation associated with logical incrementalism. Instead, the enduring and common beliefs and assumptions (central to the firm's paradigm) that were discernible from interviews with its managers, appear to have strongly influenced attitudes to the need for change.

These values centred on the view that Coopers' success in the 1970s was due to its merchandising strength. In particular, this function and its policies were such that those within the firm came to see that changes in fashion were not important, since Coopers were concentrating on 'commodity' merchandising. Indeed such was the perceived prowess at merchandising that Coopers' failed diversification and acquisition activities in the early 1970s were blamed on their complacency regarding the function. As one reflective manager said some time afterwards, 'We thought we knew enough about retailing to retail anything'.

In the early 1980s, performance at Coopers declined dramatically. However, this was seen to be to do with the economic recession of the time – internal activities were not the problem. What action there was, was within the existing paradigm: cost-cutting rather than re-examining the quality in fashion terms of the merchandise. When initial efforts here failed to make an impact, there was more response but still within the existing paradigm: major cost-cutting through massive redundancies. Finally, when an externally appointed marketing director presented findings that pointed to outdated conception of the clothing market on the part of senior management, two things happened. First, there was heavy resistance to the report that the marketing director presented; it was a heavy political attack on those who were running the company. Second, the marketing director's expertise and experience were criticized. A belated attempt at market repositioning served only to preface the takeover of Coopers in 1985.

Source: Johnson, 1991.

is primarily facilitated by gathering information from outside the organization. While this means acquiring data on the evolution of technologies, consumer tastes and competition, it does not imply that such activity should be conducted in 'planning mode', with all the pretence to comprehensiveness and objectivity that that usually implies. Instead, the role of gathering such information is to create the sense of unease mentioned above. The data that will be of issue, therefore, may be 'soft' data gleaned, say, from picking up clues about product quality from conversation with customers, as well as more 'objective' market analysis. Sources of information may be informal and stem from the day-to-day operations of the organization and from activities at its boundaries, such as its relationship with governmental institutions, competitors or suppliers, as well as customers.

Applying this notion of momentum can serve to illustrate the manner in which the seeds of new strategic directions may be planted in the garden of

Case study 5.3 Collective entrepreneurship at Jaguar

It is important to remember that the management of strategic change is often accomplished by more than one individual. Pettigrew and Whipp describe the significance of a leadership team change at the Jaguar Car company. True, it is acknowledged that the arrival of John Egan as chief executive was a turning point. However, much of what was achieved in the first half of the 1980s was due to the senior management team that was assembled. This was a team that reflected complementary skills and 'untypically wide engineering qualifications' (an especially relevant point given Egan's admitted lack of technical expertise). Another important aspect of the team was that it included a number of ex-British Leyland people – Beasley, Edwards and Johnson, in manufacturing, personnel and marketing, respectively – who had a commitment to the survival of Jaguar.

Source: Pettigrew and Whipp, 1991.

pre-existing practices and experience. This idea closely resembles the incremental and interpretative models of strategy introduced in Chapter 1. For example, the version of incrementalism elucidated by Quinn (1980) emphasizes the value (and closeness to actual practice) of gradual change built on consensus, small-scale experimentation and general scanning of the organization's environment. This approach is exemplified in Case study 5.1.

'Good' incrementalism, it is argued, should enable the continuous learning and flexibility that will help organizations to cope with environmental change. Where such learning does not occur, or where flexibility has been compromised by past commitments or investments, such as in advanced technology or failed product developments, renewal may require more thoroughgoing rethinks of strategic direction and underlying values. In other words, where the performance of the organization is endangered by inertia or excessive momentum. Here, addressing attitudes to and perceptions of the strategic position and environment of the firm may be essential if fundamental transformation is to be implemented effectively. This is where the interpretative schemes of managers and other employees within organizations become relevant. The need for learning and renewal in a firm is not given but is a matter of individuals and groups within it seeing it as such, depending on how they interpret signals emanating from inside and outside its boundaries (Johnson, 1987). Case study 5.2 exemplifies the interpretative approach.

Finally, the role of leaders and the means by which renewal can be effected need to be addressed. Much attention is given in the strategy literature to turnaround 'heroes', change agents and dynamic, charismatic leaders, who are credited with shaking up their organizations and smartening up their competitiveness. The contribution of such executives needs to be put into perspective. Yes, such leaders can have a dramatic effect in transforming outmoded attitudes and practices (e.g. Ralph Halpern at Burton Group, or Lee Iaccoca at Chrysler). However, more 'collective entrepreneurship' is often involved, as demonstrated by the example of Jaguar (Case study 5.3) (Pettigrew and Whipp, 1991).

5.5 Summary

This chapter has considered the relevance of capabilities and learning to organizational performance and the process of managing strategic renewal, the conduct of which reflects the flexibility of the firm in a fundamental sense. In contrast with the Porterian approach, it is the resources an organization owns that are said to confer the potential for strategic advantage. However, more deeply than that, the role that such resources play needs to be understood in terms of the distinction between tangible and intangible resources and of the contribution of these to the development of strategic capabilities. An important aspect conditioning the strategic relevance of such resources is the nature of organizational routines and the likelihood that capabilities can be lost, eroded or imitated. A framework for understanding the strategic significance of capabilities has been provided.

The chapter has connected this discussion of capabilities with the nature of learning and the current debate concerning the changing boundaries (or scope) of large firms. The argument that corporate restructuring can provide flexible, innovative, yet efficient responses to changes in consumer demand has been introduced. This has taken the form of outlining different forms of 'externalization' of current activities that a firm performs but has also referred to some of the potential problems that may exist for the organization that has shed labour or 'de-layered'.

Finally, the significance of organizational learning to strategic renewal has been addressed. The possibility of such learning has been connected with the nature of organizational routines, and the elements and different types of learning process have been identified. The interrelationship between learning and the concept of momentum has been indicated. Notably, where incremental approaches to strategy fail to produce the ongoing change required to hone capabilities in line with competitive needs, more fundamental attitudinal shifts may have to be attempted. It is here that an interpretative approach to understanding strategic renewal and flexibility may be of benefit, in that more radical wholesale changes in organizational routines may have to be undergone.

Study questions

1. How would you attempt to analyse the capabilities of an organization?
2. How important are intangible resources to the strategic performance of an organization (use examples)?
3. What is meant by 'externalization'? Discuss the significance of the term to strategic flexibility.
4. Consider the implications for organizational learning and renewal of the notion of 'momentum'. How does the Icarus paradox illuminate the issues raised?

Key readings

Grant's (1991) book espouses a capabilities-based perspective on the consideration of sources of competitiveness.

'The Icarus Paradox' by Miller (1992) addresses the enabling and constraining aspects of 'strong' organizational cultures.

Thompson and Wright (1988) give more detail on 'externalization' and 'intermediate governance structures'.

Readers who are interested in following up the debate on 'flexible specialization' may consult *Farewell to Flexibility* (Pollert, 1991), which provides a critique from an employment/employee relations and work organization perspective.

References

Abernathy, W. J. (1978) *The Productivity Dilemma: Roadblock to Innovation in the Automobile Industry*, Johns Hopkins University, Baltimore, MD.

Borum, F. (1990) *Organizational Learning – Variants in Theory and Dilemmas in Practice.* Revised version of paper prepared for Creativity and Innovation in Organizations conference, April 22–24, 1990, Stanford University.

Burnes, B. (1992) *Managing Change*, Pitman, London.

Clark, P. and Staunton, N. (1989) *Innovation in Technology and Organization*, Routledge, London.

Dodgson, M. (1991) Technology learning, technology strategy and competitive pressures. *British Journal of Management*, **2** (2), 133–49

Genus, A. (1992) Social control of large-scale technological projects: inflexibility, non-incrementality and British North Sea oil. *Technology Analysis and Strategic Management*, **4** (2), 133–48.

Goold, M. and Campbell, A. (1989) *Strategies and Styles: The Role of the Centre in Managing Diversified Corporations*, Blackwell, Oxford.

Grant, R. (1991) *Contemporary Strategy Analysis*, Blackwell, Oxford.

Hall, R. (1992) The strategic analysis of intangible resources, *Strategic Management Journal*, **13**(2), 135–44.

Johnson, G. (1987) *Strategic Change and the Management Process*, Blackwell, Oxford.

Johnson, G. (1991) Rethinking incrementalism. *Strategic Management Journal*, **9**, 75–91.

Legge, K. (1993) The Role of Personnel Specialists: Centrality or Marginalisation, in *Human Resource Management and Technical Change* (ed. J. Clark), Sage, London.

Levitt, B. and March, J. G. (1988) Organizational learning. *Annual Review of Sociology*, **14**, 319–40.

Lewin, K. (1951) *Field Theory in Social Science*, Harper and Row, New York.

Miller, D. (1992) *The Icarus Paradox*, HarperBusiness, New York.

Nelson, R. and Winter, S. (1982) *An Evolutionary Theory of Economic Change*, Harvard University Press, Cambridge, MA.

Pavitt, K. (1991) Key characteristics of the large innovating firm. *British Journal of Management*, **2**(1), 41–50.

Peters, T. (1989) *Thriving on Chaos*, Pan, London.

Pettigrew, A. and Whipp, R. (1991) *Managing Change for Competitive Success*, Blackwell, Oxford.

Piore, M. and Sabel, C. (1984) *The Second Industrial Divide*, Basic Books, New York.

Pollert, A. (ed.) (1991) *Farewell to Flexibility*, Blackwell, Oxford.

Porter, M. (1985) *Competitive Advantage*, Free Press, New York.

Quinn, J. B. (1980) *Strategies for Change – Logical Incrementalism* Irwin, IL.

Quinn, J.B. (1982) Managing strategies incrementally. *Omega*, **10**(6), 613–27.

Thompson, S. and Wright, M. (1988) *Internal Organisation, Efficiency and Profit*, Philip Allan, Oxford.

FLEXIBILITY BETWEEN ORGANIZATIONS

6

Learning objectives

After studying this chapter you should:

- understand how collaboration between firms can enhance flexibility and strategic performance
- appreciate the nature of and motives for horizontal and vertical collaboration, and the difference between them
- have an understanding of the concept of strategic networks
- understand the problems of managing inter-firm relationships and the requirements for success in doing so

6.1 Introduction

The central theme of this chapter is the nature of inter-firm collaboration. As discussed in the previous chapter, activities of this type are somewhat underplayed in strategy texts. The extent to which organizations collaborate with each other has been held up to represent an expression of the emergence of a new paradigm, at odds with conventional views of the nature of competition. Such co-operative activity may occur in planned or unplanned ways, be short or long-term in duration and may frustrate as well as enhance strategic flexibility. The management of relationships between firms of different objectives, size and relative power is of particular interest. For a number of reasons, which are explored below, the outcomes from collaboration may be at odds with any hoped-for benefits (Lawton Smith, Dickson and Lloyd Smith, 1991).

Section 6.2 discusses the nature of collaboration between rivals. These alliances are viewed as exemplifying horizontal collaboration, which takes place for a range of reasons that are outlined. In contrast, section 6.3 considers the changing nature of relationships between producers of end products and their suppliers and customers with reference to 'vertical collaboration' (c.f. the discussion of different transactional relationships in Chapter 5). As in section 6.2 some of the possible motivations and potential benefits of collaboration are identified.

Section 6.4 introduces the concept of 'strategic networks', partly to illustrate the multiplicity and complexity of relationships of many organizations. A number of practical examples serve to portray the nature of network relationships in a number of different national, international and industry contexts. Following on from this, some of the difficulties of managing collaborative relationships and the characteristics of effective management of co-operation between firms, are considered in section 6.5. Finally, section 6.6 provides a summary of the chapter.

6.2 Strategic alliances: horizontal collaboration with competitors

While much of the emphasis in strategic management education and research has been in the realm of identifying and outperforming industry competitors, there has been a growing awareness of the co-operative moves that firms make with respect to their rivals. In particular, there has been increasing attention on the development of strategic alliances. This section considers the nature of these collaborative efforts, the motives for instituting them and also some of the difficulties involved in their conduct. It relates these issues to the extent that strategic alliances contribute to strategic flexibility. The section looks at what may be termed 'horizontal collaboration' (Contractor and Lorange, 1988), such as that among rival car manufacturers, as opposed to 'vertical collaboration', such as that between a car manufacturer and suppliers of component parts, for example.

Strategic alliances occur when organizations commit themselves to sharing the responsibility for some of the participants' activities. In aspects other than those included in such commitments, the participants remain separate entities and will continue to compete with each other. Hence it is important to note that strategic alliances are not the same as mergers, where the merging organizations become a new single entity (Dicken, 1992). One type of alliance, the joint venture, may, however, result in the partners setting up a separate new legal entity while remaining independent of each other in other respects.

Another distinction relates to the nature of horizontal and vertical collaboration. Briefly, horizontal collaboration occurs between firms that operate at the same stage of the production process. One example of international horizontal collaboration is the world automobile industry, where developments in competition during the 1980s contributed to the emergence of a global network of co-operation involving virtually all the major competitors. These companies (such as Ford, General Motors, Honda and Rover) continue to compete with each other. However, they simultaneously co-operate by exchanging design drawings, tools and even complete vehicles to various degrees with different rivals.

According to a study by Morris and Hegert of 839 collaborative agreements between 1975 and 1986, the motor vehicle sector accounted for 24% of strategic alliances. Other major sectors included: aerospace, with 19% of the collaborative agreements studied; telecommunications (17%); computers (14%); and 'other electrical' (13%) (Morris and Hegert, 1986). Although there is nothing inherently new in this form of strategic alliance, there has been a rapid increase in the extent to which collaborations are being employed. Moreover, it is the centrality of many alliances to the strategy of firms, especially where these businesses compete globally, that is noteworthy (Dicken, 1992).

Several factors help explain the development of collaboration between rival firms and their centrality to overall strategic development. They may be grouped under the following headings according to the potential for:

- cost sharing and reduction
- sharing and improving learning for product or process development
- reduced lead times (e.g. for developing and introducing new products)
- access to complementary assets
- raising or lowering barriers to entry.

In sum, these potential benefits of horizontal collaboration relate to the capacity of firms to cope with the uncertainties of contemporary markets. They therefore also connect to the possibility of a flexible approach to managing strategy, based on the competitive benefits of collaboration between rivals.

Facilitating capital intensive projects

One of the prime motivations for the establishment of horizontal collaboration is in the area of cost reduction and sharing. The significance of costs is most dramatically demonstrated where technology development is central to activities within an industry. This is especially so where the sector is embryonic and the technology related to an industry is unproved, complex and/or potentially prone to rapid obsolescence.

In the semiconductor industry, for example, the enormous costs of research and development, allied to the increasing rapidity of technological change and the costs of installing new production facilities, have all contributed to the attractiveness of strategic alliances (Dicken, 1992). This industry is among the most capital-intensive of all industries. At the end of the 1980s, for instance, the costs for installing production facilities for 4mb microchips was put at US $150 million. Such costs are even greater for the new generation of 64mb chips. In 1994, one proposal to build facilities for producing 16mb and 64mb microchips put the cost of doing so at over US $1 billion (*Guardian*, 1994).

In the UK banking sector, the development of the EFTPOS electronic funds transfer system provides another example of how capital and operating cost factors can stimulate collaboration between competitors. EFTPOS (electronic funds transfer at the point of sale) is a scheme to enable the clearing by banks of cash and cheques to be replaced by the electronic transfer of funds. The system would be based on the use of plastic cards and the installation of terminals that could read them at the payment counter in retail outlets. The motivation to collaborate may be explained by the estimated size of the investment needed to produce a national EFTPOS network, said to be of the order of billions of pounds, and the savings on cheque clearing costs (Howells and Hine, 1991). In particular, at the outset of the venture EFTPOS was deemed to require collaboration because:

None of the banks feels . . . they can possibly afford to go entirely on their own. You can't do EFTPOS . . . on your own, it's a ridiculous concept. [To co-operate] is a way of exchanging data with your competitors: you have to have a forum.

Banker quoted in Howells and Hine, 1991, p. 401

The story of EFTPOS will be returned to towards the end of this chapter, as in this case the collaborative aspect of the project was to degenerate and it provides some insight into the management of co-operative relationships.

The potential contribution of collaboration to facilitating learning about new products and processes is worthy of some discussion. One project that is an example of effective collaboration for product development is 'Project Four'. In Project Four, Fiat, Lancia, Alfa Romeo and Saab, all European car producers, developed models sharing several of the same features, such as floor panels. Yet each manufacturer was still able to maintain the separate brand identity of its own product, which was received in the marketplace as distinct and differentiated. Another example is the development of the Ford Probe, the result of a joint development by Ford and Mazda. This car, which was developed with the US market in mind, was essentially a combination of the learned skills and capabilities of Ford and Mazda engineers. In particular, the Probe synthesized the chassis and body shell reliability of the Mazda 626 with the general qualities of Ford exterior and interior design plus suspension setting (Clark and Fujimoto, 1991).

Lead times

Matters of capital investment, cost reduction and the input of shared learning into new product development are often associated with another motive for collaboration – reduction or control of lead times. Collaboration may enable the solution of technological uncertainties, getting products to market, or the setting up of production facilities, more rapidly than can be achieved by firms acting individually. This is by no means a new phenomenon. A reminder of the historical importance of lead times is given by the example of collaboration in the US weapons systems sector. This has centred on shortening product lives, the need for reduced lead times, high technical performance and diffusion of new techniques such as computer-aided design. What is more, this has been the case since at least 1945 (Markusen in Freeman, 1992).

Access to complementary assets

In the developing biotechnology sector, access to complementary assets has been recognized as an important source of collaboration (Dodgson, 1991). These 'complementary assets' may be described as the additional capabilities that are needed for new products or processes to be sold at profit in the marketplace (Teece, 1987). In the biotechnology industry, collaboration has stemmed from the different nature of access to complementary assets possessed by academic institutions, the smaller and newer biotechnology firms and the larger, more established pharma-ceuticals companies. Thus the capability to innovate in biotechnology, at least in basic science and R&D terms, lay first with university and research institutes which transferred their expertise to the small ('dedicated') biotechnology firms. However, the larger firms tended to possess the complementary assets required to commercialize the discoveries being made, such as marketing and distribution, manufacturing and dealing with regulatory agencies and processes. This situation of differential access to complementary assets provided a powerful stimulus to collaboration, at least in the early life of the sector.

Raising or lowering barriers to entry

The advantages of horizontal collaboration cited above can be interpreted in terms of another potential motive for seeking alliances with rivals. This may be to do with creating favourable competitive conditions with regard to barriers to entry. Thus entering into partnerships can, on the one hand, be seen as a means by which the capabilities to develop and capture new markets may be enhanced. As discussed above, this may be particularly the case where the lead times or technological uncertainties involved present potentially high entry barriers. On the other hand, while allied firms can enjoy the lowering of barriers to entry, those organizations that are not party to such collaborations may find that, in relative terms, their entry barriers are raised for the sector in question.

An element of game playing may be present in this, and firms may enter into partnerships with one competitor that has particular capabilities at least partly to prevent other competitors from gaining access to these skills. In addition, the employment of cross-border alliances has become a valuable means of circum-venting barriers to entry that exist in the form of national trade tariffs or other restrictions on inward foreign investment.

As well as the academic and other contract research institutions mentioned above, an important source of collaboration may be governmental activity. Thus there may be a direct or indirect governmental impetus to horizontal collabora-tion. Examples of the role of public policy in promoting horizontal collaboration may be given with reference to development programmes in information tech-nology (Dodgson, 1993). The Japanese VLSI (very large scale integration) project was one of the early ground-breaking public policy programmes that provided a stimulus for others across the globe and in a variety of industry sectors. The VLSI project was begun during the latter part of the 1970s. It involved five computer and semiconductor firms which together received more than US $350 million dollars of public funding for collaborating on specific information tech-nology (IT) activities. VLSI was also one of the focuses of the Alvey programme in the UK, a collaborative programme spanning 1984–1990 and funded almost equally by government and industry. Evaluation of the programme has found that without governmental support and the collaborative nature of Alvey, much important 'pre-competitive' R&D would not have been conducted by industrial participants. Indeed, it has been argued that the programme has had the effect of helping industrial participants to rethink their attitudes towards the role of

R&D within the firm and the benefits of collaboration across its boundaries (Guy, in Dodgson, 1993).

The motivation behind such programmes can be explained in terms of the benefits to international competitiveness for domestic (or regional) industry sectors as a whole, and also for the individual firms within such collaborations. Thus at a regional level, for instance, the sponsoring of collaboration between European firms by the European Union may be seen as a response to the competitive threat posed by the trading blocs of South–East Asia and North America.

More generally, the nature of relationships between governmental, financial and industrial organizations may be as significant as inter-firm relations *per se*. Japan has been offered as an example of this as the nature of the *keiretsu* structures is usually considered to promote horizontal co-operation between groups of industrial firms. (The *keiretsu* are large collections of industrial and financial organizations tied together by mutual shareholdings and close links.) Instead, Dodgson (1993) claims that the extent and importance of horizontal firm collaboration within the *keiretsu* may be overstated. Rather, relationships within the *keiretsu* are characterized by similar tensions between co-operation and competitiveness as exist among groups of firms in other countries. Moreover, collaboration within the *keiretsu* has been considered more notable for the interaction of financial and governmental institutions with industrial organizations. More specifically, information exchange between industrial firms and major banks provides for a longer-term perspective on investment and (arguably) horizontal collaboration. And, although it is wise not to overplay the consistency and success of Japanese governmental activities, there seems little doubt about the role of public policy in establishing institutions that facilitate collaborative activity.

Governmental activities have evolved from being more to less direct over the years. However, despite a measure of disagreement over the actual amount of horizontal collaboration in Japanese industry, bodies such as MITI (Ministry of International Trade and Industry) have been influential on the collaboration that has occurred. This, in turn, has been held to be an important source of information and technology transfer and of the potential improvement in innovativeness capacity.

6.3 Vertical collaboration with suppliers

The nature of vertical collaboration within an industry is typified by relations between producers of final goods and services and suppliers of raw materials, components and other inputs. The discussion therefore relates to a number of variants on the theme of vertical collaboration, including subcontracting and outsourcing (where certain 'non-core' activities such as payroll management or cleaning are contracted out to external firms).

As with the horizontal collaboration that was the subject of the previous section, it is the extent of change in the quality of relationships involving suppliers, subcontractors and so on, that is noteworthy. Indeed, a number of recent studies on the topic have demonstrated that 'much new wine is poured into old bottles' so far as relationships with subcontractors or suppliers are concerned (Freeman, 1992). This is demonstrated by the practices of Japanese firms in the automobile industry, the operational processes of which have been the subject of much writing and competitor imitation.

To take one aspect of activities in this sector, the extent of supplier involvement in engineering for product development in Japanese, US and European firms may be contrasted. At the beginning of the 1990s, Japanese suppliers were performing more than four times the amount of engineering work needed for product development than their American counterparts. The amount of product development engineering performed by European automotive suppliers fell midway between that of the Japanese and the American firms (Clark and Fujimoto, 1991).

Such variations reflect differences in the nature of the relationship between car producers and their suppliers, not just in engineering and product development but with regards to other suppliers to the industry. In particular, is the contrast between Japanese and traditional US supplier systems in terms of the different nature of contracts, communication channels and incentives.

As far as contracts are concerned, the traditional US supplier system is characterized by large numbers of suppliers who deal directly with the car manufacturers on the basis of short-term contracts. In general, these suppliers have little engineering capability. Moreover, the attitude underlying the relationship between suppliers and manufacturers conforms to the playing of a 'zero sum game' (win–lose). Hence the participants behave as adversaries and communication is somewhat distant, centring on conveying limited information on prices, specifications and other requirements. Specifically:

> Suppliers are treated as a source of manufacturing capacity; auto companies establish requirements and play suppliers off against one another in a contest for one-year contracts.
>
> *Clark and Fujimoto, 1991, p. 138*

The 'typical' Japanese system is characterized by rather more emphasis on long-term relationships and by a multitiered structure of suppliers. The nature of these tiers is such that 'first-tier' suppliers provide some inputs which are subassembled from parts produced by lower-tier suppliers. The relationship of first-tier suppliers with manufacturers is one of mutual dependence and commitment (more 'win–win' than 'win–lose'). However, first-tier supplier firms may be demoted to a lower tier if their performance is deemed to be below requirements.

While it is the case that suppliers are confronted by tight quality and efficiency targets and have to incur penalties for failing to meet them, manufacturers do go some way to absorbing their suppliers' investment risks. The latter occurs, for example, where the volume of lifetime production is less than originally planned by the manufacturer, the supplier having planned its own production according to estimated cumulative figures. In such cases, suppliers have the benefit of compensation, under long-term guarantees, for the unfulfilled production. This mutuality encourages frequent contact and sharing of information, such as the detailed nature of suppliers' costs and production processes (Clark and Fujimoto, 1991). A notable example of this approach to supplier relationships is that of Toyota, usually mentioned with reference to the development of 'just-in-time' inventory management systems.

Finally, it has been noted that as the technical capabilities of subcontractors have improved, so the relationship between the larger and smaller Japanese firms has tended to become more equal. Thus, a rigid hierarchical arrangement featuring a 'parent' organization at the top and *kogaisha* (children) firms at the bottom has been transformed into co-operative networks (Freeman, 1992).

As far as the international dimension to supplier–producer relations is concerned, a similar *rapprochement* has been observed. Although it is difficult to generalize across industries and firms, one clear development is that of producers adopting closer functional relationships with their suppliers in different national locations. This signals some move away from the traditional approach to international subcontracting based on the objective of obtaining low-cost supplies or processing, but characterized by remote functional (as well as geographical) relationships. Instead, while seeking out low-cost suppliers remains important, other dimensions of supplier performance drive the motivation towards the nomination of 'preferred suppliers'. Increasingly such suppliers have greater responsibility for the quality of their outputs and play a more direct role in product design. Moreover, the diffusion of just-in-time inventory management techniques has potentially significant implications for the geographical distance between producers and their suppliers in international subcontracting. In particular, trends away from holding large buffer stock implies the need for more frequent delivery of inventory as required (i.e. 'just-in-time' to be used in production). Therefore:

> Orders to . . . suppliers and subcontractors . . . [may be] small and frequent, indeed deliveries may be made several times a day and hence [geographical] proximity to suppliers is essential.
>
> *Sayer, in Dicken, 1992*

6.4 Strategic networks

Thus far this chapter has presented a fairly general introduction to industry level collaboration and strategic alliances. What is needed now is a consideration of more of the complexity that can characterize real-life relationships between firms. In doing so, a network perspective will be useful; employing such an approach enables the multiplicity of relationships between various manufacturers, suppliers and other actors (such as universities and governmental agencies) to be better understood. In addition, it is also relevant to consider the potential for flexibility that is offered by collaboration both to networks (or clusters) of firms as a whole and to individual entities within such a web. Finally, another important element of this section is the idea that managing flexibly involves particular choices for organizations with regard to their approach to the management of collaborative relationships. The focus here is on the requirements for 'good' collaboration, relating to the role of trust and communication *inter alia*, in developing sustainable networks. However, the extent to which organizations 'mix and match' varying degrees of market, network and vertical integrated relationships, according to their (perceived) circumstances and needs, should also be recognized.

So, what are 'strategic networks' and why might they matter? To begin with, one definition views strategic networks as:

> Long term, purposeful arrangements among distinct but related ... organizations that allow those firms in them to gain or sustain competitive advantage *vis-à-vis* their competitors outside the network.
>
> *Jarillo, 1988, p. 32*

Moreover, the concept of networks can be used to define industrial markets, if one understands networks as 'complex arrays of relationships between firms'. These relationships become established through the interactions of different firms with each other, interactions that require some investment (in terms of time and commitment as well as finance). However, organizations within the network are not completely dependent on each other; they remain independent in a number of spheres of activity. If they are not, the relationship between the participants might be better described as one of 'vertical quasi-integration'. A concept related to strategic networks is that of 'dynamic networks' (Miles and Snow, 1986). This approach is not, however, discussed further here as its emphasis is more on the picturing of inter-firm relationships than on the strategic motives or requirements for sustaining network relationships (Jarillo, 1988).

The underlying basis of competitiveness in the network approach may be said to revolve around the nature of the relationships involved and the quality of co-ordination and adaptation between the collaborators. Sometimes referred to as an intermediate mode of organization somewhere between markets and hierarchies, the key feature of network relationships is therefore neither the price mechanism nor the bureaucracy of the integrated, hierarchical organization. More specifically, the role of the 'hub' firm within a strategic network has been singled out, being the entity that sets up the network and is essentially its focal point (Jarillo, 1988).

The significance of the network approach and the role of the hub organization within a network centres on the contributions that may be made to competitiveness. For instance, the hub firm may set up a network of external relationships that together may perform a set of activities more efficiently than if these same activities were performed in the context of one integrated organization. If this is the case, then it will be possible for the network to lower the transaction costs which would otherwise lead firms to perform these different activities in-house (Chapter 4). The de-integration of the activities of organizations may be facilitated by the existence of, or the potential for, efficient networks of firms that specialize in certain functions which would formerly have been internalized. Where this is so:

> The flexibility and focus that result from de-integration, made possible by the existence of a network that takes care of ... other functions, can be

extremely powerful competitive weapons, especially in environments that experience rapid change.

Jarillo, 1988, p. 38

The relevance of a network approach to the issue of flexibility can be framed in terms of the management of organizational resources. Compared with the transaction cost perspective, evolutionary network approaches focus more on the effective (as well as efficient) management of activities and relations between firms. To reiterate a central point, it is the capability to perform these activities efficiently, flexibly and at high levels of quality, that is at the heart of organizational competitiveness. These factors also pertain to other external relationships that have implications for the conduct of the activities connected with the development and delivery of products. For example, the role of financial institutions in Japan, in providing a long-term orientation to lending for investment purposes can be seen in terms of their role within certain network systems perhaps rather better than in terms of the minimization of transaction costs (Clark and Staunton, 1989).

The application of a network approach to analysing collaboration between firms can be demonstrated by reference to the following example relating to Benetton, the Italian fashion clothing firm. Benetton is a popular example of a hub firm at the focal point of a network of inter-firm relationships. It has also been argued that the Benetton network represents one of 'flexible specialization' (Piore and Sabel, 1984), although this notion should be approached with care, as mentioned in Chapter 5. In essence this describes a network in which the individual firms specialize in particular branches of activity but where the network as a whole is flexible. Benetton exemplifies this by retaining a relatively small directly employed labour force and putting out production to a number of small firms. In addition, the distribution of Benetton's products is characterized by a high degree of decentralization, with Benetton preferring to operate a system of sales agents and franchises than to manage its own high street sales points, for example. What Benetton does maintain as its core concern are key processes such as design. Overall, the effective size of the firm (i.e. taking into account its network relationships) is very large and so economies of scale are forthcoming, for instance in purchasing. Yet the mode of organization of production allows for economies of scope; the network of suppliers, subcontractors, agents and so on facilitates the ability to alter product range or volume as market requirements change. While the operation of the network can be criticized for the extent to which there is dependence on Benetton (in terms of its power over other participants and their need for information from the hub firm), it can be said to offer a degree of organizational mobility. This refers to the capacity of the firm to alter its relationships with others at its boundary (Bessant, 1991).

Figures 6.1 and 6.2 further illustrate the nature of network relationships. Figure 6.1 characterizes the multiple relationships of NYBY, a Swedish metalwork producer. In particular, the relationships shown are those that relate to the participants in NYBY's development of a new metalworking process, known as the ASEA-NYBY process. The relationships involved are a mixture of vertical and horizontal collaboration, and the parties have different expectations of the venture depending on whether their role is one of supply, end process realization or end user. Because of these different roles, the parties have differing types of expertise and principal activities. Moreover, participants vary in size, objectives and the time frame they employ in terms of the evaluation of progress. Thus the need for working around these differences has been an important factor in sustaining the network (Hakansson, in Clark and Staunton, 1989).

In Figure 6.2, network and cluster relationships are shown as they related to the telecommunications equipment industry at the beginning of the 1990s. This figure describes the relatively small number of inter-firm clusters dominating the sector at this time. Within each cluster is a pivotal group of firms surrounded by a number of satellite partners; the cluster is bound together by the partners'

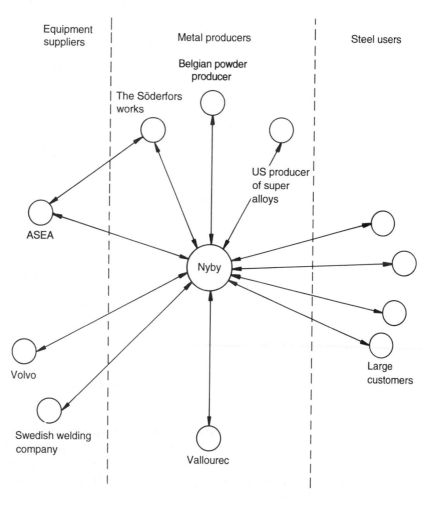

Figure 6.1 Network relationships in Swedish metalwork. (Source: Clark and Staunton, 1989, p. 169.)

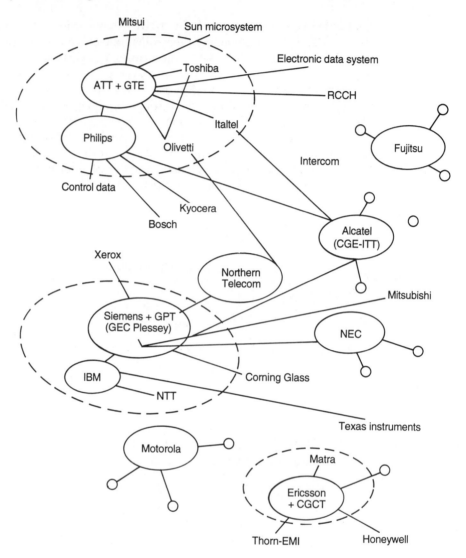

Figure 6.2   Inter-firm clusters and networks in the telecommunications industry. (Source: Dunning, 1993, p. 213.)

shared technological trajectories or activities. However, firms within a cluster may have their own, separate network relationships, which may feature other rival competitors than those within the cluster. Thus firms are able to establish alliances with competing sets of rivals in clusters which may be distinct or overlap, depending on how this serves their own interests (Dunning, 1993). Of course, there will also be relationships with suppliers and users.

Three further points may be made at this juncture. The first of these concerns the spatial dimension of networks. The nature of domestic Japanese supplier networks has been described as quite highly developed. Here, large 'hub' firms are surrounded by a 'constellation' of small and medium-sized enterprises, which act as component suppliers or perform specified processes according to the timetable and requirements of the hub firm (Dicken, 1992). This type of arrangement, it has been argued, represents localized 'industrial districts'. Second, the role of informal, personal relationships needs to be recognized (Kreiner and Schultz, 1990). Informal relationships and contacts between individuals in different organizations are often an important means of acquiring or exchanging information and expertise, at conferences or professional gatherings, for example. Third, the diffusion of information technology is a potentially powerful route by which inter-firm links may be enhanced. In particular, the advent of Electronic Data Interchange (EDI) provides an opportunity for inter-organizational communication through the link-up of computer systems (Bessant, 1991). As the next section shows, communication is but one requirement for success in collaborative and network relationships.

6.5 Managing collaboration

It should be stressed that the management of inter-firm linkages is likely to be problematic (Hamel, Doz and Prahalad, 1989). The participants in a joint R&D agreement or new supplier–manufacturer relationship enter with different histories, experiences and motives. Consequently, the specification of what is to count as 'success' and the criteria for measuring performance may present some difficulty. It is not uncommon for some parties to view a particular venture as having been a success while others involved see it quite differently. Moreover, even when the parties agree that a venture has been successful, this may well have been in ways that were unintended at the outset.

It is not necessarily the case that beneficial outputs from collaborative activity, say in terms of new or improved products or processes, will be easily internalized by the participants.

Thus to engage in collaboration for the purposes of learning about some novel application of basic science, for example, is not the same as a particular firm having the capability to take advantage of this for its own product development. Arguably, the existence of disparities in firm size and power within a network relationship reinforces the difficulties involved in achieving successful inter-firm link-ups (i.e. 'success' as perceived by all parties and not only the dominant hub organization).

Despite these qualifications and the acknowledgement that generalizations about success factors in collaboration will not fit all cases, some common features pertaining to good and not so good collaboration have been distilled from research in the area. Combining the work of a number of researchers, the key issues for collaboration management seem to be the following:

- partner selection and commitment
- trust and communication
- flexibility.

Partner selection has been seen as representing the 'most critical decision affecting the success of [technological] collaboration' (Dodgson, 1993). In particular, this refers to the advantages of finding and selecting partners who will form part of an enduring, long-term relationship. Partner selection is thus a strategic decision that should be considered in the light of the benefits accruing in the longer term rather than merely the attractiveness of an immediate project. Such a longer-term perspective can facilitate the mutual flow of information and improve the working relationships between the staffs of the protagonists, as well as facilitating the eventual transfer of marketing or production knowledge, for example. One aspect of partner selection that may be crucial to success is the values of the respective parties. The identification of prospective partners that share similar values or motivations can be valuable in promoting the longevity of a relationship by developing a climate of trust from the outset (Jarillo, 1988).

Related to a long-term orientation is the commitment of the parties to collaboration. Lack of commitment may be expressed by an unwillingness to contribute the required amount of time, trust or other resources to nurture the collaboration. The likely unevenness of commitment can be indicated where, for example, the collaboration is marginal to the business as a whole of one partner, yet central to the activities of another. This situation can be particularly acute where the relationship is between partners who are unbalanced in terms of size, financial resources or information. Indeed, one of the reasons cited for Japanese companies doing better out of their collaborations with US firms is the information gap represented by the commitment of employees in the Japanese firms to learn English, which is key to assimilating the expertise of the US partner. On the other hand, the same has not been true of employees in American firms with respect to learning Japanese (Kanter, 1989).

Another important facet of establishing alliances founded on long-term commitment is the degree of mutuality of the benefits of collaboration. For the collaboration to succeed over the longer term, the partners need to feel that the benefits they are earning from the co-operation are commensurate with the contribution they have made. For example, far from being the positive networking mechanism that has been described elsewhere in this chapter, subcontracting can also be seen as a method by which larger firms use their suppliers to protect against downturns in demand. In this way, they may be able to deflect some of the risks of production during the good times, but keep production in-house when demand slows. Such an approach may, however, be seen as rather short-sighted and scarcely conducive to enduring, good quality relationships with suppliers.

This leads on to the issue of trust in collaborative relationships. Trust and communication are vital to the success of collaboration. Trust may be defined as:

> An assumption or reliance on the part of A that if either A or B encounters a problem in the fulfillment of [her] implicit or explicit transactional obligations, B may be counted on to do what A would do if B's resources were at A's disposal.
>
> *Thorelli, 1986, p. 38*

The benefit of alliances characterized by trust is that information and potential solutions to problems encountered may be given more freely than where trust is lacking. Indeed, there is likely to be a cost (a transaction cost) to lack of trust, since monitoring systems may need to be introduced in order to show that partners are doing what they agreed or 'ought' to do.

The notion that trust can be misplaced or 'premature' is worth keeping in mind; sometimes parties to a collaborative venture have been known to behave naively in according too much trust to their partners too early in the relationship. Thus they give away sources of advantage without the protection of contractual or legal safeguards. One such example is of an American firm that had licensed the manufacture and sale of its machine tools to Mitsubishi Heavy Industries on the 'understanding' that the latter would not conduct these activities in the USA. Far from confining its efforts to Asia, however, Mitsubishi went on to establish itself on the US market. The US firm involved has since sought to protect itself by including market restrictions in its licensing agreements.

The implications of mistrust for collaborative relationships are demonstrated by the case of EFTPOS UK (initially discussed near the beginning of this chapter). The implementation of a national point-of-sale scheme had been collectively supported by the UK banks. However, disagreement over technical specifications and the move by Barclays to go ahead with its own debit card scheme undermined the development of EFTPOS, which was to have been linked to a debit card offered by all of the participating banks. Conflict over the technical features of the system were an important source of mistrust, with Barclays wanting one particular system design and some banks lining up against that option lest Barclays should 'steal a march' on them. Furthermore, the launch by Barclays of its Connect card led to coalitions of banks being formed with regard to EFTPOS according to their technical preferences and attitudes within each bank to Barclays' behaviour. The co-operative approach to EFTPOS was thus undone, and competing experimental point-of-sale systems began to emerge based on the rival debit card schemes of Visa and Switch. The national system being developed by EFTPOS UK was eventually scrapped in 1990 (Howells and Hine, 1991).

Another potential difficulty for co-operation concerns the situation where partners in a particular collaboration are also involved in other, parallel alliances, possibly including competitors. To specify an exclusive relationship in an agreement may impose extra costs, while involvement in a number of alliances might provide flexibility in that a much greater range of opportunities for learning is granted. The maintenance of outside relationships may enable one partner to drop another should it become dissatisfied with the progress of an alliance, as was reputedly the case with Olivetti and AT&T. Olivetti switched to Xerox for distribution of the Olivetti PC 6300 after having originally linked up with AT&T (Kanter, 1989).

Another of the key issues raised relates to the protection of proprietary information. The threat of information leaked through a partner, plus the general inefficacy of patent protection for innovations, further raises the significance of trust. Where this is absent, it may be prudent to ensure close relationships with suppliers, distributors and so forth. These will be particularly important for protecting access to the complementary assets that may be required to facilitate the commercialization of joint R&D, for example; assets that will be much sought after by competitors.

The point about flexibility is an interesting one. It concerns the capacity for partners to modify the objectives and day-to-day operation of co-operative relationships, in anticipation of or in reaction to new circumstances. An ability to accommodate change may pertain to a changing external market or economic conditions, or the altering of the partners' strategic objectives. However, there are certain conditions where even the most accommodating partner will feel that its flexibility is somewhat redundant. This is where a collaborator unilaterally shifts away from the line of business that the partnership is based on. This is exemplified by the ending of the alliance between the German company Siemens and RCA, when the latter suddenly pulled out of the computer business which had been the rationale for the collaboration (Kanter, 1989).

6.6 Summary

This chapter has looked at a number of aspects of flexible relations between firms. In particular, the nature of horizontal and vertical collaborative relationships has been described. Also, factors that may influence the development of inter-firm co-operation have been outlined. Benefits of collaboration can include the facilitation of technological development with shared risks or improved efficiency and quality of production. The concept of strategic networks was introduced and provides a means for understanding more of the intricacies of firms' relationships with rivals, suppliers and users. Finally, some of the requirements for good management of inter-firm relationships have been identified. While there are certain benefits to inter-firm collaboration, the difficulties of their management should not be neglected.

Study questions

1. Should firms collaborate? Why? Why not?
2. What factors are most influential in the success or failure of inter-firm collaboration?
3. What do you understand by the term 'strategic network'?

Key readings

Dodgson (1993) considers the nature of collaboration as it applies to R&D and technology development.

Kanter (1989) details some of the problems of collaborative relationships in *When Giants Learn to Dance*

Clark and Staunton's (1989) book considers inter-firm networks and their potential contribution to innovation and design capability. See Chapter 8 in particular.

Thorelli (1986) provides a useful overview of a networks perspective on inter-firm activities.

References

Bessant, J. (1991) *Managing Advanced Manufacturing Technology*, NCC Blackwell, Oxford.

Clark, K. B. and Fujimoto, T. (1991) *Product Development Performance: Strategy, Organization and Management in the World Auto Industry*, Harvard Business School Press, Boston, MA.

Clark, P. A. and Staunton, N. (1989) *Innovation in Technology and Organization*, Routledge, London.

Contractor, F. J. and Lorange, P. (eds) (1988) *Cooperative Strategies in International Business*, Lexington Books, Lexington, MA.

Dicken, P. (1992) *Global Shift: The Internationalization of Economic Activity*, Paul Chapman, London.

Dodgson, M. (1991) Technological learning, technology strategy and competitive pressures. *British Journal of Management*, **2**(2), 133–49.

Dodgson, M. (1993) *Technological Collaboration in Industry*, Routledge, London.

Dunning, J. (1993) *The Globalization of Business*, Routledge, London.

Freeman, C. (1992) *The Economics of Hope*, Pinter, London.

Guardian, The (1994) Japanese Microchip firm puts British site on shortlist. July 6, p.16.

Hamel. G., Doz, Y. and Prahalad, C. K. (1989) Collaborate with your competitors – and win. *Harvard Business Review*, January/February, pp.133–9.

Howells, J. and Hine, J. (1991) Competitive strategy and the implementation of a new network technology: the case of EFTPOS in the UK. *Technology Analysis and Strategic Management*, **3**(4), 397–425.

Jarillo, J. C. (1988) On strategic networks. *Strategic Management Journal*, **9**, 31–41.

Kanter, R. M. (1989) *When Giants Learn to Dance*, Unwin, London.

Kreiner, K. and Schultz, M. (1990) *Crossing the institutional divide: networking in biotechnology*. Paper presented at the 10th Annual Conference of the Strategic Management Society, 'Strategic Bridging', Stockholm, Sweden.

Lawton Smith, H. Dickson, K. and Lloyd Smith, S. (1991) There are two sides to every story: innovation and collaboration within networks of large and small firms, *Research Policy*, **20**, 457–68.

Miles, R. and Snow, C. (1986) Organizations: new concepts for new forms, *California Management Review*, **28**(3), 62–73.

Morris, D. and Hegert, M. (1986) Trends in international collaborative agreements. *Columbia Journal of World Business*, **22**(2), 15–21.

Piore, M. and Sabel, C. (1984) *The Second Industrial Divide*, Basic Books, New York.

Teece, D. J. (ed.) (1987) *The Competitive Challenge*, Ballinger, Cambridge, MA.

Thorelli, H. (1986) Networks: between markets and hierarchies. *Strategic Management Journal*, **7**, 37–51.

FLEXIBILITY WITHIN ORGANIZATIONS

7

Learning objectives

After studying this chapter you should:

- understand how flexibility within organizations can be developed in practice
- appreciate potential difficulties that may be associated with implementing flexibility-related moves
- be able to identify possible links between developing flexibility, learning and strategic control

7.1 Introduction

This final chapter is concerned with the means by which flexibility may be developed within organizations. Various internal areas of activity are of interest, bearing in mind the context of the increasing inter-organizational collaboration and co-operation that was the focus of Chapter 6. As with the rest of this part of the book, the connection between learning and flexibility is emphasized.

At this stage readers may wish to refer back to Chapter 1, particularly Figure 1.3, which offers the framework underpinning the book as a whole. The reason for this is that the issues considered in this chapter recall some of the earlier discussions about the notion of strategic flexibility.

Firstly, this chapter considers the ongoing notion of flexibility, which is better captured by concepts such as 'renewal' or 'learning' than by the one-off term 'adaptability'. Next, the paradox that may accompany flexibility-related moves is discussed. Thus, where Figure 1.3 identifies the potential significance of developing flexibility in terms of greater freedom of manoeuvre or readiness for change, it should be remembered that organizations have a past! Hence, the base from which such development might be attempted may be quite impoverished.

For example, a firm may have been in decline for a number of years, making a drastic turnaround effort necessary. So, while the notion of flexibility has been presented in terms of the capability for strategic renewal with the minimum of pain, cost and time, doing so in practice may be demanding in just these ways. The areas that have featured prominently in the discussions about organizational change and 'changeability' have management of human resources in common. The avenues and pitfalls of developing strategic flexibility within organizations are considered with a similar theme in mind, here. This chapter highlights various approaches for improving innovativeness, learning capability and strategic flexibility, but also tackles some of the problems that may be associated with them.

Section 7.2, for example, addresses product innovation, an important aspect of strategic flexibility. In particular, the section focuses on the conduct of new product development and research and development within an approach to strategy founded on the continual development of capabilities or competencies. Within the variants of such approaches, the creation and dissemination of knowledge can be seen as an influential factor in the conception and development of new product streams. Structural questions concerning the setting up and control of newstream ventures are also to be reckoned with, however.

In section 7.3, the focus turns to process development. Here, the nature of and potential contribution to flexible strategic performance is assessed for various types of computer-integrated technology, as well as production innovations such as just-in-time inventory management and total quality management. The question here is about the obstacles that may impede effective implementation. Such barriers include an inability or unwillingness to prepare for change by attending to issues of work organization and employee relations. Some of these are considered in section 7.4 in the context of the debate surrounding the practice (or otherwise) of human resource management (HRM), identifying HRM in its own right as an emerging practice/discipline with the potential to enhance strategic performance.

A theme of section 7.4, but also of the chapter as a whole, is the paradox that exists between implementing the various measures discussed above, which emphasize worker autonomy and responsibility, and the need for strategic control. This forms the basis of section 7.5, which serves to underline the link between learning processes, flexibility and forms of control. A summary of the chapter is provided in section 7.6.

7.2 Product innovation

A key aspect of strategic flexibility is the capability to develop new products. In common with other researchers mentioned elsewhere in this book, Adler, Riggs and Wheelwright (1989) support a capabilities-based (or resource-based) view of the sources of competitive advantage, this time with specific reference to new product development. Thus the distinction is made between 'tactical' and more 'strategic' approaches to product development and technology management, and the search for sustainable competitive advantage in general. Hence:

> [A] more strategic view of the sources of competitive advantage focuses on continuously renewed know-how and capabilities that allow the firm to out-distance competitors. Security in technological advantage or product superiority is not in having a contract, patent, or trade secret, but in having the underlying capabilities and enhancing, strengthening and extending them faster than your competitors.
>
> *Adler, Riggs and Wheelwright, 1989*

The point here is not that, for example, patent protection of new products serves no useful purpose, but rather that the issue for firms is one of nurturing in the longer-term their strategic capabilities, as opposed to relying on the temporary nature of legal provision against imitation, which is more of a tactical move. In addition, Adler, Riggs and Wheelwright note the need to link, in a strategic fashion, new product development with technology management. Thus, to help combat changes in market demand, as well as to benefit from new process technology such as flexible manufacturing systems, better interaction among product development and manufacturing operations, for example, is required. Such interaction would be at odds with a conventional approach that emphasizes clear and separable roles for an organization's departments and a 'breakthrough' mentality in the role of research and development laboratories, the output of which other operating units are meant to capitalize on.

This need to appreciate and enhance the integration between functions is demonstrated in the writings of a number of the proponents of capabilities-based competition, referred to in Chapters 1 and 5. The relevance of this issue to new product flexibility is now explored in more detail.

Outpacing

The chief architects of the outpacing approach claim that it represents a more appropriate route to competitive success than 'traditional', one-dimensional prescriptions for making strategy. Unlike Porter's generic strategy framework, for example, the outpacing approach relies on:

> The explicit capability of a company to gain product leadership and cost leadership simultaneously.
>
> *Gilbert and Strebel, 1989, p. 19*

The central theme therefore emphasizes the complementary nature of low-cost and product innovation strategies and the difficulties of those who would specialize in either cost leadership or differentiation to shift their basis of competition. Gilbert and Strebel claim that a new 'mind-set' is required that recognizes the evolutionary nature of competition. They stress the need for companies to manipulate cost and differentiation within a cluster of integrated moves that develop over time, a view that contrasts markedly with traditional one-paced strategies. It is further argued that it is the integration by leading competitors of elements that have hitherto been suggested to be incompatible that represents a major source of change in many industry sectors. In effect, these organizations have therefore been able to change 'the rules of the game' within their sector. Hence, those organizations that fail or are unable to integrate moves in this way, either in framing or responding to changing competitive conditions, are likely to be 'outpaced'.

From their observations of 100 companies in a variety of rapidly changing industries, Gilbert and Strebel note a number of common capabilities among successful competitors. Whether adopted and implemented in an offensive or more defensive, reactive manner, these capabilities are said to amount to elements of the outpacing approach. Four capabilities, in particular, should be noted:

- the capability to innovate
- the capability to put together a competitive formula
- the capability to offer the new formula at a competitive price
- the capability to perform these moves simultaneously.

Case study 7.1 exemplifies the offensive use of an outpacing strategy as observed from the strategic moves of Nintendo.

Case study 7.1 Nintendo's 'outpacing' strategy

In the 1980s, the Japanese toy manufacturer Nintendo became famous for its electronic hand-held games. Their rise to a leadership position in this sector enabled it to become the largest toy manufacturer in the world by 1988; five years previously it had not even been in the top 10. Nintendo's performance at this time has been explained in terms of its ability to pursue an 'outpacing' strategy, based on the simultaneous development of the following capabilities.

1. **The capability to innovate**. This is evidenced by the firm's development of the first computer games (such as the Nintendo Entertainment System and Gameboy) for home use not to have a keyboard but still with images of high quality.
2. **The capability to put together a competitive formula**. In addition to the equipment, Nintendo devised a competitive formula, from the design of the product to its distribution. For example, in its supplier relationships, subcontractors were chosen on the basis of their apparent motivation to enter a relatively untried market. Moreover, the suppliers selected were the recipients of large orders for integrated circuits to ensure that the costs of supplying these components would be driven down.
3. **The capability to offer the new formula at a competitive price**. Nintendo was able to price competitively as well as offering novel, high quality products. This capability can be seen to be largely a function of the above; unbundling the keyboard and the mechanisms adopted *vis-à-vis* suppliers and distribution, for example, enabled costs and the target selling price to be contained.
4. **The capability to perform these moves simultaneously**. At Nintendo this characteristic is revealed in the nature of the innovation process. The capability relates to the co-ordination of disparate organizational activities across a number of functions, at the same time, within the overall framework of strategic goals. This is in contrast to the sequential approach to innovation and strategy, where functions remain isolated and departments 'do their job' before handing the baton on to the next (e.g. from R&D to manufacturing and then to marketing).

Source: Gilbert and Strebel, 1989, pp. 19–22.

Core competencies

One of the most widely cited recent contributions to the debate about the nature of underlying sources of competitiveness is that of Prahalad and Hamel (1990) on the development of 'core competencies' within corporations. They are concerned that a fundamental source of competitiveness often fails to be recognized by organizations – the ability to 'identify, cultivate, and exploit ... core competencies'. Moreover, they argue that to benefit from such a recognition of the significance of competencies, managers will need to 'rethink the concept of the corporation itself' (Prahalad and Hamel, 1990). Thus where portfolio and Porterian approaches emphasize the targeting of 'attractive', high growth product markets in which 'stars' are grown or industry dominance secured over rivals, the core competencies view considers the 'fuzziness' of market definition and the possibly temporary nature of market dominance.

The essential distinction, observed across a number of industry sectors, is between those competitors who conceive themselves as a portfolio of competencies, versus those who adhere to the traditional approach basing strategic business units on defined market segments. In the latter view, the current performance of individual strategic business units is central, being the rationale for allocating resources across an organization's portfolio. The links or synergies between businesses, within the diversified corporation, are at best understated by such an approach. So, too, are issues connected with the role of organizational structure, senior management and, crucially, the firm's knowledge base in facilitating longer-term competitiveness.

However, in the 'long run':

> Competitiveness derives from an ability to build, at lower cost and more speedily than competitors, the core competencies that spawn unanticipated products. The real sources of advantage are to be found in management's ability to consolidate corporatewide technologies and production skills into competencies that empower individual businesses to adapt quickly to changing opportunities.
>
> *Prahalad and Hamel, 1990, p. 81*

In order to understand the significance of core competencies it is vital to understand the link between core competencies, core products and end products. Core competencies refer to expertise that may apply to the design or development of core products. For example, this might mean possessing the skills to develop superior compressors, which is a core product in end products such as air conditioners and refrigerators. Enjoying such competence can therefore be seen as a way of conferring upon a firm the capacity to shape the evolution of future end products, based on these core products and competencies.

An important facet of developing core competencies relates to the notion of building the 'strategic architecture' of the organization. This is a means of linking emerging customer needs, potential technological developments and the core competencies that are required in order to bridge the two. Further, the strategic architecture is said to provide a basis for more operational, day-to-day

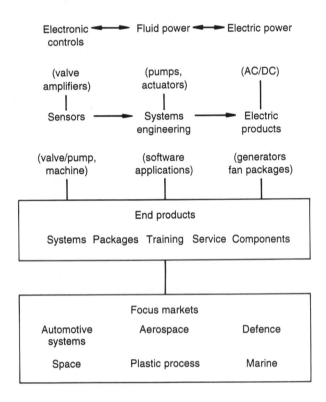

Figure 7.1 Strategic architecture at Vickers – Vickers' map of competencies. (Adapted from Prahalad and Hamel, 1990, p. 88.)

decisions, within the framework of an approach that seeks to map out possible longer-term linkages. In order to illustrate strategic architecture, a map of competencies may be drawn for a particular business. In the example that follows, this is done with reference to Prahalad and Hamel's own illustration of competencies at Vickers in the USA (Figure 7.1).

Vickers supplies various control systems and packages to a range of markets including the aerospace, automotive and defence sectors. In the Vickers example, the core competencies are related to the design and development of electronic, mechanical and electric controls and components. In addition, the integration of the hardware and software relevant to these activities, within the context of developing service-related competencies, may be noted. The linkages and integration between the various areas of activity shown in Figure 7.1 permit a range of core products to be developed, in the form of specific components such as electronic sensors, electric generators or fans, and the application of systems engineering in the form of control software, for example. The end products that emanate from the development of core competencies and core products relate to complete control systems or service and training for users.

Core capabilities

Perhaps a more rounded view of the potential contribution of a capabilities-based approach to understanding the underlying sources of competitiveness may be gained by considering the nature of 'core capabilities'. Although there is a measure of overlap and ill-definition among those employing the terms core competencies and core capabilities, a broad distinction can be made. Hence while proponents of competency-based (or 'competence'-based) approaches tend to emphasize the role of distinctive skills, knowledge and managerial and technical systems in providing competitive advantage, relevant issues of values are neglected. However, the insight of capability-based views is to recognize the importance of values and norms to various types of knowledge within organizations and to the process of creating and controlling such knowledge. Indeed, values and norms have been seen as jointly representing one dimension of core capability that, as well as being either ignored or isolated in much of the managerial literature, is crucial to understanding and managing core capabilities (Leonard–Barton, 1992, p. 113). The four dimensions of core capability and the centrality of values and norms to managing capability are presented in Figure 7.2.

A view of capability-building that focuses on the process of knowledge creation comes from Nonaka (1991). Nonaka suggests that in successful organizations, the capability to respond to changing customer requirements, create new markets and products and to dominate emergent technologies owes much to organization-wide knowledge creation. This 'knowledge' is not merely a matter of 'processing objective information'; it is more to do with tapping the tacit or intuitive knowledge that individual employees have and making this available and usable across the company as a whole. As such the management of knowledge is not the sole province of R&D, for example, but a strategic, organization-wide concern.

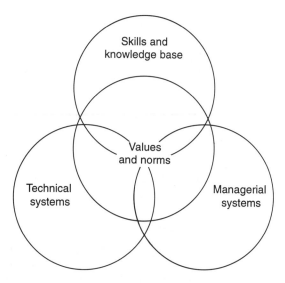

Figure 7.2   Four dimensions of core capability. (Source: Leonard–Barton, 1992, p. 114.)

In particular, the use of figurative language, i.e. metaphors or analogies, is cited as playing a crucial role in the conversion of tacit to explicit knowledge. Metaphors 'trigger' the knowledge creation process, while the use of analogies helps to complete it (Nonaka, 1991). Nonaka employs 'metaphor' to mean:

> A way for individuals grounded in different contexts and with different experiences to understand something intuitively through the use of imagination and symbols without the need for analysis.

Examples of the use of this type of figurative language include Honda's late-1970s product development effort in its automobile business, partly promoted by project team leader Hiroo Watanabe's coining of the phrase 'theory of automobile evolution'. This developed a metaphor of the automobile as a living organism and encouraged thinking about the nature of the evolution of car design. The debate this use of metaphor helped to spark undoubtedly contributed to the design of cars with a spherical image, in contrast to the low elongated shapes favoured by American competitors (Nonaka, 1991).

Canon's development of the personal copier exemplifies the use of analogy in product development. The essence of the problem faced here was how to eradicate the main source of maintenance difficulties in the copier – the photosensitive drum. In order to provide this reliability, a throwaway drum was proposed, creating another problem of how such a drum could be manufactured. The analogy that was employed stemmed from team leader Hiroshi Tonaka 'wondering aloud' about the manufacturing cost of beer cans (the team members had ordered some drinks and were consuming them as they talked through various design issues). This led to the development team speculating whether the same process of manufacture for aluminium beer cans could be used to make aluminium copier drums, and about the extent to which the two products were analogous. By considering the similarities and differences between copier drums and beer cans, the Canon team was therefore able to consider and shape the appropriate product and process developments necessary to provide reliability and low-cost in the new minicopier (Nonaka, 1991).

One other component of the process of knowledge creation has yet to be dealt with – the nature of the conversion of tacit and symbolic knowledge into more explicit forms capable of being transferred for use throughout the organization. This is represented in Case study 7.2, which relates to product development at Matsushita where, in 1985, efforts were being directed at developing a new home bread-baking machine. The case study shows that the process of knowledge creation is not linear, i.e. one should not be concerned only with the tacit–explicit process of knowledge conversion. The manner in which new explicit knowledge reframes others' tacit knowledge may also be of significance to the well-being of product development capability, as may the sharing of tacit knowledge with others in the organization. Important, too, is the role of employee commitment to the knowledge creation process, as witnessed in Tanaka's willingness to go outside of Matsushita to learn the tacit skills that later contributed to the development of the bread-maker. This is related to the context and climate of the organization, which may facilitate or detract from such commitment depending

Case study 7.2 From tacit to explicit knowledge: product development at Matsushita

The process by which tacit knowledge can be converted into more explicit forms capable of being transferred throughout the organization is demonstrated in Matsushita's development of a bread-making machine. In the earlier development of this new kitchen appliance there had been many apparently intractable problems. At the heart of it all, the bread-maker would not knead the dough correctly and the bread was cooked unevenly.

The resolution of these difficulties stemmed from a proposal by one of the development team – Ikuko Tanaka – who suggested that, rather than continue with unproductive analysis of the faults, an effort should be made to learn from the practical skills of a leading baker. So Tanaka trained with the head baker at a leading hotel in Osaka, near the home base of Matsushita in Japan.

She learned that the baker stretched the dough in a quite distinctive way and Tanaka sought to emulate this, with help from the project's engineers, by adding special ribs inside the machine. In effect this was the source of the 'twist dough' feature that was integral to the eventual successful launch of the bread-maker.

What this example shows is the movement between tacit knowledge and explicit knowledge as represented in the product specifications of the bread-making machine. In particular, four patterns of knowledge creation and transfer can be identified based on this movement between tacit and explicit knowledge:

- from tacit to tacit: such as when Tanaka learns the baker's tacit skills through observation and imitation
- from tacit to explicit: for example when Tanaka is able to articulate the fundamentals of her newly-gained tacit knowledge in a form that can be assimilated and shared by product engineers
- from explicit to explicit: this can be said to occur when the project developers codify the above into a manual or workbook, embodying the specifications of the new product
- from explicit to tacit: where the new explicit knowledge is shared and internalized by employees throughout the organization, such that it becomes intuitive to them.

Source: Nonaka, 1991, pp. 96–104.

on the nature of its structures, approach to employee autonomy and other human resource practices (section 7.4).

Another perspective on the product development issue, which notes a move away from the conventional role of the R&D department, is that of Kanter in her work on newstreams (Kanter, 1989). This relates to the setting up of new product development units (or new business streams) and their role (compared with that of existing 'mainstream' activity) in generating inventions and innovations. As Kanter sees it, the pressures to innovate that confront businesses result in a delicate balancing act. This can be expressed in terms of the need to benefit from activities to which organizations are already committed, while concurrently striking out into new areas that will be of benefit in the future. Moreover, she notes:

> The era in which corporations could operate by ... a single management system for everything is over ... corporations cannot succeed by valuing uniform treatment over flexibility, adherence to procedures over fast action, and rules over results. Instead, they must recognise that the ability to invest in new opportunities means letting internal enterprises go their own ways.
>
> *Kanter, 1989*

Achieving this in practice is not a straightforward matter. As well as the lack of operational autonomy referred to above, there is a number of other potential difficulties. Where newstream projects are put in place, they may be the subject of too much strategic autonomy, under- or over-funding of projects, and too much or insufficient distance of the newstream from the mainstream. The claim is made that failure of much needed innovation projects may be due to poor strategic control on the part of senior management, which blunts the incentive to achieve efficient results. Essentially, this relates to the degree to which newstreams pursue their own, rather than overall, organizational objectives and the need to integrate newstream and mainstream activities strategically without undue day-to-day interference. Such a condition may be exacerbated where new ventures are especially large and well funded.

In this type of situation there may be a temptation for top management to leave the newstream to its own devices once a significant financial commitment has been made; the feeling may be that the fact that resources have been provided signals the fulfilment by senior management of their responsibilities. However, such riches may be frittered away on dead ends, the embarrassment of funding denting participants' awareness of the need to use resources as efficiently as they might do when funds are more scarce. Should failure occur, then not only will the immediate project have suffered but the trauma associated with extensive losses may endanger future newstream ventures. The use of multistage commitments (Stevenson and Gumpert, 1985) has been proposed as a means for avoiding this problem of over-funding, and sharpening the entrepreneurial edge of newstream projects. In short, this means the provision of relatively small amounts to newstreams, but at frequent intervals. The benefit of such an approach is to maintain the hunger that is necessary to motivate participants to clear successive hurdles (Kanter, 1989).

The issue of distance between newstream and mainstream activities may involve questions about the size of investment and potential contribution of new projects, as well as their geographical relationship to existing activities. Hence where investment in newstreams is marginal (or perceived as such) to the organization as a whole, new ventures may be endangered, even where they perform successfully. The closure of Colgate–Palmolive's venture operation in 1988, which had been set up four years previously as a vehicle for new ideas, may be noted. This unit had consumed about US $10 million of funding and contributed less than 1% of corporate revenues to a company worth $5 billion at that time. It was seen therefore as being too trivial and too remote to such a large corporation's mainstream innovation needs (Kanter, 1989).

In terms of the spatial location of newstreams, the danger that being situated close to the mainstream may result in the new venture being suffocated through political tensions has to be recognized, as does the difficulty for the newstream of establishing its own identity or style. Then again, too much physical distance may endanger the integration of objectives as discussed above, and the transfer of newstream findings into the mainstream.

The key to resolving these various potential difficulties involves the management of the autonomy of particular newstream efforts and their integration (or re-integration) with the mainstream. In these respects, the role of senior management may be to set the initial context and strategy-related goals for the new project, as well as to allocate appropriate resources for efficient experimentation. Later, it will be necessary to re-integrate the new venture into the mainstream, in order to facilitate transfer of any knowledge gained in the form of new or improved products. Hence, in the intervening period, newstream units are allowed the autonomy required for experimentation in the development of new product ideas but without the potential loss of strategic direction and relevance that was indicated previously (Kanter, 1989). This issue of autonomy versus control, and its relevance to flexibility, is one that requires further discussion as it applies to other aspects of strategic management in organizations in addition to new product development (section 7.5).

7.3 Process innovation

This section addresses the role of advanced technology in developing flexibility in organizations. It should be noted that this involves a consideration of technology that is not necessarily reliant on developments in computerized information processing as well as those that are. Thus process innovations such as just-in-time inventory management and total quality management and their relevance to competitiveness are discussed within this section. However, for the time being, attention is directed towards developments that might be grouped under the umbrella term 'computer-integrated technology' and their potential role in contributing to strategic performance.

The contribution of flexible manufacturing systems, computer-aided design and manufacture (CAD/CAM), and other forms of reprogrammable technologies lies with the extent to which they provide the means for improved competitiveness. In the context of this chapter, this issue is presented in terms of possibilities for resolving the 'productivity dilemma' and for managing economies of scope and scale. The centrality of the management of technology to competitiveness in organizations deserves to be emphasized at this point. Thus Clark considers that:

> Investment in new technology involves the development, nurturing and replenishment of the firm's productive and creative capabilities ... its application requires a thorough understanding of the business and the way that the firm competes and the way that it intends to compete over the longer term.
>
> *Clark, quoted in Loveridge and Pitt, 1990*

A contrast may be made with approaches such as those in the earlier work of Michael Porter, at least, where the role of technology and innovation therein appears to be subordinate to strategic decision-making. Thus, where Porter's generic strategy framework considers the development of a strategy for technology within the business as necessary to the subsequent implementation of previously decided generic strategies, the perspective adopted here differs. Instead, the role of technology is seen as integral to strategic decision-making and to organizational competitiveness. Indeed, much of the debate over the potential of advanced technology relates to the extent to which production activities, for example, may be integrated, firstly with each other but, more crucially, in such a way as to permit the satisfaction of what are often seen as contradictory strategic objectives.

As mentioned elsewhere, dimensions of competitiveness such as efficiency and innovation are examples of objectives that may need to be simultaneously pursued for strategic purposes but that have tended to be considered as conflicting and therefore difficult to attain operationally. Other 'false' trade-offs have been made between achieving low costs and the delivery of high quality, and the flexibility of operations versus the dependability of production systems, it is suggested by Wheelwright (1981).

As far as the supply of computer-integrated technologies (CITs) is concerned, the potential for avoiding such unnecessary dichotomies and thus developing capability along the full range of dimensions may be outlined. The benefits of CITs may be stated as applying to strategic and operational flexibility, quality and efficiency and also organizational innovativeness. CITs may enhance flexibility through co-ordination of different 'spheres of activity' within the organization, such as, for example, the better integration of design and manufacturing activities through the implementation of CAD/CAM technology, activities that separately may have been automated but where the link between functions was not. Also, increased flexibility and productivity may be granted in the sense that the greater life span of CITs enables the equipment to be used over successive generations of products, rather than becoming obsolete at the end of any one product life cycle. In this way they can permit production of more products with less overall investment in fixed assets, essentially offering economies of scope. In addition, such flexibility may be demonstrated by the capacity of flexible manufacturing systems, which allow for great variations in the range of products and volumes of production supplied, at relatively low cost (i.e. to make required changes in product mix, redesign or batch quantity). Furthermore, the reprogrammability of computer-integrated manufacturing equipment allows these machines to act as back-ups for each other in case of malfunction or breakdown.

Advantages in quality terms include greater uniformity of production and therefore an increase in the conformance of production with design specifications. Hence the incidence of defects should be expected to decline. Benefits of computer-integrated manufacture include reductions in waste or the need to rectify errors, but also the redeployment of quality inspectors to other activities. Such improvements can contribute to the reliability or 'fitness of purpose' of products or services offered. Moreover, these internal quality benefits have strategic implications externally since claims on warranties may be reduced and customer satisfaction may be generally improved.

As far as efficiency is concerned, the benefits of advanced technology in manufacturing are reductions in throughput processing and lead times. Throughput processing, in terms of the average amount of time necessary to process a piece of work, can be reduced by up to 95%. A reduction in the lead time required to realize new product innovations, or to make modifications to existing ones, is another potential operational benefit of CIT that has a strategic bearing. The latter may be especially advantageous where firms have the capability to envision or anticipate market trends as they develop.

These same benefits have also been associated with the successful implementation of just-in-time inventory management (JIT) and total quality management (TQM). JIT and TQM are processes that do not necessarily require a high degree of investment in advanced applications of information technology (IT) (Bessant, 1991). They are both likely to require a significant shift in organizational philosophy if they are to be effective, however. For example, JIT is an approach to the management of inventory that emphasizes the desire to eliminate waste. Conventionally, organizations have kept stock in order to provide a buffer in the event of a rise in demand for goods or their components, or to replace defective parts. (This can be seen as an 'old-style' flexibility manoeuvre where holding large inventory serves to cover up for what would now be seen as uncompetitive low quality.) JIT means ordering stock only when necessary for production or delivery to customers, in one version through the use of the *kanban* system. (*Kanban* means 'card' and, as exemplified by retailers' bar codes, identifies individual parts, quantity held, their destination and so on).

In a JIT system, inventory is 'pulled' through the production process (Figure 7.3) in contrast with traditional 'push' approaches, where stock is ordered according to a forecasted schedule of future demand. Under JIT, operators may only order or produce new stock when a signal to do so is given, for example when a supermarket bar code indicates that an item on the shelves needs to be reordered. JIT can thus permit low-cost flexibility since inventory is held on demand, as it were, and the expenses involved in handling or storing excessive amounts of stock are avoided. This is especially important since such savings relate to work-in-progress, which has typically accounted for 30% or more of total assets in company balance sheets (Hill, 1985).

Evidence of the experience of managers who have witnessed the benefits of JIT is presented in Table 7.1. JIT is said to be able to provide the benefits of holding minimal stock without the extra costs that might be expected from repeatedly having to set up production equipment as new machinery tools and parts are fitted and removed. So, although reductions in set-up time do not figure highly in Table 7.1, to be able to reduce inventory without additional set-up costs is a benefit that counters hitherto conventional thinking about economic order quantity and set-up costs. One other important aspect of the possible benefits of this approach concerns the relationship between assembling and supplying firms which, as Chapter 6 showed, can be vital. Indeed 'JIT2' has been coined to describe an approach to managing suppliers that is more co-operative than hitherto.

TQM may offer cost savings as well as improvements in product performance. Like JIT it is associated with early best practice in Japanese organizations. The chief architects of the approach (Crosby, 1979; Deming, 1985; Juran, 1989) agree that, like JIT, the philosophical emphasis of TQM is on continuous improvement

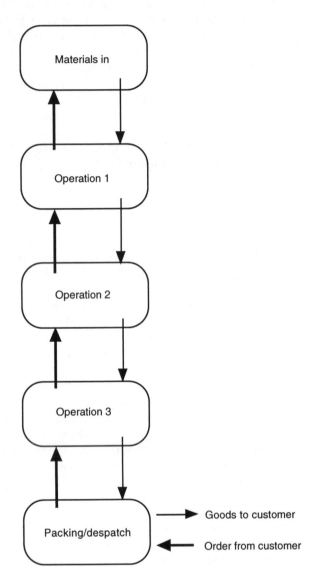

Figure 7.3   Ideal *kanban* flow in a JIT system. Thick arrows, *kanban*; thin arrows, material flow. (Source: Bessant, 1991, p. 210.)

and a 'zero defects attitude'. TQM represents a company-wide pursuit of quality improvement with a long-term orientation, something more than just quality circles. TQM can help to reduce costs and improve productivity drastically, through attention to the prevention of errors and defects in production and away from costly and time-consuming inspection of product (lack of) quality. Indeed, many firms can now count defects in production in terms of hundreds

Table 7.1 Experience with just-in-time*

Factor	Percentage responding
Reduced inventory/work in progress	74
General financial benefits	26
Reduced lead time	23
Improved quality	19
Reduced waste or scrap	16
Improved supplier relationships	12
Reduced space requirements	11
Flexibility (faster response)	11
Improved customer service	10
Better control of production	9
Increased worker motivation	5
Increased productivity	5
Less handling required	3
Better labour utilization	3
Reduced set-up times	3

* Source: Bessant, 1991, p. 225.

of parts per million produced rather than whole percentages. In addition, from the customer's point of view, the benefits may be expressed in terms of lower warranty claims and the general enhancement of customer care. A vital aspect of achieving such benefits is therefore to emphasize the (changing) nature and requirements of customer satisfaction. Moreover, quality becomes the preserve of everyone, not just production, emphasizing the responsibility of individuals for the quality of their own work. Thus the extent to which effective TQM is beneficial but also requires employee commitment is another important issue.

It is very important to note the difference between the potential benefits of such technologies as described above, and their actual performance within specific organizational settings. In particular, certain problems of implementation need to be addressed, an understanding of which may help to explain why expected benefits can fail to be (or are only slowly) realized in practice.

For example, certain technical aspects of the supply and initial adoption of CITs may be considered. Bessant (1991) notes, for instance, a shortage of supplying firms that have a 'turnkey' capability, i.e. that are able to supply a full range of the products and services necessary to install a package of computers, hardware, software, machine tools, robots, and so on. This continues to be the case. This condition has not been helped by suppliers overselling their capability in order to win business, thus exaggerating the benefits of the product(s) in question and inviting problems of implementation in specific organizational contexts. Problems of supply are exacerbated where the managers and others in the client organization are lacking in the technical know-how needed either to vet or simply understand the claims or advice offered by suppliers or consultants. Of course, 'computer-fright' among user participants, not least more senior managers, is not likely to be helpful in steering the adoption of CITs in line with the competitive needs of the organization, never mind their actual implementation.

So questions about the nature of the supply of CITs cannot be divorced from ones concerning the demand for computerized production technologies (nor should they be). Problems of supply are not minimized when managers or operational users are unsure or ignorant of what it is that they require technically or what role the new facility plays in the wider fulfilment of strategic objectives. With reference to this point, Hill and Chambers (1991) view investment in one type of CIT – flexible manufacturing systems and equipment – as often being 'manifestly inappropriate'. Three types of problem are specified involving misunderstandings about:

- the market requirements to which the new technology should contribute
- the actual or potential capability of the manufacturing/operations function to deliver benefits to competitiveness on adoption or implementation of new technologies
- the extent to which technology implementation generates unforeseen restrictions to future management options, hence serving to reduce the flexibility that was supposed to be enhanced.

In terms of the implementation of CIT, a number of further points may be made, some of which will relate to the preceding discussion about the initial decision to adopt or invest. Leonard–Barton (1988) refers to the technical mismatches, or 'misalignments', that reflect some of the implementation issues involved in the introduction of CITs. Technical misalignments may be defined in terms of the mismatch between a technology and its original specifications, or with the production process involved. In terms of the 'specifications gap', it is clear that laboratory testing cannot always be expected to replicate the environment of the user completely. In particular, there may be problems of 'scale-up' in moving up from laboratory prototype to the fully implemented system. What is more, it is not unknown for pressure of time to force the implementation of technology before some of the potential performance hiccups have been ironed out (Leonard–Barton, 1988).

The principle underlying the 'sailing ship' effect may also be invoked to explain the likelihood of technical misalignment where production technologies based on developments in computerized information technology are concerned (Clark and Staunton, 1989). In essence, the sailing ship effect describes the phenomenon of new technological solutions to operational problems being diffused rather unevenly into widespread use over time. For example, the dominance of steam ships (rather than sailing ships) in freight transportation evolved over a period of more than four decades. In part, this can be explained by reference to a number of technical improvements that had progressively to be made to enable steam ships to be competitive with sailing ships over long freight distances. A similar argument may apply to CITs. The degree to which CITs will supersede (or have superseded) existing modes of production or knowledge transfer is likely to vary according to improvements in their technical specifications and reliability still to be made. Substitution will also depend on the capability of suppliers to provide what specific users require and of users to appropriate particular technologies effectively (Clark and Staunton, 1989).

These issues are related to the ability of organizations to surmount what has been termed the 'integration barrier' (Bessant, 1985). If the benefits of CITs are to be achieved in practice, then certain technical problems need to be ironed out (or 'debugged'), as mentioned above. However, the implementation issues are wider than those to do with the complexity and compatibility of the equipment involved. One issue concerns the strategic control of the investment, related but not exclusive to the financial appraisal methods applied to the evaluation of relevant costs and benefits. Another important area involves work organization and employee skills. These are areas where crucial strategic decisions may need to be made that will be influential in the facilitation, modification or outright failure of the implementation of advanced production technologies. Such issues tend to have strategic implications that are not related to the adoption and implementation of new advanced technology only. And, to return briefly to JIT and TQM, these issues are particularly pertinent to their implementation.

One of the most common factors to inhibit diffusion in both areas is that of lack of commitment, of senior managers and employees in general. This may, in part, be to do with the difficulties of envisaging or 'proving' the likely benefits and, as with CITs, may also be explained by fear of the new. The radical nature of these processes, compared with what many organizations have traditionally done, is expressed by the change of mind-set and devolution of responsibility that may be required to make them work effectively. It is not therefore surprising when only partial efforts are made at implementation – this could be interpreted as either a sensible measure designed to minimize the shock of installation, or as a means by which management can keep its hands firmly on the reins of power. Furthermore, a tendency to a preoccupation with 'quick fix' techniques rather than considering more thoroughgoing change, detracts from the achievement of the possible benefits of new processes. For example, instead of travelling along the long, winding road to TQM, some firms find it easier (and quicker) to take the short cut of quality circles, which is merely one technique within the TQM approach. Not surprisingly, quality circles introduced in isolation, and without the necessary workforce autonomy and support (e.g. in training terms), tend to be the subject of failure and abandonment (Bessant, 1991). Issues related to the management of human resources are more closely considered in the following section.

7.4 Managing the human side of the enterprise

The purpose of this section is primarily to tackle issues of work organization and employee relations that are likely to be of significance to strategic flexibility, including those that apply to managing new process technologies. To begin with, it is necessary to consider the nature and emergence of human resource management (HRM). HRM is of interest because it is an approach to employee management that is claimed to be more appropriate to the requirements of organizational strategy than traditional personnel management practices. HRM is of particular interest because of the role it has been said to play in the post-war success of Japanese corporations, and also in the improvements that have been made more recently in US and UK firms, among others.

As a number of commentators have noted, the growing interest in HRM has arisen out of the failings of traditional personnel practices and, more optimistically, the potential benefits of such an approach for strategic performance (Beer *et al.*, 1984; Guest, 1987; Storey, 1992). In terms of what has already been discussed in this chapter, the potential benefits of HRM relate fundamentally to the strategic use of employees as assets and their relationship to, say, the strategic implementation of technological change. The HRM approach may be considered to contribute to the conduct of strategy by involving employees and thus raising their level of commitment to the aims, objectives and changing requirements of the organization. Further, discussions of HRM approaches are often related to the need to develop a philosophy welcoming continual change within organizations, the autonomy and innovativeness of employees and the flexibility of human resources and organizations more generally. It is useful to consider further the meaning and nature of human resource management before moving on to discuss its relevance to strategic flexibility.

Human resource management has been defined as:

> A set of inter-dependent personnel policies to maximise four objectives: organizational integration, employee commitment, flexibility and quality.
>
> *Clark, 1993, p. 3*

These four objectives may be explained as follows. Organizational integration refers to the harnessing of strategic and operational activities; in this respect, it relates to the recognition of the role of human resources (and their management) in contributing to both functional/operational and strategic performance. Moreover, the commitment of senior management to the development of a coherent HRM strategy to facilitate such integration is usually referred to. Moves to enhance organizational integration may include the design (or redesign) of the structure of an organization. This is likely to be with the aim of facilitating HRM moves at both the strategic and operational level, and permitting horizontal and hierarchical interaction between employees in different functions and at various organizational levels.

The objective of employee commitment can be seen as central to HRM as a strategic phenomenon. The contrast with 'traditional' personnel management is marked, particularly if a 'soft' view of HRM is considered. This would imply taking the development of employees seriously and would require a shift from a low-trust to a higher-trust basis for employee relations policies (Clark, 1993). Such commitment refers to employees identifying with and supporting the goals and objectives of the organization. It also concerns developing the commitment of managerial groups to organization-wide objectives (whereas traditional personnel policies would tend not to focus on this particular grouping).

As well as the enhancement of managerial and non-managerial commitment to organizational aims and work in general (for instance by reducing labour turnover or absenteeism), the development of receptivity to organizational change may be seen as a defining and characteristic aspect of strategically-inclined HRM. This development of an attitude to change, which sees the redesign or restructuring of an organization as a normal aspect of life, has occupied much of the strategy literature recently and contrasts with more traditional approaches to personnel, where change is seen as exceptional – an occasion for renegotiation of terms and conditions (Clark, 1993).

Flexibility relates to various types of labour flexibility (e.g. functional, numerical, temporal, wage and distancing) which may have a bearing on the strategic flexibility that is at the heart of this book. Functional labour flexibility relates to the enhancement of the range of tasks that individual employees are able to perform and is often associated with the blurring of job descriptions or boundaries. Numerical flexibility refers to the capacity of an organization to adjust the number of employees according to variations in consumer demand – by use of shorter working hours or short-term contracts, for instance. Temporal flexibility refers to the variability of hours worked, again as demand changes; as with the above the goal of management will be to make the fullest utilization of labour. Wage flexibility may be considered in terms of the ability to develop individual rather than standardized, uniform payment systems, with greater variations in the performance-related element. Distancing flexibility describes the possible use of external personnel for particular tasks, say contractors for cleaning or catering. The benefits from pursuing these types of flexibility may be in the form of increased productivity or an improved response to changing external conditions. However, the potential contradiction of this objective of HRM with, say, maintaining employee commitment, should be acknowledged (Blyton and Turnbull, 1992).

The objective of quality concerns the skills and training of employees, not just, as Clark notes, the general quality of working life in organizations that might involve job satisfaction, for example (Clark, 1993). This objective is associated with techniques such as TQM, of which the quality circle is but one manifestation.

It is possible to identify ways in which the term human resource management has been employed and possible contrasts (or similarities) between HRM and traditional personnel management. Storey (1992) discusses four meanings that apply to various uses of the term HRM. First, he suggests that the term human resource management has been employed as if it were synonymous with 'personnel management'. Thus HRM is employed to refer to traditional employee management activities, either through some wish to use a more modern phrase, or because usage of the term is rather 'loose'.

Secondly, HRM is used to refer to a set of integrated personnel management techniques. Here, the activities that characterize the management of employee relations (namely selection, appraisal, reward and employee development) are pursued in a more interrelated than isolated fashion.

Thirdly, HRM is coined to capture a more strategic orientation of employee relations practice. Indeed, the management of human resources is viewed as integral to strategic needs: employees are seen as representing a resource that needs to be harnessed to the wider objectives of the organization, as might other resources such as technology or finance.

Fourthly, the most striking use of the HRM concept (in comparison with personnel management) is where the contribution of human resources to overall strategy is seen as requiring fundamentally different responses from those that apply to other types of measure designed to integrate personnel practices. These interventions often claim to have increasing employee commitment or the

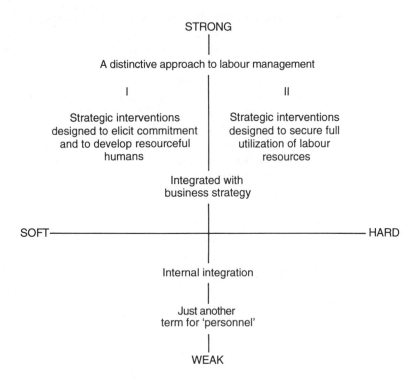

STRONG
|
A distinctive approach to labour management

I   II

Strategic interventions   Strategic interventions
designed to elicit commitment   designed to secure full
and to develop resourceful   utilization of labour
humans   resources

Integrated with
business strategy
|
SOFT————————————————————+————————————————————HARD
|
Internal integration
|
Just another
term for 'personnel'
|
WEAK

Figure 7.4   A 'map' of various meanings of HRM. (Source: Storey, 1992.)

development of the individual as their aim, and so reflect a more philosophical basis. For some the latter provides a sterner test of whether a 'genuine' HRM approach is being adopted or implemented.

The various meanings of HRM may be mapped to reflect a continuum of employee relations practices that vary from being essentially similar to old-style personnel, to representing the more significant departures of either 'soft' or 'hard' HRM. Figure 7.4 presents such a mapping of meanings of HRM, while Table 7.2 lists a number of differences between HRM and personnel management.

The pursuit of the four objectives described above may necessitate attention to issues connected with the structure and design of the organization. They may also relate to the scope of autonomy, the innovativeness of employees, and the development of a philosophy welcoming and, indeed, capable of instigating continual organizational change. The remainder of this section considers these issues as they serve to connect the practice of human resource management with strategic flexibility and organizational performance.

The principal areas here include the overall shape of the organization. In addition to this question about the appropriateness of alternative structural forms to uncertain environments, the matter of the integration of different organizational activities or departments is also of importance.

A number of mechanisms and conditions have been seen as appropriate for encouraging internal organizational co-ordination and are therefore related to

Table 7.2   Points of difference between HRM and personnel management*

Dimension	Personnel and industrial relations (IR)	HRM
Beliefs and assumptions		
1 Contract	Careful delineation of written contracts	Aim to go 'beyond contract'
2 Rules	Importance of devising clear rules/mutuality	'Can-do' outlook; impatience with 'rule'
3 Guide to management action	Procedures	'Business-need'
4 Behaviour referent	Norms/custom and practice	Values/mission
5 Managerial task *vis-à-vis* labour	Monitoring	Nurturing
6 Nature of relations	Pluralist	Unitarist
7 Conflict	Institutionalized	De-emphasized
Strategic aspects		
8 Key relations	Labour-management	Customer
9 Initiatives	Piecemeal	Integrated
10 Corporate plan	Marginal to	Central to
11 Speed of decision	Slow	Fast
Line management		
12 Management role	Transactional	Transformational leadership
13 Key managers	Personnel/IR specialists	General/business/line managers
14 Communication	Indirect	Direct
15 Standardization	High (e.g. 'parity' an issue)	Low (e.g. 'parity' not seen as relevant)
16 Prized management skills	Negotiation	Facilitation
Key levers		
17 Selection	Separate, marginal task	Integrated, key task
18 Pay	Job evaluation (fixed grades)	Performance-related
19 Conditions	Separately negotiated	Harmonization
20 Labour-management	Collective bargaining contracts	Towards individual contracts
21 Thrust of relations with stewards	Regularized through facilities and training	Marginalized (with exception of some bargaining for change models)
22 Job categories and grades	Many	Few
23 Communication	Restricted flow	Increased flow
24 Job design	Division of labour	Teamwork
25 Conflict handling	Reach temporary truces	Manage climate and culture
26 Training and development	Controlled access to courses	Learning companies
27 Focuses of attention for interventions	Personnel procedures	Wide ranging cultural, structural and personnel strategies

* Source: Storey, 1992, p. 35.

issues of innovativeness and flexibility. Some of these include matrix structures, teamworking, broad job definitions, empowerment and employment security supported by open communication channels (Kanter, 1983). These are considered below by addressing issues connected with the development of matrix structures and teamwork, in particular.

Writers such as Kanter (1983) and Galbraith and Kazanjian (1986), for example, assert that there is some role for matrix structures in developing collaboration between parts of organizations, a view somewhat at odds with that of critics of matrix configurations, while Mintzberg (1979) and Quinn (1980) offer a variation on the theme in terms of the adoption of *ad hoc* structures.

Kanter's view is that matrix designs can help to legitimize integration between organizational units, although they are 'not essential' for doing so. The manner in which this legitimization may be achieved lies in the symbolic significance of an organizational chart that shows a number of links from each position within an organization to others (Kanter, 1983). She describes the nature of a matrix structure at General Electric Medical Systems as follows:

> 'Matrixed' managers ... typically reported to both the function where the manager had traditionally worked (generally the stronger and more direct tie) and a connected department, or the office where tasks would be integrated for a particular product (often a less direct 'dotted line' tie). Although the 'dotted line' relationship was often ill-defined, it benefited the manager by providing him or her with access to another powerful upper-level manager (generally a department head). Managers were thus able to use their dotted line reports to secure support, resources or information, gaining an additional route to vital organizational commodities. There were also important implications for sponsorship; if a manager was unable to obtain sufficient backing from his direct superior, then there was an alternative in the dotted line boss.
>
> *Kanter, 1983, p. 168*

Here legitimacy was provided in the sense that managers could go across formal lines and levels in the organization without the feeling that they were breaching 'protocol'. Moreover, such a structure serves to recognize the complex ties and need for inter-unit contact in organizations while at the same time countering narrow identification with departmental rather than organizational aims and the politics often associated with this. Finally, although 'managers nearly everywhere' in Kanter's study complained of the time-consuming nature of the meetings involved, these occasions did provide opportunities for developing both formal and informal working relationships with people from various other functions. In short, the employment of matrices can contribute to the avoidance of 'segmentalist', non-innovative (and less flexible) organizations (Kanter, 1983).

The work of Galbraith and Kazanjian (1986) also helps to put some of the criticisms of matrix (or 'simultaneous') structures into perspective. Thus the accusation that 'matrix doesn't work' receives a balanced response. These authors say that critics of matrix structures are justified in asserting their poor contribution to organizational performance for a number of reasons. In some companies, for instance, the matrix form was adopted because it was fashionable (rather like other organizational innovations such as quality circles or portfolio management). In 'many cases', matrix structures were adopted where they did not 'fit' the business situation and resulted in operational difficulties.

Acknowledging that there are problems with the concepts of 'fit' and 'structure', it is still instructive to consider aspects of the implementation of matrices that have given cause for concern, even where their proposed adoption did appear to fit the business. Two principal factors help to explain the abandonment of matrix structures in apparently appropriate situations (Galbraith and Kazanjian, 1986). The first of these relates to the manner of implementation, for example where the matrix, which is intended to facilitate collaboration and participation, is imposed centrally or autocratically. Similarly, implementation of the matrix suffered where the organization involved tried to force the pace and scale of change such that radically new structures were given insufficient time to realize the desired effects. The second factor relates to changes in the external environment that may render matrix forms less appropriate strategically. Here, a change in competitive conditions may see a reduction in lead times for developing and introducing new products, which might put a premium on new product flexibility. In terms of achieving the latter, Galbraith and Kazanjian suggest that, in the electronics industry, the matrix used to integrate parts of large organizations has become less appropriate to strategic needs than the establishment of small, self-contained and faster-responding organizational units.

However, this is not to say that matrix forms *per se* do not work. Rather, Galbraith and Kazanjian claim that failures associated with the matrix form have more to do with the way in which they are implemented than with any intrinsic faults with the structural form. In particular, attempts to install matrices, rather than to adopt a more evolutionary approach, are viewed as susceptible to failure. They go further and suggest that the matrix form is the most appropriate form for the conduct of effective strategy in global and diversified companies, although it is difficult to support or refute this claim categorically.

As mentioned above, Kanter does not view the matrix organization as being, of itself, a necessity – it is merely one way to accomplish the integration necessary for achieving innovativeness or facilitating flexibility. It may represent a 'transitional' step in an ongoing process of decentralization or integration.

Team building is seen by Child (1984) as an aid to integration in organizations and a central focus of the work of the 'organizational development' movement. In addition, teamwork has also been discussed in terms of its relevance to other objectives of HRM, namely employee commitment, flexibility and quality (Delbridge and Turnbull, 1992; Martinez Lucio and Weston, 1992; Sewell and Wilkinson, 1992). An example of the centrality of teamworking is provided by the case of negotiations between management and unions in a UK plant of a multinational vehicle manufacturer (Martinez Lucio and Weston, 1992). A new agreement that was 'overwhelmingly' accepted by the workforce emphasized the introduction of teamworking and team leaders as 'a critical part of the new system'. As Martinez Lucio and Weston report, an essential aspect of this new system is that:

Employees 'have an opportunity to impact on the success of the business through their own decision making, pride in their work and co-operative efforts among each other'. This meant a change from a traditional section composed of 60 employees to teamworking consisting of between 10 to 15 employees.

Martinez Lucio and Weston, 1992, p. 226

More specifically, in terms of securing employee commitment to the task in hand and to wider organizational objectives, the structure and organization of work teams and the interpersonal relations that develop within them have been cited as being crucial (Delbridge and Turnbull, 1992). Delbridge and Turnbull illustrate this with reference to UK truck manufacturer Iveco-Ford and its introduction, in 1989, of a new supervisory structure in place of the old foreman arrangement. An attempt by management to 'tap into' the detailed operational knowledge of employees on the shopfloor included the introduction of a new 'co-ordinator' position. The function of co-ordinators was:

To bridge the role of foreman and hourly-paid operatives, with each Co-ordinator (team leader) responsible for volume, quality, minor mainte-nance, operator training, process checks, allocating jobs at the start of each shift and reporting on lateness, sickness and absenteeism. Team leaders become the 'eyes and ears of management on the shopfloor and provide a direct means of communication with the workforce. The aim is to keep the teams small . . . so that they develop their own identity and pull together to solve problems – management's problems.

Delbridge and Turnbull, 1992, pp. 62–3

This example of a team-based approach may be said to reflect a 'hard' form of human resource management, being more concerned with the maximization of the use of human resources and less to do with the improvement of employee capabilities and autonomy implied in a 'soft' type of HRM. A more positive example of team working can be given, however, with reference to both lower- and higher-order employees. Research into organizational changes associated with the introduction of CITs has noted the development of teamworking in conjunction with changes in employee responsibility, reward and supervision (Bessant, 1993).

Bessant's study looked at the 'successful' implementation of CITs in 28 manu-facturing organizations between 1988 and 1990. Chief among the changes in work organization that have accompanied and facilitated the introduction of the new technology was the establishment of multiskilled, autonomous operator teams. A number of variations on the theme are described by Bessant, including quality circles, task forces, multidisciplinary teams and cross-functional teams. 'Significant' increases in employee responsibility through greater autonomy are reported and, together with operator flexibility, are seen as key to realizing the skills and potential of the workforce. In addition, changes in the reward system were viewed commonly as being of 'high priority' for achieving the new work structures. In particular, the Bessant study highlights shifts in the basis of payment from 'output achieved' to payment for 'skills and quality'. The role of the new type of reward system is described as 'the bedrock on which the attainment of extra flexibility rests' (Bessant, 1993, p. 200). Changes in the role of supervision were also identified as being critical. In most cases, sample companies provided evidence of a shift in supervisory role that permitted the level of responsibility to be shifted down to the operators in order to allow them to do what they saw as necessary to perform the job. This shift was seen as reflective of a fundamental change in the managerial approach to employee relations, from one emphasizing monitoring and control of the labour force to a more supportive and collaborative role.

In terms of the middle and upper managerial levels in organizations, Kanter notes the use of integrated teams at innovative, entrepreneurial companies both in high-tech and more mature industries. The point made is that what appeared to be effective is not the adoption of teams *per se*, but rather the existence of norms of collaboration and consultation and a tradition of teamworking. In innovative companies, the acceptance over time of the need for 'a marketplace of ideas', was in recognition of the benefits to problem-solving or creativity of the pooling of diverse talents, skills and perspectives. This type of team-based integration, says Kanter, is in marked contrast to the 'caution of committees', where the spreading of responsibility serves to dull risk-taking and innovativeness (Kanter, 1983).

A number of researchers note that team approaches are unlikely to work where structural and other organizational conditions are inappropriate, for example where objectives are set for different departments that mutually conflict, or where interpersonal relationships are not conducive to collaboration (Child, 1984). Another important influence lies with the recruitment of staff into organizations and their deployment into teams, for which organizations such as Nissan in the UK have been noted. Finally 'employability security' (if not security within one particular place of employment) has been viewed as a factor enabling sustained commitment and the longer-term development of employees. Here, the value of workers' skills to any future employer is enhanced and provides a means of resolving possible tensions between corporate flexibility and individual employee security (Kanter, 1989).

7.5 The dilemma of strategic control

This chapter and the two that preceded it have all been concerned with various aspects of the transition to a new set of organizational practices, deemed appropriate for contemporary competitive conditions. Within firms, these have been considered in terms of the move towards the enhancement of flexibility through organizational restructuring, new patterns of human resource management and the implementation of process innovations. In addition, new perspectives on the management of organizational boundaries have brought into focus the relationships that organizations have with their customers, suppliers, competitors and governmental or other institutions. Whether such changes, in practice, add up to a new 'post-Fordist' paradigm is debatable. An important aspect of whether or how organizations introduce technological and organizational change relates to issues of strategic control.

The dilemma of strategic control can be expressed in terms of the need to monitor and improve performance without imposing undue rigidity about the setting of objectives and reporting mechanisms. This issue is especially relevant where organizations operate within uncertain environmental conditions, in which flexibility will be vital. In certain areas, the dilemma of control may be presented differently, although the two aspects are related to each other. This second type of dilemma concerns the extent to which the benefits associated with departures from the status quo can be acquired without undue costs. In the latter, manoeuvres that might significantly alter organizational routines include decisions to implement advanced manufacturing technology, or other organizational innovations such as TQM or fully-fledged HRM.

Implementing innovations in these areas, within specific organizational contexts, can be something of a double-edged sword. On the one hand, the benefits of doing so may be great in competitive terms (although difficult to measure given conventional investment appraisal techniques). On the other hand, the costs of implementation may be high – even where the project is adjudged 'successful'. Particularly where computerized technology is involved, capital investment can be especially high (again allowing for problems with evaluation techniques). Moreover, failure (or the perception of the likelihood of it) can mean partial implementation of the manoeuvre, high costs of reversing the policy and low morale or loss of face, which might impede future moves in a given area.

In outline, the requirements of an effective formal control system are that it should facilitate the co-ordination of various organizational activities, enhance the clarity of strategic direction, motivate employees and highlight areas where intervention is necessary for objectives to be achieved. Goold and Quinn (1990) found little evidence of the existence of formal strategic controls in practice. Thus informal strategic controls best reflect the nature of practice, even where many of the largest firms are concerned. Moreover, informal control processes appear to offer a better hope for achieving the types of outcomes that have been associated with the operation of an effective control system, especially in uncertain environments.

The practice of informal strategic control accords well with behavioural models of the process of strategic management in general. Recalling logical incrementalism (Quinn, 1980), research evidence shows that strategy evolves on the basis of tentative and broad commitments. Major moves in strategic development tend to occur piecemeal, emphasis being placed on keeping options as open as possible, countering political opposition to change and creating commitment and consensus.

Research into companies that have more informal strategic control processes has shown that, although long-term performance objectives are not made explicit, the dialogue between the centre and the rest of the organization may facilitate quite a clear mutual understanding of where the priorities lie. Examples of this include BOC, Philips, Toshiba and General Electric (Goold, 1991).

Making this informality work puts effective two-way communication at a premium. Moreover, learning to interpret the feedback from this dialogue is an important capability. As well as informal contacts, a variety of other means can be used to monitor and control performance. These may include more formal periodic strategic reviews and task force reports. However, the absence of explicit milestones means that, overall, formality is low and intervention can be based on broad assessments of progress. This is a feasible method of control since the triggers for intervention that managers need (i.e. the early warning signs that all may not be well) tend to be provided informally. As one BOC manager puts it:

> You need a control system, but the really early warnings will never come from the formal control system. They will come from your feel for the business.
>
> *Quoted in Goold, 1991, p. 73*

As well as stemming from managerial intuition and judgement, it is important to appreciate strategic control as an organization-wide phenomenon, an activity that is not only the preserve of senior managers. This is accomplished more easily if linear views regarding the strategic management process are dispensed with. Hence, environmental assessment becomes something other than the first step in formulating a strategy to be implemented later. Instead, as with the example of Jaguar, environmental assessment is being facilitated when deeper relationships between purchasing departments and component suppliers are developed. These relationships simultaneously enable control in the sense that feedback (or 'feedforward') about supplier performance or difficulties can be obtained. In the Jaguar case, the deepening of relationships between the purchasing function and suppliers is complemented by databases covering existing and potential supply firms (Pettigrew and Whipp, 1991). Together, these provisions enhance the learning capability of the organization.

The link between strategic control, flexibility and learning is an important one. Many of the avenues that typically feature in discussions of the enhancement of strategic flexibility, learning or innovativeness require what for many organizations are fundamental changes in organizational philosophy and conduct. As mentioned previously, great uncertainty surrounds the performance of such 'leaps in the dark' associated with implementing advanced technology, new programmes or structures. To avoid disastrous investments, efficient and effective experimentation is required, forms of ongoing trial and error that enable low-cost learning about the performance of the innovation. Where complex technology is involved, for example, it has been found that analysis and control of performance is made more traumatic and costly when implementation is hasty or 'lumpy'. What is more, the problems of radical technological change, for example, tend to be exacerbated by lack of participation in decision-making by those who are likely to be affected, such as those who have to work with or maintain equipment (Collingridge, 1992).

Hence, there appears to be a tension: gradual change seems more appropriate for retaining flexibility of manoeuvre than fundamental decisions. Yet, gradual or partial implementation may be thought of as legitimizing the status quo, so that moves towards adopting HRM, for example, become seen as attempts by management to control employees better, rather than as part of any transition to a new outlook on employee relations.

Another aspect of this dilemma of control is that fundamental change, implied by the adoption of the measures described above, is what appears to be required if organizations are to benefit fully from the implementation of advanced techno-logy, TQM and so on. This is as much a matter of fundamental reorientation of attitudes within organizations as it is about the introduction of a new technique or technology. This includes the recognition by managers that what counts as 'improvement' or greater 'flexibility' from their viewpoint is not necessarily going to be seen that way by their employees (who may interpret improved strategic flexibility as greater work load with less job security).

Yet, the implementation of such moves and the sustainability of any benefits arising from them is likely to be weakened without the commitment and involve-ment, at a strategic level, of those most likely to be affected by such decisions. There is, therefore, a tension between maintaining strategic control where funda-mental decisions are involved, which requires organization-wide support, and the generally unbalanced nature of employer–employee control relationships. Sustained commitment from the latter may well need to be considered in terms of how and to what extent their interests are likely to be at odds with those of management, not in terms of identification with unitary organizational objec-tives. It may be difficult, over the longer term, for employees to accept greater autonomy or to respond to calls for greater creativity in the absence of such recognition. (This is in addition to wider issues concerning the training and development that may be needed.) Without such consideration, wholesale attempts to implement strategies for flexibility seem only likely to be more, not less, precarious.

7.6 Summary

This chapter has considered various means by which flexibility may be enhanced to the benefit of general strategic performance. The areas deemed of primary importance include the management of product and process innovation and human resource management. In all of these activities there may be performance benefits associated with the introduction of new practices and structures. Flexibility of production and product development is claimed to be a key benefit, so too is the ability of organizations to enhance their learning capabilities. However, a paradox exists. In order to ascertain the likely strength of improve-ment from new practices, some mechanism for controlled learning needs to take place. Without this, management will not be likely to give the commitment required to implement radically different processes fully, let alone choose to cede authority over vital areas, as the effective introduction of such innovations would seem to require.

Study questions

1. Consider the relevance of innovation and creativity to developing strategic flexibility.
2. What measures may be taken to enhance organizational flexibility and learning?

3. What factors constrain and facilitate attempts to improve strategic flexibility through implementing advanced technology or changes in employee relations?

Key readings

Nonaka (1991) provides a less technical, more knowledge- and cognition-oriented view of the capabilities approach than others.

Steven Wheelwright (1981) develops the issue of the interaction between strategic and operational concerns.

The book edited by Blyton and Turnbull (1992) contains a number of articles that address the extent to which (strategic) human resource management has emerged in practice. Similarly, the volume edited by Clark (1993) contains a number of articles related to empirical and theoretical work on the interactions between strategic objectives, human resource management and technical change.

References

Adler, P. S., Riggs, H. E. and Wheelwright, S. C. (1989) Product development know-how: trading tactics for strategy. *Sloan Management Review*, **31**(1), 7–17.

Beer, M., Spector, B., Lawrence, P. *et al.* (1984) *Managing Human Assets*, Free Press, New York.

Bessant, J. (1985) The integration barrier: problems in the implementation of advanced manufacturing technology. *Robotica*, **3**, 97–103.

Bessant, J. (1991) *Managing Advanced Manufacturing Technology*, NCC Blackwell, Oxford.

Bessant, J. (1993) Towards Factory 2000: Designing Organizations for Computer-integrated Technologies, in *Human Resource Management and Technical Change* (ed. J. Clark), Sage, London.

Blyton, P. and Turnbull, P. (eds) (1992) *Reassessing Human Resource Management*, Sage, London.

Child, J. (1984) *Organization: a Guide to Principles and Practice*, Harper and Row, London.

Clark, J. (ed.) (1993) *Human Resource Management and Technical Change*, Sage, London.

Clark, P. A. and Staunton, N. (1989) *Innovation in Technology and Organization*, Routledge, London.

Collingridge, D. (1992) *The Management of Scale*, Routledge, London.

Crosby, P. (1979) *Quality is Free*, McGraw–Hill, New York.

Delbridge, R. and Turnbull, P. (1992) Human Resource Maximization: The Management of Labour under Just-in-time Manufacturing Systems, in *Reassessing Human Resource Management* (eds P. Blyton and P. Turnbull), Sage, London.

Deming, W. E. (1985) The roots of quality control in Japan. *Pacific Basin Quarterly*, Spring/Summer.

Galbraith, J. R. and Kazanjian, R. K. (1986) *Strategy Implementation: Structure, Systems and Process*, West, New York.

Gilbert, X. and Strebel, P. (1989) From innovation to outpacing. *Business Quarterly*, Summer, 19–22.

Goold, M. (1991) Strategic control in the decentralized firm. *Sloan Management Review*, **32**(2), 69–81.

Goold, M. and Quinn, J. J. (1990) The paradox of strategic controls. *Strategic Management Journal*, **11**(1), 43–57.

Guest, D. (1987) Human resource management. *Journal of Management Studies*, **24**(5), 503–21.

Hill, T. (1985) *Manufacturing Strategy*, Macmillan, Basingstoke.

Hill, T. and Chambers, S. (1991) Flexibility – a manufacturing conundrum. *International Journal of Operations and Production Management*, **11**(2), 5–13.

Juran, J. (1989) *Juran on Leadership for Quality*, Free Press, New York.

Kanter, R. M. (1983) *The Change Masters*, Unwin, London.

Kanter, R. M. (1989) *When Giants Learn to Dance*, Unwin, London.

Leonard–Barton, D. (1988) Implementation as mutual adaptation of technology and organization. *Research Policy*, **17**(5), 251–67.

Leonard–Barton, D. (1992) Core capabilities and core rigidities: a paradox in managing new product development. *Strategic Management Journal*, **13**.

Loveridge, R. and Pitt, M. (1990) *The Strategic Management of Technological Innovation*, Wiley, Chichester.

Martinez Lucio, M. and Weston, S. (1992) Human Resource management and Trade Union Responses: Bringing the Politics of the Workplace back into the Debate, in *Reassessing Human Resource Management* (eds P. Blyton, and P. Turnbull), Sage, London.

Mintzberg, H. (1979) *The Structuring of Organizations*, Prentice-Hall, New York.

Nonaka, I. (1991) The knowledge-creating company. *Harvard Business Review*, **69**(6), 96–104.

Pettigrew, A. and Whipp, R. (1991) *Managing Change for Competitive Success*, Blackwell, Oxford.

Prahalad, C. K. and Hamel, G. (1990) The core competence of the corporation. *Harvard Business Review*, **68**(3), 79–91.

Quinn, J. B. (1980) *Strategies for Change: Logical Incrementalism*, Irwin, IL.

Sewell, G. and Wilkinson, B. (1992) Empowerment or Emasculation? Shopfloor Surveillance in a Total Quality Organization, in *Reassessing Human Resource Management* (eds P. Blyton and P., Turnbull). Sage, London.

Stevenson, H. and Gumpert, D. (1985) The heart of entrepreneurship. *Harvard Business Review*, **64**(2), 84–94.

Storey, J. (1992) *Developments in the Management of Human Resources*, Blackwell, Oxford.

Wheelwright, S. C. (1981) Japan – where operations really are strategic, *Harvard Business Review*, **59**(4), 67–74.

INDEX

Advanced manufacturing
technology, *see* Computer-
integrated technology
Ansoff, H. I. 93–7
Aldrich, H. E. 18–19
Alvey programme 131
Automobile industry
horizontal collaboration in
128
import penetration in USA 41
scale/scope economies in
114
vertical collaboration in 133–4

Banking industry 129–30, 141
Barriers to entry 61
BCG, *see* Boston Consultancy
Group
Bessant, J. 136, 159, 161, 168–9
Biotechnology industry 130–1
Body Shop 44, 45
Boston Consultancy Group 69
Bounded rationality 11
British Coal 39–40
Buyers, bargaining power of
60–1

'Cadbury Report' (on corporate
governance) 9
Canon 152
Capabilities, core 151–3
Capabilities, *see* Strategic
capabilities
Car industry, *see* Automobile
industry
Chandler, A. 4, 98–9
Change, management of 121
see also Strategic renewal
Checkland, P. 17–18
Clark, K. B. and Fujimoto, T.
130, 133
Clark, P. and Staunton, N. 114,
136, 137

Co-contracting 115
see also Horizontal
collaboration
Collaboration, inter-firm
partner selection and 139–40
trust and 140–2
success factors in 139–42
see also Horizontal
collaboration; Strategic
networks; Vertical
collaboration
Collective entrepreneurship 19,
124
Collingridge, D. 171
Competencies, core
as source of competitiveness
149–50
strategic architecture and
149–50
as Vickers 150
Competition
experience curve 69–71
globalization and 62–4
intensity of 62
market share leadership and
71–2
product life cycle and 66–9
strategic groups and 72–6
structural analysis of 58–62
see also Competitive
advantage, sources of
Competitive advantage, sources
of
core capabilities 151–3
core competencies 149–50
cost leadership 90, 93
differentiation 90–1, 93
focus 91, 93
'outpacing' 147–8
Computer industry 69
Computer-integrated technology
156–7, 159–61
Consolidation strategy 95

Contracting out 115
see also Vertical collaboration
Contractor, F. and Lorange, P.
128
Core capabilities, *see*
Capabilities, core
Core competencies, *see*
Competencies, core
Corporate governance 9
Cost efficiency
economies of scale and 81–3
experience curve and 81
Cost leadership 90, 93
Cultural differentials 111–13
Culture, *see* Organizations,
culture and
see also Capabilities, core;
Human resource
management; Organizational
learning; Total quality
management

Decentralization 117–18
De-integration, of activities
economies of scope and 115
organizational routines and
98
transactions costs and 97
see also Contracting out;
Externalization
De-layering 117–18
Differentiation 90–1, 93
Diversification 94
Dodgson, M. 119, 132
Downsizing 117–18
Duncan, R. 37

Economic conditions 38–41
Economies of scale
cost efficiency and 81–3
interplay with economies of
scope 114
Economies of scope 114–15

EFTPOS (electronic funds transfer systems) 129–30, 141
Emergent strategies 5
Empowerment 168–9
Entrepreneurial mode of strategy-making 19
see also Collective entrepreneurship
Environment, the business, see Industries; Organizations; Macro-environment
Environmental awareness 44
Environmental fit 98–9
see also Strategic fit; Structural fit
Ethics, of business 8, 43–4
European food processing industry 75–6
Evans, J. S. 20
Exchange Rate Mechanism (ERM) 40
Exnovation 85
see also Unlearning
Experience curve 69–71, 81
Externalization 97

Five force model (Porter) 58–66
Flexible specialization 25, 116
Focusing strategy 91, 93
Franchising 115
Freedom of manoeuvre 22–3, 145, 170–1
Freeman, C. 42

Galbraith, J. R. and Kazanjian, R. K. 166–7
'Garbage can' model 18
Gilbert, X. and Strebel, P. 147–9
Globalization 41, 61–4
Goold, M. 170–1
Governance structures
de-integration and 97–8
integration of activities and 97
Government policy
impact on industries 64–5
and renewable energy 65
Grant, R. 110, 113–14
Growth strategies 93–5
see also Consolidation; Withdrawal

Hall, R. 110–12
Hamel, G., Doz, Y. and Prahalad, C. K. 139
Harrigan, K. R. 20

Harrison, J. and Taylor, B. 37
Honda 49–50, 152
Horizontal collaboration
automobile industry 128
banking sector 129
barriers to entry and 131
biotechnology industry 130
competition and 127–8
complementary assets 130
EFTPOS (electronic funds transfer system) 129–30
factors in development 129–32
information technology development 131
in Japan 132
lead times and 130
research institutions and 131
semi-conductor industry 129
VLSI (very large scale integration) project 131
see also Research and development; Vertical collaboration; Strategic networks
Howells, J. and Hine, J. 129, 141
Human resource management (HRM)
definition 162
at Iveco-Ford 168
matrix structures and 166–7
new technology and 168–9
objectives of 162–3
and personnel management compared 163–4, 165
team building 167–8

'Icarus Paradox' (Miller) 99–102
Incrementalism 12–13
Industries
analysis of 58–76
definitional issues 59, 62, 84
evolution of 66–8
Industry life cycle, see Product life cycle
Industry organization economics 57–8
Innovation, see Process innovation; Product development/innovation
Institutional economists
routines and 98
transactions costs and 97
Intangible resources 110–12
Integration, of activities, see Internalization
Intended strategies 5

Internalization 97
Interpretative approach (to strategy) 14
Italian textiles industry 116

Japan/Japanese firms
Canon 152
collaboration with US firms 140
Honda 49–50, 152
keiretsu 132
Matsushita 152–3
role of MITI (Ministry of International Trade and Industry) and horizontal collaboration in 132
Nintendo 148
public policy 131, 132
supplier systems in 133–4
Johnson, G. 14, 123
Just-in-time (JIT) (inventory management)
experience of 157
implementation and 161
kanban system 157–8

Kanter, R. M. 141–2, 153–5, 166–7, 169
Keiretsu 132
Knowledge creation 151–3
see also Intangible resources; Organizational learning

Labour flexibility 163
Learning, see Organizational learning
Levitt, T. 62–4, 66–8
Lewin, K. 121
Lindblom, C. E. 12
Linear planning 10–12
Logical incrementalism 13, 122
Long range planning
evolution of planning styles and 38
nature of approach 46
see also Planning styles

Machine tool industry 41
Macro-environment
analysis of factors in 45–55
economic conditions 40–1
ethical issues 43–5
and forecasting 50–4
political issues 38–9
socio-cultural issues 43–4
technological change 42–3
uncertainty in 35–45

Market
    development strategy 94
    penetration strategy 93
    see also Industries
Market share
    performance and 71–2
    and portfolio analysis 84
Mass production 118
Matrix structures 166–8
Matsushita 152–3
Miller, D. 99–103, 122
Mintzberg, H. 4–5, 19
Models
    of strategic decision-making
        10–19
'Muddling through' 12
    see also Incrementalism
Multinational companies 63–4

Nelson, R. R. and Winter S. G.
    22, 98
Neo-Fordism 29
Nintendo 148
Nonaka, I. 151–3

Oil crisis 38–9, 40
OPEC (Organization of
    Petroleum Exporting
    Countries) 38–9, 40
Organizational learning
    collaborative 120–1
    contexts of 120
    definitions 118
    horizontal collaboration and
        130
    incrementalism and 122, 123–4
    interpretative schemes and
        123
    nature of 119
    routines and 119
    sources of 119
    strategic capability and 118–19
    strategic renewal and 121–2
Organizations
    culture and 14, 99–103
    human resource management
        in 161–9
    post-Fordism and 24, 29, 127
    routines in 22
    structure 98–103
Outpacing strategies 147–8

Pavitt, K. 119
Peters, T. 117–18
Pettigew, A. and Whipp, R. 124,
    171

PIMS, see Profit Impact of
    Market Share
Piore, M. and Sabel, C. 25, 116
Planners, specialist 53
Planning styles 37–45
Political factors
    and uncertainty 38–40
Population ecology 18
Porter, M. 58–62, 86–9, 89–93
Portfolio analysis 83–5
Post-Fordism/post-Fordist
    paradigm 24, 29, 127
Prahalad, C. K. and Hamel, G.
    149–50
Process innovation
    and competitiveness 155–6
    computer-integrated
        technologies, supply of
        156–7
    implementation issues 159–61
    Just-in-time inventory
        management 157–9, 161
    product innovation and 85,
        147
    strategic control and 161
    total quality management
        157–9, 161
    see also Human resource
        management
Product
    development/innovation
    at Canon 152
    control of 'newstreams' and
        152–5
    'core capabilities' and 151–5
    'core competencies' and
        149–50
    as growth strategy 94
    knowledge creation and 151–3
    at Matsushita 152–3
    at Nintendo, 148
    'outpacing' approach 147–8
    process innovation and 85, 147
Product life cycle
    computer industry and 69
    definition of 'product' 68
    extension of 68
    stages 66–7
    and technological dematurity
        68
Profit Impact of Market Share
    (PIMS) 69

Quality, management of, see
    Total quality management
Quinn, J. B. 13, 122, 124

R&D, see Research and
    development
Rational planning, see Linear
    planning
Realized strategies 5
Renewable energy 65
Renewal, strategic 21
    see also Change, strategic
Research and development
    Alvey programme 131
    banking industry and
        129–30
    biotechnology industry 130–1
    complementary assets and
        130–1
    government policy 131–2
    horizontal collaboration and
        129–32
    semiconductor industry and
        129
    VLSI (very large scale
        integration) project 131–2
Resources
    choice of generic strategy and
        92, 93
    nature of strategy and 8
    relationship to capabilities
        108–14
    SWOT analysis and 81–8
    see also Capabilities, core;
        Competencies, core;
        Knowledge creation;
        Outpacing strategies
Reverse engineering 120
Rumelt, R. 65

Scenario building 52–3
Semiconductor industry 129
Senge, P. 21
Simon, H. 11–12
Slack, N. 26–7
Social responsibility, see Ethics
Socio-cultural/demographic
    factors 43–4
Stakeholders 8, 11
Starkey, K. 23–4, 28
Strategic capabilities
    analysis of 80–9
    as basis of competitiveness
        108–14
    development of 109
    organizational boundaries and
        108–9
    routines and 112–13
    sources of 109–13
    sustainability of 113–14

178 **Index**

Strategic control
  dilemma of 169–72
  formality/informality of 170–1
  at Jaguar Cars 171
  of 'newstreams' 153–5
  as organization-wide issue 171
  process innovation and 161
Strategic fit 7, 167
  see also Environmental fit;
    Structural fit
Strategic flexibility
  aspects of 23–6
  dimensions of 26–7
  nature of 19–23
  see also Learning,
    organizational; Renewal,
    strategic
Strategic groups
  European food processing
    industry and 75–6
  and 'strategic space' 73–4, 76
Strategic management (linear
    model)
  stages of 11
  strategic analysis 10–12, 35–89
  strategic choice 89–98
  strategic implementation 98–9,
    100
  see also Models, of strategic
    decision-making
Strategic networks
  Benetton 136
  competitiveness and 135
  definition of 135
  hub firms in 135–6
  industrial districts 139
  Swedish metalwork 136–7
  telecommunications equipment
    sector 137–8
Strategic planning
  evolution of planning styles
    and 38–9
  techniques of 46–54
  see also Planning styles
Strategic renewal 21, 120

Strategy
  characteristics of 5–10
  defined 4–5
  nature of 4–10
  structure and 97–103
Structural fit 98–100, 167
  see also Environmental fit;
    Strategic fit
'Stuck-in-the-middle' 91–2
Substitute products, threat of
    61
Sugiara, H. 49–50
Suppliers
  automobile industry
    133–4
  bargaining power of 60
  vertical collaboration and
    132–4
SWOT (strengths, weaknesses,
    opportunities, threats)
    analysis 45, 48–9, 80,
    88–9
Synergy 93–4
Systems thinking 14

Team building 167–8
Technological change
  types 42
  uncertainty of 41
Technological dematurity
    68
Technology, development
    and management of,
    see Computer-integrated
    technology; Horizontal
    collaboration; Just-in-time
    inventory management;
    Process innovation;
    Product development/
    innovation; Research and
    development; Strategic
    networks; Technological
    change; Total quality
    management; Vertical
    collaboration

  see also Alvey Programme;
    Automobile industry;
    Biotechnology industry;
    Computer industry; EFTPOS
    (electronic funds transfer
    system); Human resource
    management; Research
    institutions; VLSI (very large
    system integration)
Textile machinery industry 41
Thorelli, H. 140
Total quality management
    (TQM) 157–9, 161
Tottenham Hotspur 6–7
Transactions costs 97

Uncertainty
  as characteristic of strategy 10
  macro-environmental 35–45
United Kingdom (UK)
  decline in manufacturing 41
United States of America (US)
  import penetration
    (automobiles) 41
Unlearning 85, 120
Utterback-Abernathy framework
    85

Value chain
  activities 86
  analysis of 86–9
  linkages in 88
Values
  and stakeholders 8
Vertical collaboration
  see also Horizontal
    collaboration; Strategic
    networks
VLSI (very large scale
    integration) project 131

Williamson, O. 97
Wilson, D. 102
Withdrawal strategy 95
Woo, C. 71–2